Building Procurement Systems

Third Edition

Building Procurement Systems

A client's guide

3rd edition

James Franks
with additional material provided by
Peter Harlow

'The basic decision on the procurement route
(is difficult) . . . inexperienced clients need advice.'

Sir Michael Latham
Constructing the Team

Longman

The CHARTERED
INSTITUTE OF
BUILDING

Please note: references to the masculine include, where appropriate, the feminine.

Addison Wesley Longman Limited
Edinburgh Gate
Harlow, Essex CM20 2JE, England
and Associated Companies throughout the world.

Co-published with The Chartered Institute of Building through
Englemere Limited
The White House, Englemere, Kings Ride, Ascot
Berkshire SL5 7TB, England

First published 1984
Second Edition 1990
Third Edition 1998

ISBN 0 582 31926–9

British Library Cataloguing-in-Publication Data

A catalogue record for this book is
available from the British Library

Set by 35 in 9/13 pt Palatino
Produced through Longman Malaysia, TCP

Contents

Foreword

A major conclusion of the report *Constructing the Team* was that the basic decision on the building procurement route should precede the preparation of the outline project brief. Obtaining the right balance of priorities (value for money, early completion date, initial: running cost, risk avoidance etc) is so important for clients of the construction industry.

Constructing the team suggested that inexperienced clients need advice on decision making, particularly during the crucial early stages of a project's development. *Building Procurement Systems* provides clients with a guide to the contractual arrangements which are available for them and it offers a simple method of rating the alternative procurement routes. The earlier editions proved very successful and it is to be hoped that this revised and extended edition, sponsored by the Chartered Institute of Building, will also provide clients of the construction industry with advice, thus enabling them to determine their real needs and devise a project strategy before taking that important initial decision on any construction project – which procurement option to adopt.

Sir Michael Latham
September 1997

Acknowledgements

Many people contributed to the three editions of this book. Thanks are due and gratefully given to:

- Peter Harlow at the CIOB whose contribution is mentioned in the fore-word; colleagues at South Bank University who assisted in various ways; and Julian Vickery whose contribution is mentioned in the text;
- Ron Denny, former deputy director, British Property Federation; John Newton, Christopher Hogg and Ross Shute at Bovis; Jeff Wild at Costain Project Management; Graham Love at Jones Lang Wootton; and David Wheater at Balfour Beatty, each of whom provided facts regarding the activities of their respective organizations;
- Nigel Bentley and the fifty firms listed in the Appendix who provided information for the survey which provided the material for the Appendix; and to Simon Ralf of Peat Marwick McClintock with whom findings of mutual interest were exchanged;
- The editors of *Architects Journal, Building, Building Design, Building Today, Chartered Builder, Chartered Quantity Surveyor, Chartered Surveyors Weekly, Contract Journal* and *Estates Gazette* who kindly published an open letter which provided many points of contact with people with similar interests and concerns whose contributions have influenced the text;
- Derek Beck, consultant to both government and private consortia on private finance iniative projects, and Robert Longley, a director of contractor James Longley, whose knowledge of private finance initiatives and partnering was invaluable;
- Roger Waterhouse at the College of Estate Management for his comments on the role of the project manager; and the editorial and production teams at Addison Wesley Longman Ltd who converted new text to its final form in record time.

Preface

In the early 1980s The Chartered Institute of Building received numerous enquiries about the proliferation of alternative contractual arrangements for the procurement of buildings. As Head of Information, Peter Harlow suggested the publication of a guide to procurement systems using as the starting point my series of articles which had recently been published in the magazine *Building Trades Journal*. The articles, which had been coordinated and provided course notes for a seminar for construction industry clients held at South Bank University in February 1984, were extended with Peter Harlow's comprehensive bibliography (abstracts) and glossary of terms to form the first edition of Building Procurement Systems which was published in 1984.

The first edition achieved a worldwide readership and was used as course notes for numerous courses. The abstracts provided countless students with material for research. The second edition, published in 1990, extended the original text in a number of respects and was twice reprinted. This, the third, edition incorporates developments which have occurred since 1990, brings up to date the bibliography and extends the glossary. It also takes into account recommendations contained in *Constructing the Team* (Latham 1994), more commonly known as *The Latham Report* insofar as the recommendations refer to the initial stages of building procurement.

Much of the text is concerned with so-called *fast-track* alternatives to the traditional client–architect–contractor selected by competitive contractual arrangement. Figure 4.1 indicates the alternative types of 'system' and some of the terms in current usage. The essence of fast-track arrangements lies in overlapping the design and construction stages as a means of reducing project time. Section 5 contains a case study of the time and cost effects of carrying out a commercial project using both traditional and fast-track contractual arrangements. Figure 5.2 demonstrates the time-saving and commercial advantages of the fast-track approach. The construction cost is shown to be £0.5 million *more* if the fast-track approach is used, yet by the end of month 24 the total project cost of the fast-track approach is almost £2 million *less* than the project which adopted the traditional contractual arrangements. In many respects this is the most significant aspect of alternative procurement systems.

The operation and characteristics of the alternative systems are discussed in Section 4, with Section 6 providing a basis for their comparison. Selecting the most appropriate procurement path is largely a matter of determining which of the client's performance requirements head the list of priorities. Other sections are concerned with the role of the client and the incidence of use of the systems (Section 7), a brief review of systems in Europe (Section 8) and clients' needs and expectations of project organizations (Appendix).

For the serious student of building procurement systems the bibliography provides an extensive source of reference.

1 Background to change

In the government-initiated report *Constructing the Team* (see Latham 1994), more commonly referred to as *The Latham Report*, Sir Michael Latham described 'formulation of a project strategy by the client' as 'the first building block to a successful and cost effective scheme'. He described the basic decision on the procurement route as difficult and suggested that '. . . *inexperienced clients need advice*'. This book provides an introduction to making 'the basic decision'.

Until the 1960s a client with a need for building works would usually commission an architect to prepare drawings identifying all requirements. These drawings would provide the basis for competitive tenders by builders for the execution of the works. It is a system that was established early in the nineteenth century and has continued. It is customarily referred to as the 'traditional system'.

Towards the end of the 1960s alternatives to the traditional system evolved. The main reasons for change were the failure of the construction industry to satisfy its clients' needs. Too many projects ran over their contract periods and cost significantly more than clients anticipated. These failures were identified by the government-sponsored Banwell Committee, which reported in 1964 (HMSO 1964). The failures were particularly troublesome on exceptionally large and complex projects. Many of the key issues identified by Banwell were still evident when the Latham Report was being prepared some thirty years later.

There had, however, been some changes. Banwell had encouraged public sector clients to use 'unorthodox methods' of appointing the contractor. At that time some 60 per cent of the construction industry's work was commissioned by central and local government. They were the industry's major clients and were in a strong position to dictate the contractual arrangements to be adopted. So, the existence of a government-commissioned report, which encouraged government departments and local authorities to consider alternative approaches to building procurement, made them less liable to charges of misconduct, failure to obtain the lowest tender, etc., etc. The relevant departments took a wider view of public accountability – a view that was concerned not just with which tender submitted in competition was the lowest but also with which contractual arrangement facilitated the optimum overall result.

The most significant catalyst was, however, the collapse of the economy of the Western world which followed the 'oil crisis'. During the period 1973–74 many of the oil-producing states combined to bring about massive increases in the price of crude oil. The outcome was immediate, with massive increases in the borrowing rate and in inflation. The economy of the Western world was in disarray – a disarray that continued for more than a decade.

The essence of almost all the alternative systems for the procurement of buildings is reducing the time taken from the client's briefing to his occupation-day by overlapping the design and the construction periods rather than going to tender with completed drawings and specifications.

The cost effect of undertaking the design stage in parallel with the construction stage is demonstrated in the case study in Section 5. Parallel working can produce significant reductions in the total cost of a project, and these reductions are particularly pronounced when interest rates are high and when obtaining a return on investment made in the project is an important feature.

The increase in public and construction industry interest in the systems was remarkable. Clients and their advisers realized that for many projects time was now the main priority. The sooner a project was completed, the less the client paid in interest on the money used to finance it and the effect of inflation was less. Most of the new 'alternative' procurement arrangements claimed to facilitate shorter project periods, making earlier occupation possible and allowing the client to obtain an earlier return on investment. The winds of change reached gale force.

The recommendations of the Latham Report most closely concerned with building procurement and the client's part in it were:

- A Construction Clients Forum should be formed with a commitment to promoting excellence.
- The Construction Industry Council should issue a guide to briefing for clients.
- The Department of the Environment should publish a construction strategy code of practice dealing with project management and tendering issues.
- A set of basic principles for forms of contract should be prepared.
- Clients should begin to use the New Engineering Contract (NEC) which has been designed to meet many of the basic principles. (The NEC has been renamed *The Engineering and Construction Contract* (ECC) and ECC is the abbreviation used below.)
- The role and duties of project managers need clearer definition.
- Tenders should be evaluated by clients on quality as well as price.
- Advice should be given on partnering arrangements.
- A productivity target of 30 per cent real cost reduction by the year 2000 should be launched.
- A Construction Contracts Bill should be introduced by the government.

Many of the recommendations have been or are in the course of being adopted.

Latham recognized that clients should be the driving force in a construction project. It is therefore important that those involved in such projects, not least the clients, should appreciate the clients' needs, expectations and role they should play.

2 The client

Strategy

A finding of the Latham Report was that clients are insufficiently prepared before they embark on building procurement. Formulation of a project strategy by the client, states Latham, is 'the first building block to a successful and cost effective scheme'.

A recommended route for a client to take is:

- that he satisfies himself of the need for a building (or refurbishment),
- that he makes an internal assessment which considers benefits, risks and financial constraints,
- that he ranks options in order of benefits and feasibility, and
- that he makes a decision in principle as to whether the project is necessary and feasible.

The Latham Report suggests that clients who are unable to undertake their own project strategy/need definition in-house should 'retain some external expert (a professional adviser), but not necessarily in the title of *project manager*. Such an adviser is there to help the client decide if the project is necessary.' If the adviser has been retained in the expectation of becoming lead consultant for the project, it places a substantial strain upon that individual to advise the client that the project is not needed at all or, if it is, that it could be a very small scheme which required no further consultant advice. Any client who wants external advice on project strategy and need definition should, then, retain an adviser on the express understanding that the role will terminate once the decision has been formulated on whether or not to proceed.

The report suggests that once the client is satisfied about real need and feasibility within overall budgetary constraints, the instinctive reaction is to retain a consultant to design the project – the 'ring up an architect/engineer' syndrome. That takes a crucial step too quickly and closes off potential procurement options.

The next step should be the use of internal risk assessment to devise a project strategy. The client should decide how much risk to accept. No construction project is risk free. Risk, however, can be managed, minimized, shared, transferred or accepted. It cannot be ignored. The client who wishes to accept

Table 2.1 Rating private sector clients' 'wants'

| | Clients | | | |
Wants	Domestic	Commercial	Industrial	Total 'stars'
Value-for-money	*****	***	****	12
Timely delivery	****	****	****	12
Pleasing to look at	****	***	***	10
Fit for purpose	****	**	***	9
Reasonable running cost	****	**	***	9

little or no risk should take different routes for procuring advice from the client who places importance on retaining detailed 'hands-on' control.

The basic decision on the procurement route should precede the preparation of the outline (project) brief, since it also necessarily affects the decision on who shall assist with the design brief. That choice of route must be determined by the nature of the project and the client's wishes regarding acceptance of risk. Such decisions are difficult, and this is where inexperienced clients need advice.

The allocation of risk between client and contractor when alternative procurement systems are used is discussed in Section 6 below.

The description of the operation of the British Property Federation system (see p. 24) has much in common with the strategy outlined above.

Needs

Clients, Latham reported, commission projects which contribute to their wider objectives. Their 'wants' from the completed building are that it:

- provides value for money
- is pleasing to look at
- is free from defects on completion
- is delivered on time
- is fit for the purpose
- is supported by worthwhile guarantees
- has reasonable running costs, and
- has satisfactory durability.

The 'type' of client influences the priorities placed on wants. A summary of the five most important 'wants' in order of priority is shown in Table 2.1. This table, adapted from Table 1 in the Latham Report, shows that domestic, commercial and industrial clients all placed high priority (four out of five stars) on 'timely delivery' – a total of twelve stars for the three client types. Equal in importance to the clients taken together was 'value-for-money' (twelve stars), but whereas this rated five stars for domestic clients it only rated three for commercial clients and four for industrial clients. None of the other wants rated more than two stars in the opinion of the commercial and industrial clients but domestic clients were more demanding. They rated 'guarantee' at four stars against only one from the other clients.

Although the table does not claim to be a scientific statement, it provides some indication of clients' priorities. Furthermore, it accords with the findings of a survey detailed in the Appendix (see Table A.4) in which 'economy' and 'time' are equal-first priorities and 'price certainty' ranks highly.

Preparations

Having satisfied himself that he has a need for a building, has made an internal assessment of benefits, risks and financial constraints, has ranked options in order of benefits and feasibility, has decided in principle that the project is necessary and feasible and has prioritized his wants, the client has then to decide whether he has the skills and resources, including time, to manage the project himself or needs to employ an independent project manager.

3 Project manager/client's representative

The role of the project manager

The findings of the survey in the Appendix (p. 56) indicate that the needs of clients in terms of contractual organization vary widely. The more experienced and knowledgeable the client, the more he tends to identify a single point of contact, i.e. a person to act as his representative, and leave that person to manage the project. For most clients that person is not an architect. The first-time client for one of the smallest projects referred to her architect as 'a great designer but lacking in management skills'. One of the largest and most sophisticated property owners in Britain even referred enquiries in connection with the survey to the company's consultant project managers.

Increasingly, clients look to a manager rather than an architect to manage their projects. This applies to large clients such as the PSA, to developers and to many of the occasional clients with some experience of building. The exceptions are local authorities and, to a lesser extent, housing associations which are bound by 'standing orders'.

The majority of clients expect to be involved in running the project during both the design and the construction stages. The extent to which they are involved, because work on site is frequently commenced before the design is completed, is difficult to ascertain. Whatever the reason for their involvement, the experience of many clients leads them to expect involvement at both design and construction stages. They may not *wish* to have involvement over such a long period but they *expect* it. Table A.2 in the Appendix indicates the extent of clients' involvement in their projects.

Project management, in itself, is not a building procurement system. A project manager may be employed as an integral member of the procurement team regardless of the procurement path taken. During the 1960s and 1970s construction projects tended to become larger and more complex. It became apparent that the time-honoured client–architect–builder relationship was sometimes inadequate as a system for constructing buildings within cost budgets and tight time schedules. There was a need for the project to be managed by a separate, distinct member of the construction team – a project manager or client's representative.

There is nothing new in the concept of a project manager. Before the end of the seventeenth century when architecture, as a profession, was established in Britain, virtually all major building projects for Church and Crown – the principal clients of the building industry – were designed by craftsmen and managed by an influential 'clerk' who was frequently known as the Clerk of Works or the Master of Works. This person was the client's representative. He held the purse-strings and had overall management of the project. The emergence of project managers for major projects in the 1960s marked the return to a system which had existed for some six hundred years in Britain.

The essence of the appointment of a project manager or client's representative is that a single person acts as surrogate client. The title 'project manager' is most generally employed but 'client's representative' is becoming increasingly used. Whichever title is used, the role is to ensure that all the client's needs are satisfied and to act as the contact point between the client and the building procurement team. It is the direct relationship between the client (whose interest the project manager represents) and the project manager that distinguishes his role from other 'managers' in the construction process who frequently have the word 'project' affixed to their 'manager' title.

The Wood Report (HMSO 1964) suggests that the project manager's prime task is one of coordinating client requirements such that clear instructions from a single source can be provided to the other parties involved. The importance of the client identifying a single person to represent his interests (before he has a firm commitment to actually build), and to assist him with drafting the brief for the project, is recognized in *Thinking about Building* (NEDO 1985), which provides a guide to the selection of the most appropriate procurement path to meet a potential client's specific needs.

A vital feature of the role of the project manager/client's representative is that he is concerned solely with managing the project. Because he is not involved in designing or constructing the building works he is able to take an objective overview of the activities of all concerned.

In 1988 the NEDO report *Faster Building for Commerce* (NEDO 1988) identified the need for the client (referred to in the report as the 'customer') to appoint a 'customer representative' with experience in working with the construction industry if his in-house project executive was insufficiently experienced. The report suggested that such a person can be found among architects, engineers, surveyors, project managers or in contracting companies with management and/or design skills as well as those of construction. Such a representative must have sufficient status and authority to act on the client's behalf in the dialogue between the client's organization and the team appointed to procure the building. There is no reason to believe that the requirements of clients for commercial buildings differ greatly from those of clients for other types of building. Indeed, the Latham Report recommended that if the client does not have 'in-house' a person capable of undertaking the role of project manager, a separate (independent) project manager should be employed.

The report's recommendations were similar to those contained in earlier reports regarding the need for the project manager's duties to be clearly

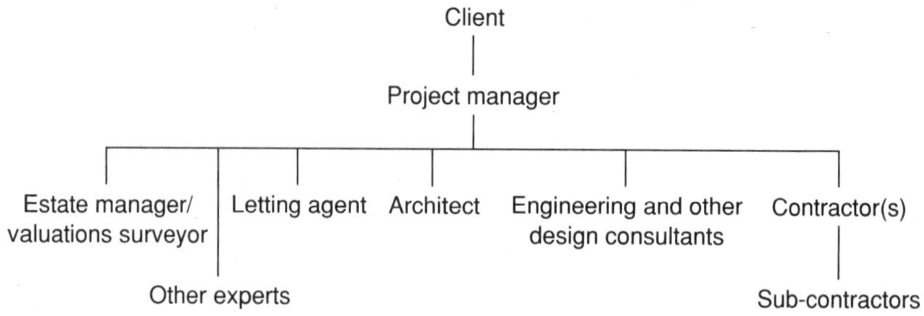

```
                              Client
                                |
                         Project manager
```

Fig. 3.1 Relationship between parties for project management systems

| Estate manager/ valuations surveyor | Letting agent | Architect | Engineering and other design consultants | Contractor(s) |

Other experts   Sub-contractors

defined. He had to produce evidence of practical experience in the industry and prove that he had the specific management skills necessary to carry out the duties.

The Engineering and Construction Contract describes the project manager's duties and authority in the clauses of the contract. The guidance notes to the ECC state that the project manager is 'the key person involved in the management of the contract'. None of the standard forms of contract precludes the employment of a project manager.

The relationship between the parties to the contract when a project manager or client's representative is employed is shown in Figure 3.1.

An indicative sequence of the project manager's activities is:

1. Coordinate the relevant experts to appraise alternative proposals, adopting that which is most appropriate, and prepare the project brief.
2. In consultation with the client, assemble the design team.
3. Decide on the most appropriate procurement path.

The composition of the expert team should be determined by the nature of the client's needs. If, for example, the aim of the project is to maximize the client's return on his investment, the project manager might well consult the letting agents or undertake extensive market research. On high-technology projects such as nuclear power stations, the appraisal might be between alternative energy sources. The magnitude of many projects requiring the engagement of a project manager is such that his task at this stage would be as 'coordinator of expertise'. He would then present the experts' collective recommendations to the client for his decision regarding the project which best suited his needs. In practice, the 'client' would more usually be the board of directors of a corporation or the council of a public authority.

When the client's needs have been fully determined the project manager may assemble the design team best suited to the specific features of the project and coordinate preparation of the project brief which provides the basis for the contract documentation. The precise role of the project manager varies with the type of procurement system.

Characteristics of a project manager

*   Project managers were used with increasing frequency and success during the 1970s and 1980s for complex and large projects.

- They were popular because of the dissatisfaction of some clients with the traditional system and its associated delays and excessive costs.
- The project manager is a 'professional', surrogate client with experience of identifying and stating the client's needs and requirements.
- A project manager will often have a professional background appropriate to the type of building to be constructed.
- The project manager is able to act as a leader who can take into account all aspects of the project – finance, feasibility, design and time – and hold a balance between them.
- The engagement of a project manager releases the client from the need to delegate a member of his staff (often a member without previous experience) to act as the intermediary between client and project team.
- The management function is separated so that the manager is able to act in an independent capacity.
- The client incurs an additional cost from the project manager's fee but this cost is offset to some extent by savings in his own 'management' involvement.
- The design and construction functions are separated so that those involved can act as partners on equal terms.
- A 'them and us' confrontation may be avoided as a result of this separation.
- Overall project planning and control which results from the engagement of the project manager ensures that both design and production are planned and coordinated to give as short an overall design and construction duration as possible.
- The architect and other consultants are released from the tasks and problems associated with managing a project, enabling them to concentrate on design matters.
- The quantity surveyor carries out cost estimating and planning and control throughout the overall project period.
- The system is able to combine the advantage of the traditional system, which is understood by most clients, with improved management methods.
- The system provides for alternative means of selecting the contractor.
- Reduction of the overall project period provides consequential cost reductions as the client is able to utilize the building, or obtain a return on his investment, more promptly.

Whether or not the client decides to employ a project manager, the building procurement systems which are available are the same and a decision must be made on that which is most appropriate for the client's needs and expectations of a specific project.

4 Procurement systems

Alternative systems, types and terms

Figure 4.1 illustrates the various systems that have evolved. The principal types of system are:

- Designer-led, competitive tender
- Designer-led, construction works managed for a fee
- Package deal
- Partnering.

Various terms have emerged to identify the systems in current use, some of which are shown in Figure 4.1. A project manager/client's representative may be employed in conjunction with any of the systems.

Standard forms of contract are used for the management of the majority of building procurement systems. In Britain, and for many building contracts undertaken by British firms overseas, the standard forms produced by the Joint Contracts Tribunal (JCT) are those most used. The JCT has published a 'family' of contract forms for use with the various procurement systems discussed below.

Reference is made on page 2 to the recommendation of the Latham Report that construction industry clients should begin to use the ECC forms which were published by the Institute of Civil Engineers in 1995.

'Architect' is the title most generally used to identify the party who acts as the designer and/or contract administrator for the client. The ECC forms refer to 'architect', 'engineer', 'supervisor' and 'project manager' when identifying the person who is responsible to the client for the conduct of the contract. The title used in the relevant form of contract stated below should be substituted for 'architect', as appropriate. The forms of contract appropriate for a particular procurement system are listed after the characteristics of the system.

Designer-led competitive tender

Because many clients for construction work initially seek someone who can express their needs in the form of a design, the designer is traditionally the

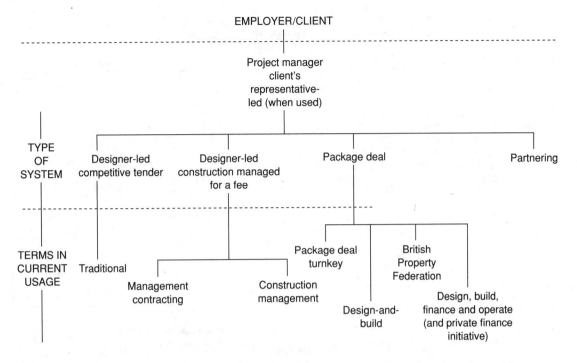

Fig. 4.1 Systems for building procurement

leader of the construction process. This 'traditional' approach provides a useful datum for consideration of the other systems available.

Traditional system

The traditional system has evolved and developed over the centuries. The role of the architect was established in more or less its present form by the end of the eighteenth century, by which time he was recognized as the independent designer of buildings and manager of the construction process.

Early in the nineteenth century bills of quantities began to be used as the means of providing a number of different contractors with a common basis for tendering. By the middle of the century the quantity surveyor was established as an independent compiler of bills of quantities and an expert in building accounts and cost matters.

There is considerable evidence, extending over several centuries, of building craftsmen acting as contractors for complete building projects embracing the work of all crafts. Nevertheless, the general contractor in his present form is frequently regarded as coming into his own at the beginning of the nineteenth century. The present traditional system, which involves the parties mentioned above, is enshrined in the Standard Form of Building Contract.

Operation

The components of the traditional approach may be seen in a simplified form in Figure 4.2. The process starts, as for all such processes, with a client having a need for a building (nodes 1–2). He briefs his architect on his needs, as he sees them, and by node 3 the cost ceiling for the project has been decided.

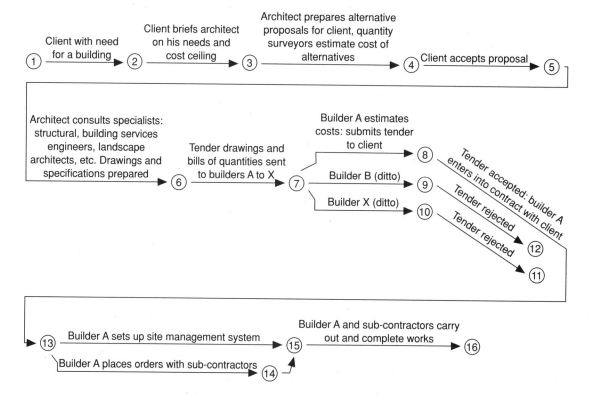

Fig. 4.2 The 'traditional' system (using Standard Form of Building Contract with quantities)

The quantity surveyor should have provided preliminary cost advice by this stage.

Between nodes 3 and 4 the architect prepares alternative drawings/proposals so that the client may select that which he prefers; the quantity surveyor estimates the cost of the alternatives.

Between nodes 4 and 5 the client accepts a proposal.

Between nodes 5 and 6 the architect develops the design of the accepted proposal. This will probably entail consultations with specialist engineers and negotiations with specialist contractors. Drawings and specifications are prepared and the quantity surveyor provides regular monitoring of the alternative designs to ensure that the cost implications of the design decisions are known to all concerned. The quantity surveyor then prepares bills of quantities.

Between nodes 6 and 7, tender drawings, bills of quantities and forms of tender are sent to selected builders (contractors) in order that they may submit tenders for the work. Beyond node 7 the builders estimate the costs of the operations involved in the project. The duration of the project is assessed from the pre-tender plan prepared by each builder's production planners and managers. Management decisions determine the margin to be added to the tender for profit.

In Figure 4.2 the tender submitted by Builder A is accepted by the client and he and the builder enter into a contract (nodes 8–13). The other tenders are rejected (nodes 9–12 and 10–11).

Between nodes 13 and 15, Builder A sets up his site management system, plans and organizes the works, schedules material deliveries, etc. Concurrently, he also places orders with his own sub-contractors and those nominated by the architect (nodes 13–14).

Between nodes 15 and 16 Builder A and the sub-contractors carry out and complete the works.

Characteristics of the system

- The system has operated in Britain, the Commonwealth and other parts of the world reasonably satisfactorily. It has stood the test of time.
- It is understood by most clients and they know their financial commitment when they accept the builder's tender, if the design has been fully developed at time of going to tender.
- The architect has considerable freedom to conceive and develop the design without excessive time or economic pressures, provided the cost ceiling is not exceeded and the client's requirements are generally satisfied.
- The project cost can be estimated, planned and monitored by the quantity surveyor from inception stage through to completion of the project.
- The system makes it possible for the architect to introduce consulting engineers, landscape architects and other experts to advise on or design 'sub-systems' of the project.
- The architect is able to consult specialist contractors and suppliers who he believes to be appropriate for the project or who manufacture and/or install components for sub-systems which would be compatible with the system as a whole at design stage, with a view to nominating them subsequently as sub-contractors or suppliers for the project.
- Sub-contractors may be invited to submit competitive tenders to the architect for the sub-system in which they specialize, thus ensuring that the most economic price is obtained.
- Drawings and bills of quantities provide a common basis for competitive tenders from selected main contractors.
- In the event of the client requiring the project to be varied during the course of construction, the bills of quantities contain prices for items of work which may be used to adjust the contract sum to take into account the variation(s).
- The design should be fully developed before bills of quantities and, subsequently, tenders are prepared. If not, excessive variations and disruption of the works are likely to occur.
- The need for the design to be fully developed before tenders are prepared leads to an 'end-on' design/build arrangement. Frequently, such an arrangement requires a longer overall project period than is necessary if both design and construction are able to proceed concurrently.
- As the length of the project period increases so does the project cost, because the client usually incurs financing charges on the sum he has

invested in land purchase, interim payments to the contractor and other members of the building team.

- Many contractors are of the opinion that their ability to organize and control the work of nominated sub-contractors is undermined by the nomination process, because such sub-contractors have less loyalty to the contractor than to the architect who nominated them.
- The separation of the design and construction processes tends to foster a 'them and us' attitude between the designers and contractors. This reduces the team spirit that experience has shown to be vital for the satisfactory conclusion of a building project.
- Lines of communication between the parties tend to be tenuous and the interests of all may suffer as a consequence.
- The traditional system has been proved to be unsatisfactory for some large and complex projects which require advanced management systems, structures and skills.

Standard forms of contract
- JCT 80 and IFC 84 may both be used with quantities and are appropriate for the traditional system.
- Standard forms of sub-contracts are used for nominated sub-contracts under JCT 80 and for named sub-contracts under IFC 84.
- The standard domestic (DOM) form of sub-contract is used with both JCT 80 and IFC 84.

The Joint Contract Tribunal's Practice Note 20 recommends the use of bills of quantities for larger and more complex projects. If a specification is used as a tender and contract document, rather than bills of quantities, omit reference to 'quantity surveyor' and to 'bills of quantities' between nodes 3 and 4 and 6 and 7 above and in Figure 4.2 and substitute 'specification' for 'bills of quantities'. If bills of quantities are not used, JCT 80 and IFC 84 forms 'without quantities' or JCT Minor Works 94 may be used.

The ECC may be used with Options A and B. If option A (fixed contract with activity schedule) is used, reference to 'quantity surveyor' and to 'bills of quantities' between nodes 3 and 4 and 6 and 7 in Figure 4.2 should be omitted. Between nodes 3 and 4 the architect or engineer prepares proposals. Between nodes 6 and 7 the competing contractors prepare a schedule of activities which provide the tender and contract documents which are priced between nodes 7 and 8, 9 and 10. The ECC sub-contract with appropriate options should be used.

If option B (priced contract with bill of quantities) is used, the operations shown in Figure 4.2 are followed. The ECC sub-contract with appropriate options should be used.

Fast-track

The term 'fast-track' has been more subject to varying definitions than others, but overlapping of design and construction as a means of reducing project time is a generally recognized characteristic of the term. This overlapping, often referred to as 'parallel working', can be achieved by using a modified version of the traditional system or by adopting a form of construction management or management contracting.

Designer-led, construction works managed for a fee

Under this heading are included the various management fee and construction management systems. There are almost as many variations on different systems as there are firms offering management services. The vast majority of the variations have one feature in common: the management contractor or construction manager offers to undertake the management of the works for a fee. He is, in effect, in much the same relationship with the client as the architect or any other consultant. The actual construction work is undertaken by specialist contractors, each of whom contracts to carry out and complete one or more of the work packages which make up the whole of the works.

Those firms who adopt the title 'management contractor' are often divisions of major construction contractor companies. Some management contractors and construction management firms are concerned solely with management contracting, having abandoned their original, traditional, contractor activities. The management contractor almost invariably employs the specialist contractors who undertake the work packages as his sub-contractors. It is the employment of the specialist contractors that typically distinguishes the management contractor from the construction manager. When a construction manager firm is employed, the specialist contractors and suppliers are generally in direct contract with the client rather than being sub-contractors to the construction manager.

A two-stage tender agreement (see glossary) is used for management contracting and for projects using a construction management approach. Some construction management firms have developed from the ranks of the consultants (rather than from contractors), and they manage the construction process as part of the team of consultants.

Operation

The process of a typical management contracting system is shown in Figure 4.3. The construction manager's role is similar to that of the management contractor but he is less likely to be appointed by competitive tender. When a construction manager is appointed the works package contractors will most usually be in direct contract with the client. For practical purposes 'construction manager' may be read for 'builder', 'contractor', and 'management contractor' in the text in this section and in Figure 4.3.

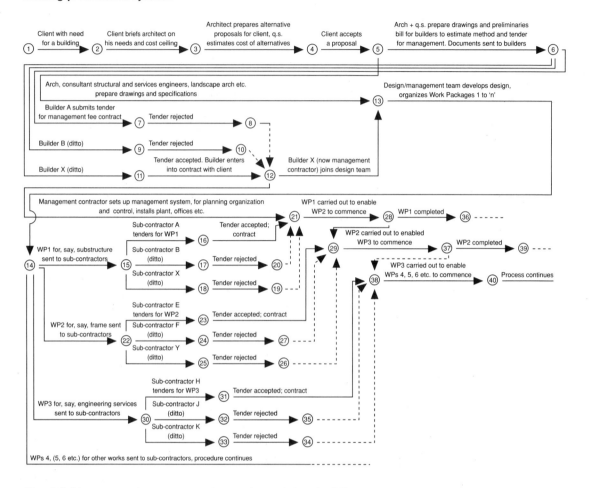

Fig. 4.3 Management (fee) contract system using two-tier tendering approach

It must be emphasized that the following 'operation' notes should be regarded as merely indicative of such systems.

Referring to Figure 4.3 it can be seen that between nodes 1 and 5 the system is similar to that of the traditional system. Between nodes 5 and 6, however, the architect and quantity surveyor concentrate on preparing drawings and a 'Preliminaries' bill of quantities in sufficient detail to enable the prospective fee contractor(s) to determine the method to be used for construction and to prepare a firm fee tender. At the same time the architect and other members of the design team develop the design generally and prepare drawings and specifications.

Beyond node 6 the contractor (or contractors if the client seeks competitive tenders) prepares the first-stage tender for the management fee. It is unusual for more than two or three contractors to be invited to tender. By the time node 12 is reached, Contractor X enters into a fee contract with the client and the other tenders are rejected. The most competitive tender is often regarded as of less importance than a credible construction programme and a sound track record.

Extensive interviews with the staff of the contractors who are tendering are usually regarded by client and design team as an essential aspect of the selection process. This ensures compatibility between design team and contractor's staff who will, if the tender is accepted, be working closely together as a design-and-management team.

Between nodes 12 and 13 the management contractor, as he has now become, joins the design team. Concurrently (nodes 12 to 21), he establishes a management system for planning, organizing and controlling the project. He installs the plant, site offices, etc.

Between nodes 12 and 13 the design-and-management team continues to develop the design and organizes a series of work packages for all aspects of the work. The work packages provide the basis for a number of contracts which are placed as soon as the necessary information is available.

Beyond node 14 the work packages are put out to tender and contracts entered into. Drawings and bills of quantities or specifications may be used as the documentation for the sub-contract tenders. It is by no means unusual to have between thirty and forty work packages, and for major projects the number of work packages may be much larger.

The works contained in the work packages are frequently commenced almost as soon as the contracts have been placed. Project completion is achieved with completion of all the work packages.

Characteristics of the system

- Management contracting has been used successfully to a limited extent since the 1920s and with increasing frequency since 1970.
- Clients and contractors often adopt the system on a regular basis once they have gained experience, which suggests that it has merits. It is generally recognized that its adoption requires mutual trust.
- Work can commence as soon as design proposals have been accepted by the client and drawings have been approved by the local authority.
- The management contractor (or construction manager) is appointed much earlier than would be possible with the traditional system. He is able to become a member of the design team and contribute his construction knowledge and management expertise.
- Management contractors (or construction managers) frequently compete at first-stage tender, ensuring that an economical fee is charged for management.
- 'Them and us' attitudes are reduced and lines of communication are improved.
- The management contractor (or construction manager) finds it easier to identify with the client's needs and interests and 'integration of the team' becomes possible and practical.
- Decisions regarding appointment of sub-contractors are made jointly (by designers and construction manager or management contractor), thus making use of wider experience.

- Specialists (or sub-contractors) compete at second-stage tender ensuring economical tenders.
- Contracts are entered into near the time of commencement of the works making firm-price tenders possible.
- Tenders submitted near the time of commencement of work are frequently more competitive than those submitted several months or even years ahead.
- When a construction manager is employed the client enters into contracts with numerous specialist contractors instead of with a general contractor, as would be the case if the traditional system were adopted. He usually has a closer involvement in the project throughout its whole life.
- Lines of communication between clients and specialist contractors are shorter than with the traditional system. Advantages which stem from this factor are:

  - the client is enabled to make prompt decisions which can be implemented without delay; it makes possible a prompt response by the client to unforeseen site problems and by the contractor to changes required by the client;
  - the cost implications of design changes can be promptly assessed and cost control for the client is thereby facilitated.

- Specialist contractors frequently prefer to be in contract with the client rather than with a management contractor because interim payments are usually made more promptly when paid direct.
- When contracts are made direct between client and specialist contractor, conditions of contract can be adopted which are appropriate to the needs of the works to be undertaken.
- The total project completion period is reduced by parallel working.
- A reduced project completion period produces a corresponding reduction in financing charges on the sum invested in land purchase, interim payments to contractors and other members of the building team. Inflation has less effect.
- The client takes delivery of the building earlier because the project completion period is reduced. He thus obtains a return on his investment more quickly.
- The client is usually given an approximate estimate of the final project cost by the quantity surveyor and/or contractor early in the project life, but he does not know the final project cost until the last sub-contract is entered into. On other projects he is given a guaranteed maximum cost.
- The architect may have less time to develop the design because he is under greater pressure from client, contractor and sub-contractors. The design may suffer as a result.
- During the 1980s and 1990s a significant number of disputes arose, particularly on construction management projects, which led some clients away from the use of this procurement system.

Standard forms of contract

- The JCT Standard Form of Management Contract, 1987 edition (MC 87), may be used for contracts between the employer (client) and management contractor.
- Works Contracts, WC/1 and WC/2, are used for contracts between the management contractor and the various works (sub-)contractors.
- The ECC forms with appropriate options may be used.
- The ECC sub-contract with appropriate options should be used.

Package deal/ design-and-build

Under this heading are included terms such as turnkey, package deal, contractor's design, design-and-build, British Property Federation (BPF), design, build, finance and operate (DBFO) systems and private finance initiatives (PFI).

The range of services offered by package deal contractors varies greatly. Some will find sites, arrange mortgages, sale-and-leaseback and similar facilities, in addition to designing and building to meet the client's requirements. Others contract to design and build a unique building on the client's own site. The feature that the systems have in common is that the 'contractor' is responsible for the whole of the design and construction of the building. As responsibilities are not split between designer and builder, the client is not involved with separate 'parties' in the event of a building failure. The systems offer 'single-point-responsibility', a feature that commends itself to clients frustrated by the traditional system.

The package deal approach is taken as far as it can go with DBFO systems, several versions of which are discussed below. Package deal contracts involve direct negotiation between client and contractor (or several contractors if the client seeks competitive tenders). The client states his requirements and the contractor prepares design and cost proposals to meet the requirements. Initially, the contractor produces only sufficient by way of design proposals to demonstrate his 'package' to the client. The design is fully developed when both parties have reached and agreement regarding specification and price.

Experience indicates that clients are frequently able to procure buildings more quickly when these contractual arrangements are adopted. Time savings tend to result in cost savings.

Design-and-build is a more refined form of package deal which obtained recognition from the Joint Contracts Tribunal in 1981 with the publication of the JCT Standard Form of Building Contract with Contractor's Design (CD 81). This recognition followed changes in British architects' codes of practice which allowed architects to become directors of construction firms. Hitherto, they were able to be salaried employees but director status had been denied. Figure 4.4 shows the stages in the operation of CD 81.

There is evidence that package deal design standards have improved as architects have taken up senior appointments in design-and-build firms or, as is by no means unusual, founded firms which are predominantly designer-led.

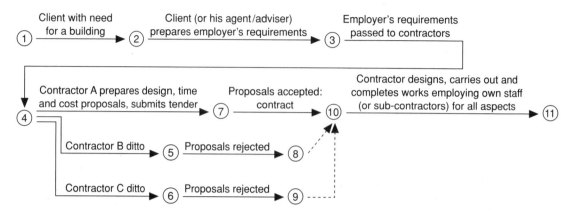

Fig. 4.4 Design-and-build system

Most types of building have been constructed using a package deal approach but industrial and office buildings in new development areas are the most typical examples of building types which are frequently built using a package deal system. Some package deals involve a type of proprietary building system. Package dealers frequently advertise their services and/or product in the pages of selected newspapers and journals that are apt to be read by people who make decisions regarding their firm's future building needs. Package deals provide buildings rather than designs and the dealer may offer to find a site in the part of the country where, for example, government grants are available to the client, in order that he has an incentive to expand his business in that area – for example, a high unemployment area.

The package dealer will usually undertake to obtain planning permission and building regulations approval.

Novation

The recession in the construction industry in the first half of the 1990s facilitated the clients' quest for the 'best' design *and* single-point responsibility. With work in short supply architects and contractors were amenable to risk-taking and contractors accepted the principles of novation even though they reduced their freedom of action and at the same time gave them increased responsibility in the event of building failure.

Novation occurs when, in the context of building procurement, the client employs consultants to design and specify the proposed building to the extent that the client's needs and intentions are clearly stated. On the basis of these drawings, specifications, etc., competitive tenders are sought and a contractor is selected. The client then *novates* his agreements with the consultants to the contractor who takes responsibility for the project to completion.

This contractual arrangement is similar to that used at Stage 5 in the British Property Federation system (see Figure 4.5).

Operation

For purposes of illustration, the contractual arrangement and terms used in CD 81 have been used. The components of the system may be seen in

Figure 4.4. It starts when the client identifies his need for a building between nodes 1 and 2, and states his requirements between nodes 3 and 4. In practice, he may ask an 'agent' to prepare his *Employer's Requirements* – the term used in CD 81. The client might employ an architect, quantity surveyor, building surveyor or similar competent person to state his requirements but such a person's task would be complete when he had prepared the statement.

The client's requirements are passed to the design-and-build contractors (nodes 3–4), each of whom prepares a design and ascertains the time it will take to carry out the works. At the same time each prepares an estimate of the cost of his 'proposals' and submits a tender (following node 4). No further details are given than are necessary for tender purposes.

The client's requirements need to be submitted only in sufficient detail to enable the contractors to ascertain needs and submit their proposals. In Figure 4.4 three contractors are shown to be submitting proposals, but it is by no means unusual for a client to negotiate with only one contractor.

In Figure 4.4 the proposals of Contractors B and C are rejected but those of Contractor A are accepted (between nodes 5 and 10). Contractor A now prepares a detailed design and carries out and completes the works employing his own staff or sub-contractors.

The contractor's proposals normally include a *Contract Sum Analysis*, which takes the place of bills of quantities. It is generally accepted that the Contract Sum Analysis should contain sufficient pricing data to enable the cost of 'changes in the Employer's Requirements' to be calculated, should changes occur.

There is provision in CD 81 for the client to nominate an 'employer's agent' whose role is to receive or issue applications, consents, instructions, notices, requests or statements or to otherwise act for the employer. This agent will probably, but not necessarily, be the person who prepared the statement of client's requirements. He has a much more restricted role than that enjoyed by the architect or supervising officer when the traditional system is used.

Characteristics of the system

- It is used increasingly as a means of managing the building process at home and abroad.
- It provides single-point-responsibility so that in the event of a building failure the contractor is solely responsible. There can be no question of 'passing the buck' between architect and builder as has so often been the case in the past. The client's interests are safeguarded in this respect.
- The client knows his total financial commitment early in the project's life, provided he does not introduce changes during the course of the works.
- The client has direct contact with the contractor. This improves lines of communication and enables the contractor to respond and to adapt more promptly to the client's needs.

- The contractor is responsible for design, construction planning, organization and control. These activities can proceed concurrently to a greater extent than is generally possible using the traditional system.
- The package dealer may provide a comprehensive package comprising site seeking and purchase, obtaining planning permission and building regulations approval, financing facilities, leasing, etc.
- The package dealer may use a proprietary building system or modular building form which reduces design time and the time required for approval of the building components.
- The client is frequently able to see examples of the package dealer's product when his proposals are being made. Most clients can visualize their needs more readily in three dimensions (by moving within and 'sampling' an actual building) than by the study of drawings and specifications. Quality, a feature which it is difficult to specify, may be more easily indicated by comparison with a sample.
- Many systems used by package dealers have been tested over a period of years and are less prone to 'teething troubles'.
- There have been some serious failures among building systems.
- The package dealer's components are often readily available so that manufacturing time is minimal and construction time may be correspondingly reduced because manufacture of components and work on site can proceed concurrently.
- Work on the building can commence as soon as local authority approvals have been obtained and sufficient information regarding the earlier site operations is available. The design does not need to be finalized before some, at least, of the work may be commenced.
- The package dealer is familiar with the construction methods to be used for his product and work proceeds more quickly.
- Some proprietary package deal products lack aesthetic appeal.
- The range of designs available from some proprietary package dealers is sometimes limited.
- Competition between the contractors' proposals should ensure economical tenders and alternative design concepts.
- The relaxation of the architects' code of practice makes it possible for them to become full partners in design-and-build firms.
- This relaxation should lead to the construction of buildings which reflect the senior status of the designer in the team and lead to more aesthetically pleasing buildings than may have been built in some instances in the past.
- The nature of the system should promote the creation of an integrated design-and-construction team.
- The closer involvement of architects in the building process should lead to designs which have a greater appreciation of construction methods; 'buildability'.

- The integrated nature of the team improves communication between designer and builder, which encourages prompt decisions.
- A prompt response is achieved in the event of materials or labour shortages.
- Design costs are built into the package but because the design input and 'detailing' required are less than when using the traditional system the costs involved are frequently less.
- There is no independent architect or similar 'professional' available to the client to advise on the technical quality of the designs at time of tender, although he is not precluded from seeking such advice if he so wishes.
- The employer's agent may supervise the works and ensure that the contractor's proposals are complied with and that the work is not skimped.
- The nature of the contract tends to reduce changes (variations) from the original design and disruption of the works is less likely to occur.
- The reduction of changes and disruption produces time and cost savings which benefit the client.
- The total project completion period is reduced.
- Time savings reduce the employer's financing charges, inflation has less effect and the building is operational sooner which, in a commercial context, produces an earlier return on the capital invested.

If the design is novated
- The client has the advantage that he is able, from the drawings and specifications prepared by the consultants, to satisfy himself that his needs and intentions are adequately expressed for tendering purposes.
- The contractors tendering for the works are provided with more detailed information on which to base their tenders.
- The contractor has less design work to carry out before tendering, so his tendering costs should be less.
- The contractor accepts responsibility for risk of building failure due to inadequate design and his increased responsibility will be reflected in his tender.
- An advantage of the design-and-build system is that the contractor has some control over the design and is able to introduce components, materials and systems with which he is familiar and which he knows are more economical to construct. The further the design has been developed at tender stage the less flexibility is available to the contractor. This may be reflected in higher tenders.
- Many of the characteristics of the BPF system, outlined below, apply to novated design-and-build contracts.

Standard forms of contract
CD 81 is intended for use on projects where the client provides the site which is the subject of the contract. Many design-and-build projects use conditions

of contract drafted for specific purposes. The diverse nature of these projects leads to correspondingly diverse conditions of contract.

- DOM forms of sub-contract may be used between contractor and the various sub-contractors.
- The ICE Design and Construct 1992 form may be used.
- The ECC forms with appropriate options may be used.
- The ECC sub-contract with appropriate options may be used.

The British Property Federation system

The British Property Federation (BPF) is a powerful client body which has recognized the importance of the client appointing a single person to represent his interests. The BPF has done much to promote the term 'client's representative'.

In November 1983 the British Property Federation published a manual of the BPF System for building design and construction. The manual comprises ninety-nine pages of which thirty-six are appendices providing schedules of responsibilities, checklists and proformae.

The manual excited considerable interest and criticism because it proposed radical changes to established procedures. Some members of the building team saw their traditional roles threatened.

The BPF system 'unashamedly puts the client's interests first'. It attempts 'to devise a more efficient and cooperative method of organising the whole building process . . . to the genuine advantage of everyone concerned in the total construction effort'. The reason for this enterprise is that 'to build in this country costs too much, takes too long and does not always produce credible results'.

The BPF represents substantial commercial property interests and thus it was able to exercise considerable influence on the building industry and its allied professions, particularly at a time when the industry was working at much less than its optimum capacity.

The BPF manual provides the definitive document and the 'operation' described below should be regarded simply as an introduction to the system. This disclaimer is significant because the manual is at pains to offer a system which can be used with various methods of contracting and one which 'although consisting of a series of precisely described steps, can be used flexibly'. In many respects the system is an amalgam of those discussed above.

The system's contribution to the building industry's output is not great. Nevertheless, the system has made a significant contribution to developing the industry's attitudes and approaches to building procurement.

Operation

The components of the system may be seen in simplified form in Figure 4.5. The process commences at node 1, when a client plans to build. BPF members

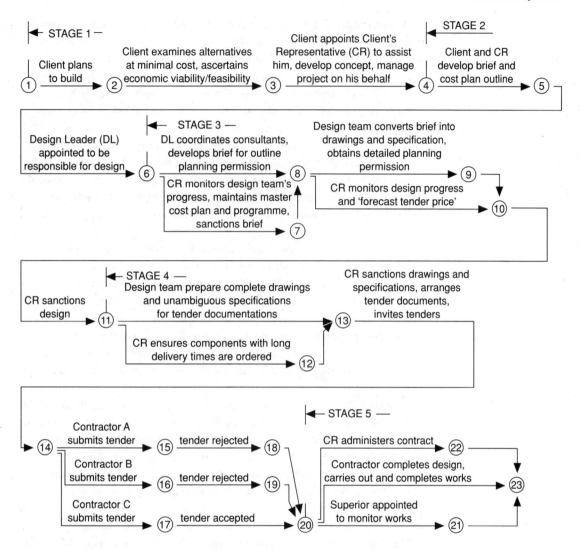

Fig. 4.5 BPF system for building design and construction

are largely 'commercial', but the Federation's system should be capable of adoption by a wider range of clients.

The manual suggests that the client should explore the many courses open to him 'at minimal cost' and appoint a 'client's representative', who is defined as 'the person or firm responsible for managing the project on behalf of and in the interests of the client'. The client's representative may be an employee of the client or an architect, chartered surveyor, engineer or project manager.

At node 3 the client appoints the client's representative whose first tasks are to help the client develop the concept and manage the project on his behalf. Obviously, the extent to which it will be necessary for the client's representative to become involved in ascertaining the economic viability and technical feasibility of the project will depend on the client's in-house skills and expertise.

Between nodes 4 and 5 the client and the client's representative develop the outline brief and the outline cost plan to the point where the client is satisfied and to the extent that the full brief may be specified. The activities between nodes 1 and 4 comprise 'Stage 1 – Concept' in the BPF manual.

Node 4 is the commencement of 'Stage 2 – Preparation of the brief'. It is possible that the 'design leader' may have been appointed in Stage 1 but, if not, he will be appointed at node 5.

The design leader is defined as 'the person or firm with *overall responsibility* for the pre-tender design and for sanctioning the contractor's design'. The design leader might be an individual, a multi-disciplinary firm, or a consultant with specialist consultants contracted to him. The words 'overall responsibility' have been printed in italics above to emphasize the 'unique' role of the design leader.

'Stage 3 – Design development', commences at node 6. Between nodes 6 and 8 the design leader coordinates consultants and develops the brief to the point where an application for outline planning permission may be obtained from the local authority. Concurrently, the client's representative monitors the design team's progress and prepares and maintains the master cost plan and the master programme. The former is 'a schedule prepared by the client's representative of the expenditure required to implement the project' and the latter is 'a schedule prepared by the client's representative of the main activities to complete the project'.

By node 8 the client's representative will 'sanction' the design leader's brief and, subject to obtaining outline planning permission, the design should progress to the point where an application for detailed planning permission may be obtained (nodes 8–9). The glossary of terms in the manual refers to 'sanction' as 'the process by which the client's representative successively agrees the work of the design team to ensure that it meets the requirements of the brief'. The contractor's design is similarly sanctioned by the design leader to ensure that it complies with the contract documents.

The client's representative continues to monitor design progress and at node 10 agrees the 'forecast tender price' which is a 'forecast made by the design leader of the likely cost of construction'. The forecast tender price forms part of the master cost plan, referred to above.

Between nodes 10 and 11, the client's representative sanctions the design as far as it has advanced at this point.

Between nodes 11, 12 and 13 the design leader and the client's representative work together towards the provision of tender documentation. The design team prepares what are referred to in the manual as 'complete drawings', but this term may be misleading if the reader is accustomed to the traditional system in which design is entirely the province of the design team. Complete drawings in the context of the BPF system means that the drawings, together with 'clear unambiguous specifications', are sufficient as a basis on which contractors might tender without 'being justified in claiming for omissions or inadequate descriptions'. The manual points out that the quality of the information will control the standard of the buildings.

Between nodes 13 and 14 the client's representative sanctions the drawings and specification, arranges tender documents and invites tenders. 'Stage 4 – Tender documents and tendering' commences at node 11 and is completed at node 20 when a tender is accepted and a contract is entered into between the client and the contractor.

There will probably be a need for clarification of sundry items by all concerned with the project, and the prospective contractor may be required to provide further information, costs, calculations, etc., before contracts are finally exchanged.

Tender documents consist of:

- invitation to tender with its appendices
- specifications
- drawings
- conditions of contract
- bills of quantities, should the client decide to use them.

The contractors' tenders are submitted to the client's representative, and the tenders should include:

- outline priced schedule of activities
- organization chart
- details of personnel
- method statement
- list of declared sub-contractors
- schedule of time charges.

The tender may also contain alternative proposals for the design and construction of the building.

'Stage 5 – Construction' is carried out between nodes 20 and 23. A particular feature of the BPF system is that the contractor 'completes the design, providing coordinated working drawings. He obtains approval of his design from statutory authorities should this be necessary and coordinates the work of statutory undertakers.' The building agreement between the client and the contractor states that the contractor's design is to be sanctioned by the design leader to ensure that it complies with the tender specification.

The client's representative administers the building contract, approves payments to the contractor, decides on the need for variations and issues instruction. It is he who decides if the services of the design leader should be retained during the construction stage (nodes 20–23). It will be appreciated that the design team tasks should have been completed by node 20; or perhaps by node 14.

A supervisor is appointed to monitor the works (nodes 20–23); his duties are detailed in the appendices in the manual. They are similar to those of a clerk of works but more comprehensive in their scope.

Characteristics of the system

- It was devised, almost unilaterally, by one party to the building contract – the client – so it lacks some of the compromises inherent in agreements devised by bodies such as the Joint Contracts Tribunal. It is concerned primarily with the client's interests.
- It is designed to produce good buildings more quickly and at lower costs than the traditional system.
- It is designed to change attitudes and alter the way in which members of the professions and contractors deal with one another, with a view to creating a fully motivated and cooperative building team and to removing as much as possible of the overlap of effort between designers, quantity surveyors and contractors, which is prevalent under the traditional system.
- It is designed to redefine risks and re-establish awareness of real costs by all members of the design and construction team and to eliminate practices which absorb unnecessary effort and time and obstruct progress towards completion.
- It provides for an independent 'client's representative' who manages the project as a whole and who is not involved as a designer or contractor. He provides single-point-responsibility for the client and by virtue of his non-involvement in details he is able to concentrate on management.
- It creates a design leader with overall responsibility for the pre-tender design and for sanctioning the contractor's design.
- The contractor's knowledge and experience of the cost implications and buildability of design variables may be utilized to good effect because he contributes to the design.
- It provides financial incentives which encourage contractors to undertake design detailing economical to construct.
- The arrangement by which the contractor undertakes detailed design should reduce 'pre-tender' time and so enable the client to have earlier occupation of the building and an earlier return on his investment. He should incur lower financing costs because of a reduction in the overall project period.
- The system makes provision for the design team and contractor to negotiate upon and alter the pre-tender design before entering into a binding contract. This should reduce variations once the works are in progress.
- There is provision for the design team to name sub-contractors and suppliers who they would require (or prefer) to be invited by the contractor to tender for part of the works. There is no provision for nominated sub-contractors as with the traditional system.

- It supports the use of specifications, rather than bills of quantities, as the basis for obtaining competitive tenders from contractors, despite the preferences of contractors and others for bills of quantities.
- The contractor is required to provide, as a tender document, a priced schedule of activities which supplants bills of quantities and may be used for managing the construction works, monitoring progress, ascertaining the amounts of payments on account to the contractor and negotiating the value of variations.
- Consultants' fees for their services are subject to negotiation rather than being determined by closely defined 'scales' as has been the custom with the traditional system.
- An adjudicator is appointed to decide impartially disputes which may arise in the implementation of the project arrangements. His task is to carry out a prompt investigation and give a decision which is implemented forthwith. There is provision for reference to arbitration 'after the taking over of the works' if the dispute cannot be resolved by the adjudicator.

Form of contract

The ACA form of building contract, BPF edition, is available for use with the BPF system.

DBFO and PFI systems

The term 'private finance initiative' (PFI), used in the context of building procurement, gained recognition in the United Kingdom in the 1980s, but PFI refers only to the procurement of government accommodation and/or facilities. It is one of several similar approaches in a 'family' which includes 'design, build, finance and operate' (DBFO), 'build, own and operate' (BOO) and 'build, own operate and transfer' (BOOT). The transfer in the last-named version refers to the transfer of the completed project to the client. There are several versions of DBFO which are listed above, but DBFO is the acronym used below when referring to this 'family' of systems.

The principle of DBFO systems is that the promoter designs, builds, finances and operates the project for the benefit of the client who is sometimes referred to as the 'purchaser' or the 'principal'. 'Client' is the word used below.

'Private' finance applies when the project is commissioned by a *public* client such as the government or a local authority, but there is no reason why the client should not be a private enterprise. The principle of DBFO systems is not new and has been adopted universally. PFIs in the United Kingdom received major boosts in 1989 and 1992 when the British government sought to involve the private sector in public projects to a greater extent than before. The government's commitment to PFI increased over the years. In 1995 the government introduced changes to regulations to facilitate PFI in the local authority sector. The description 'local authority', in this context, includes bodies such as police, fire and national park authorities.

PFIs are part of a government policy of 'privatization' which was designed to take services which are not directly concerned with government, outside the public sector. In a privatized service the private sector takes complete control subject to a system of regulation laid down by statute. Almost all risk is taken by the private sector.

Simplified, when DBFO is used the promoter provides accommodation and/or facilities (using those words in the broadest sense), together with air-conditioning, lighting, cleaning, catering, communications systems, etc., and maintaining and renewing plant and equipment as and when necessary; a complete 'service'. This releases the client from accommodation problems and enables it to concentrate on its proper 'business' of government, commerce, manufacturing, etc., as the case may be.

In the context of construction industry projects, DBFO is concerned with providing the client with performance-specified accommodation facilities for a given period of time rather than with providing a building which will be the property of the client. Providing the client with a service which gives value for money is at the centre of PFI, in particular, and of other DBFO systems generally.

Authoritative explanatory notes and essential guides have been published on PFI and HM Treasury has published a series of documents concerned with progressing PFI, sharing of risk and structuring of PFI contracts, writing an output specification, the part of PFI in government accommodation, etc. (The Bibliography refers.) The following notes on the operation of DBFO systems do nothing more than provide an introduction to a complex and evolving approach to building procurement.

Operation

An indicative flow chart, derived from various models, is shown in Figure 4.6. Between nodes 1 and 2 the client identifies its needs for accommodation and/or facilities. It should at this stage consider the type of service it needs, its social benefits and the respective parts to be played by client and promoter organizations.

The cost of preparing a tender for a DBFO project is high, so between nodes 2 and 3 the client invites a small number of prospective promoters to pre-qualify. The invitation may outline the scope of the project, its location, programme, concession period, etc. The client may ask the promoter to provide, in order to pre-qualify, information on the organizations which would comprise the promoter, sources of finance, past work, present workload and resources generally.

Between nodes 3 and 4 the client prepares a concession agreement which identifies risks, rewards and responsibilities. It also includes the legal agreement and project conditions which cover construction, operation and maintenance, finance and revenue generation packages.

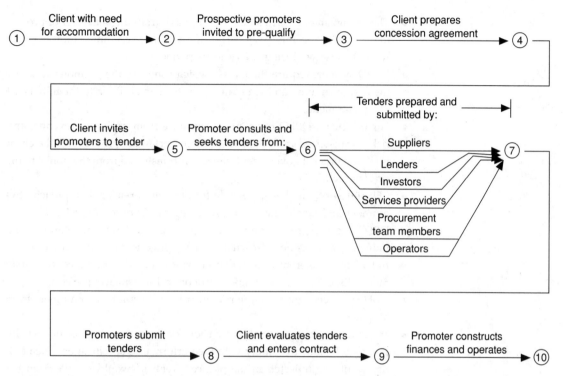

Fig. 4.6 Design, build, finance and operate

Between nodes 4 and 5 the promoters are invited to tender. The documentation should include the concession agreement, instructions to tenderers, criteria for award and arrangement for transferring risk from client to promoter. Each promoter comprises a number of specialist organizations which contribute to the tender, and between nodes 5 and 6 the promoter consults with appropriate organizations. Their individual contributions are assessed and coordinated into the promoters' tenders (nodes 7–8).

The client then evaluates the tenders and, between nodes 8 and 9, enters into contract with a promoter which constructs, operates and finances the project (nodes 9–10). Experience suggests that evaluating the tender is the most time-consuming stage. The time between nodes 1 and 9 may be measured in months or years.

Characteristics of the system

- Many of the characteristics of the package deal systems outlined above (pp. 19–24) are those of DBFO systems. DBFO is the ultimate form of package deal.
- All DBFO systems require fundamental changes in the approach of client and the parties which comprise the promoter. The change is from the procurement of a building to the provision of accommodation and/or facilities to predetermined standards for a period of time – typically, a span of years.

- The change in approach shifts the emphasis from the *initial cost* of procuring a building to the *life-cycle cost* of providing accommodation together with all services during the contract period.
- DBFO systems require the parties which comprise the promoter to know the cost of running and maintaining systems in addition to the initial cost of procurement.
- For the client, DBFO transfers expenditure from capital to revenue, and risk is transferred from the client (purchaser) to the promoter. If the client is central or local government, the risk is transferred from the public to the private sector.
- PFI philosophy makes it possible for any entrepreneur to approach government and take initiative in proposing provision of a service.
- DBFO projects provide an increasingly large market for the construction industry which is not restricted to major projects, but legal and administrative costs inherent in negotiation prior to entering into a contract may make DBFO and PFI systems uneconomical for smaller projects.
- DBFO projects require long-term rather than short-term commitment from all parties.
- Many DBFO contracts make provision for the promoter to incur 'penalty points' if he fails to comply with the performance specification. Such failure would be reflected in the reduced 'rent' he would receive from the client until the failure is remedied.
- The traditional construction team – engineers, architects, contractors, etc. – are employed by the promoter not the client.
- The quality of 'architecture' may suffer as emphasis is on the provision of accommodation rather than provision of a building, but Town Planning regulations should provide a safeguard against poor design.

Forms of contract

The nature of DBFOs tends to preclude standard forms of contract, but HM Treasury publications provide guidelines in *Basic Contractual* Terms for PFIs. Many of the standard forms of construction contract, sometimes with modifications, may be used for contracts between the parties which comprise the promoter.

Partnering

The Latham Report recommended that 'specific advice should be given to public authorities so that they could experiment with partnering arrangements where appropriate long-term relationships can be built-up'. This was an endorsement of the earlier Banwell Report which approved 'serial contracting' or 'negotiation', both of which had much in common with 'partnering'.

Partnering is a contractual arrangement between two parties for either a specific length of time or for an indefinite period. The parties agree to work together, in a relationship of trust, to achieve specific primary objectives by maximizing the effectiveness of each participant's resources and expertise. It is not limited to a particular project.

Partnering is not a new concept but it is an approach which has not achieved wide acceptance in the United Kingdom. In the context of construction proced-ure the partners might be the client, design team, principal contractors, spe-cialist contractors (including sub-contractors) and leading suppliers. Objectives might include improved quality standards, reduced project delivery time, reduc-tion in incidence of accidents and claims, projects completed within budget, streamlining administrative procedures and maximizing value engineering potential.

Any partner may initiate a partnering arrangement, but experience of suc-cessful working with the prospective partners on previous projects should improve future prospects of successful partnering. In practice the client is most likely to be the initiator. A firm contemplating partnering should, before making an approach to other partners, prepare its own personnel for the change. People with experience of successful partnering suggest that partnering differs from a simple legal partnership agreement in that partnering requires 'business culture adjustments' by all partners to achieve common beliefs, values and norms, shared assumptions and similar expectations. Initiatives should come from 'top management' who must have a commitment to the prospect of partnership.

Education should include all personnel in the organization and the inten-tions of top management should be established at an early stage. The commit-ment should be shared at all levels in the organization. Workshops should involve all key players.

Operation

The sequence of events may be seen in abbreviated form in Figure 4.7. Having ascertained interest in the concept of partnering from others, the prospective partners (nodes 1, 2, 3, 4, 5 and 6) aim to create a viable partnership.

Between nodes 6 and 7 the partners, jointly, determine mutual objectives, goals and equity interests at top management level. Between nodes 7 and 8 the partnership 'charter' is created. This may include objectives similar to those suggested above. Publication of the charter may be marked with a cere-mony to emphasize the significance of the charter to the partnership.

Development of trust among the newly formed team between nodes 8 and 9 might be fostered through joint 'workshops' at which a training programme is devised for joint education and training at all levels (nodes 9–10). Strategies will be implemented and tested and problem-solving and dispute resolution mechanisms introduced between nodes 10 and 11.

Joint evaluation processes will be developed and milestones or benchmarks put in place at all management levels in the organization to facilitate joint interim evaluations (nodes 11–12). The final evaluation (nodes 12–13) might mark the completion of a specific project and provide data for future benchmarks.

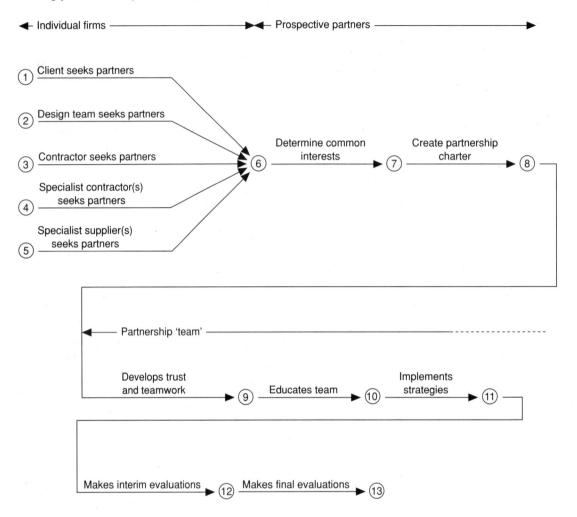

Fig. 4.7 Partnering

Characteristics of the system

- Partnering has had a well-established success in Japan, the USA and Australia and has been operated on some projects in the United Kingdom.
- The Latham Report created a favourable business climate for partnering.
- Partnering depends for success more on cultivation of receptive attitudes of mind and willingness to succeed than on legally enforceable conditions of contract in a partnership agreement.
- Partnering requires an 'open-book' approach.
- When setting up a partnership charter the partners should take care to avoid agreements which are contrary to EU regulations. Such regulations are concerned with long-term agreements which run contrary to the spirit of competition. The avoidance of collusion between designers and individual suppliers resulting from specification of materials available from a single supplier, so that that supplier is automatically awarded the con-

tract, provides an example of 'running contrary to the spirit of competition'. Non-exclusive relationships should be avoided.

- Experience from successful partnering arrangements demonstrates that cost savings in excess of 25 per cent are available and that innovation is more easily obtained when the parties work in partnership.
- Exposure to litigation and time and cost over-runs should be reduced.
- Quality management, value engineering and efficient problem resolution are simplified.
- Provision should be made to ensure that mechanisms are in place to share the burden of cost and time increases caused by changes.
- Lawyers have expressed doubts as to the feasibility of agreements based entirely on 'mutual trust'. It has been suggested that it is essential to identify targets for all the personnel before commencement.
- Prompt payment of all parties is an important ingredient of successful partnering.
- Every effort should be made to foresee and forestall problems and disputes and to deal with them at the lowest level.
- Partnership will not succeed if there is no provision for the partners to make a profit.

Forms of contract

No standard forms of contract have been published by ECC or JCT.

5 Project time–cost relationships

This publication contains numerous references to the time and cost advantages of various systems for the procurement of buildings, and this section aims to illustrate the extent of the relationship of time to cost.

The report *Faster Building for Industry* (NEDO 1983) states that the traditional methods of design and tendering can give good construction times but, on average, the use of non-traditional routes tends to produce overall times shorter than those produced by the traditional routes. Figure 5.1 provides a 'pre-construction timetable' which demonstrates the relative times of the options.

From this figure 5.1 it may be seen that the use of a negotiated contract enables construction work to commence some seven months earlier than would be possible with the 'end-to-end' traditional system. It is reasonable to assume that whichever approach is used for the design, the construction periods will not differ significantly so that the total project period will be reduced if one of the non-traditional or 'fast-track' approaches is used. What effect does this have on the project cost?

Case study

The following case study relates to a commercial project in a city centre, and illustrates the relationship between time and cost.

Figure 5.2 shows alternative expenditure plans for the project assuming use of (a) the traditional system and (b) a 'fast-track' approach. The data have been provided by a client body specializing in such projects. Some of the data cannot be more than indicative but the study provides a reasonably reliable basis for cost comparison.

Figure 5.2(a), the expenditure plan for the traditional system, shows an estimated design period prior to commencement of construction of 12 months. Some design will continue for a period of 3 months after construction commences. Construction will take 12 months. The total project period is 24 months. Figure 5.2(b), the fast-track expenditure plan, shows design and construction periods which are similar to those required for the traditional system. The total project period is 15 months.

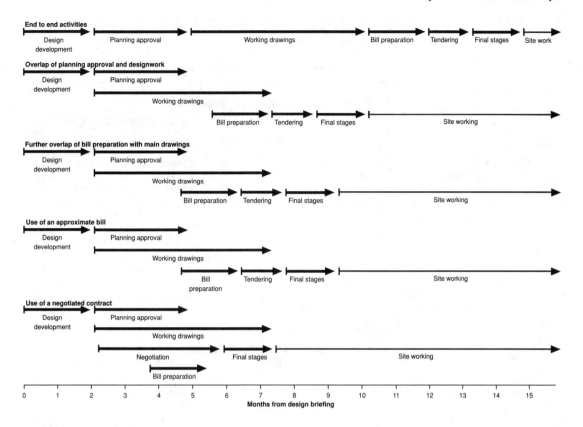

Fig. 5.1 The preconstruction timetable (source: *Faster Building for Industry*, NEDO, HMSO, 1983)

The cost of the elements which comprise the project (site, design, construction, etc.) are shown in the expenditure plans. Site acquisition cost (the property itself and associated fees) and design cost are the same for both alternatives.

The construction cost shown in Figure 5.2(b) is estimated at £0.5 million more than that required when the traditional system is used. That sum may be regarded as an allowance for the additional cost of construction management, accelerated progress, less competitive tendering and similar factors. Some contractors question if the cost of construction is, in practice, higher where a fast-track approach is used.

A significant factor in the cost comparison is the timing of expenditure and the associated financing costs. The design team is to be paid as the design is developed. The contractor is to be paid monthly on the basis of the value of work executed. Financing charges follow those payments. For purposes of the case study an interest rate of 12 per cent p.a. has been used. Charges have been calculated quarterly.

To demonstrate the advantage of early completion on a commercial project Figure 5.2(b) shows a rental income for the period between the estimated completion date using a fast-track approach and the estimated completion date using the traditional system, namely, 9 months.

	Cost (£'000)	Cost (£'000)							
	Cost (£'000)	3 months	6 months	9 months	12 months	15 months	18 months	21 months	24 months
Site acquisition	6000	6000							
Design	1200	250	250	250	250	200			
Construction	10000					2500	3000	3000	1500
Quarterly total		6250	250	250	250	2700	3000	3000	1500
Cumulative total		6250	6680	7123	7579	10499	13733	17055	18977
Financing cost (quarterly)		180	193	206	220	234	322	422	524
Totals	17200	6430	6873	7329	7799	10733	14055	17477	19501

(a) Expenditure plan – traditional system

	Cost (£'000)	Cost (£'000)							
	Cost (£'000)	3 months	6 months	9 months	12 months	15 months	18 months	21 months	24 months
Site acquisition	6000	6000							
Design	1200	300	300	300	150	150			
Construction	10500		3000	3000	3000	1500			
Quarterly total		6300	3300	3300	3150	1650			
Cumulative total		6300	9780	13274	16723	18780			
Financing cost (quarterly)		180	194	299	407	514			
Rental income (£2.3m p.a.)							(575)	(575)	(575)
Totals	17700	6480	9974	13573	17130	19294	18719	18144	17569

(b) Expenditure plan – fast-track approach ▇ peak activity ▇ some activity

Fig. 5.2 Time–cost case study for commercial project

It may be seen that although the construction cost of the fast-track approach is shown as £0.5 million more than that of the traditional system, at the end of the two-year period, when the traditional system would produce a completed building, the fast-track approach shows a saving of £2 million over the traditional system.

In practice, the rent would not be shown as coming back as a saving. A trader developer would sell the development and so accrue a profit, whereas an investment developer would renegotiate medium-term finance, say 25 years (similar to a mortgage), so that construction finance could be paid off and, from the rent derived, he would be able to pay the interest on his medium-term finance.

The other benefit to a developer is that by the building being completed sooner it can be valued as a complete development and shown in his accounts as an asset against which he can borrow further money to carry out further developments and grow more quickly.

6 Comparison of procurement systems

It should be emphasized that the systems as described are subject to great variation.

Client's needs

The first component in each of the figures which has been used to illustrate the systems has read: 'client with need for a building' and the following assessments are concerned with that need. The client's viewpoint has been adopted for purposes of the comparison which follows.

The first comparison of the alternative systems should be made when the client decides the extent to which he is prepared to take risk – at the time when he is making fundamental decisions such as whether or not to build and when assessing benefits and risks.

The Latham Report contains a table which identifies four types of risk:

- fundamental – war damage, nuclear pollution, etc.
- pure – fire damage, storm
- particular – collapse, subsidence, vibration, removal of support
- speculative – ground conditions, inflation, weather, shortages and taxes.

The table suggests that package deal/design-and-build systems provide the client with minimal risk. Traditional projects offer rather more risk for the client but management contracting and construction management projects place virtually all the risk with him.

The above allocations of risk should, however, be regarded with reservations. The package deal/design-and-build systems and the traditional system, for example, provide minimal risk for the client only if the works are not varied after contracts have been placed.

Once the decision to proceed or not to proceed with the project has been made, selecting the most appropriate procurement path is largely a matter of determining which performance requirements head the client's list of priorities. These might include:

(a) technical complexity

(b) aesthetics/prestige

(c) economy

(d) time

(e) exceptional size or complexity involving input from numerous sources and/or to satisfy the requirements of several users

(f) price certainty at an early stage in the project's design development

(g) facility for the client to change/vary the works during the project's construction stage.

In Table 6.1 each of the requirements listed above, together with risk, is rated insofar as it is able to satisfy the requirement. Ratings have been given on a

Table 6.1 Rating the systems

Client's performance requirements/expectations	Traditional	Management contracting/ construction management	Package deal/ design-and-build
* Minimum risk	4	1	5
(a) Technical complexity: the project has a high level of structural, mechanical services or other complexity	4	5	4
(b) High aesthetic or prestige requirements	5	3	3
(c) Economy: a commercial or industrial project or project where minimum cost is required	3	4	4
(d) Time is of essence: early completion of the project is required	2	4	5
(e) Exceptional size and/or administrative complexity: involving varying client's/user requirements, political sensitivity, etc.	2	4	4
(f) Price certainty: is required at an early stage in the project's design development	4	2	4
(g) Facility for change/variation control by client, users or others during the progress of the works	5	5	1

1 to 5 scale, with 1 the minimum and 5 the maximum capacity to meet the requirement. The ratings are the author's assessments of 'satisfaction'. It is assumed that the competence of the personnel involved is similar in all instances – only the systems are being compared. The following comparisons do not take into account all the characteristics of the systems that have been discussed.

Risk, the initial decision

As risk is assessed earlier than the other requirements it should be considered separately. The highest rating, 5, is given to the package-deal/design-and-build system when 'least risk' is the client's requirement. Almost as safe is the traditional system. Management contracting, with a rating of 1, is the least attractive system for the client seeking freedom from risk. The other performance requirements may be compared system by system.

Traditional The traditional system rates 4 for projects with high technical complexity and/or with high aesthetic standards because the design team is not submitted to pressure, provided the design is essentially complete before competitive tenders are sought. In this event the team is able to develop the design rationally. It is the system which has provided the majority of designs in the past.

Competitive tenders ensure that the client obtains the benefit of the lowest building cost. The system should produce a high rating for economy but the rating is reduced because the need to complete the design before commencing construction extends the overall project period. The interest paid by the client on the capital invested during the relatively long project period adds to the total cost of the project.

The sequential nature of the system and the experience gained by a significant number of clients of poor performance on exceptionally large or complex projects has prompted the low ratings for performance requirements (d) and (e).

Price certainty should be capable of achievement provided the project has been fully designed and documented before tenders are sought. Priced bills of quantities facilitate the measurement and valuation of variations during the progress of the works; hence the high ratings for requirements (f) and (g).

Management for a fee A rating of 5 has been given to requirement (a) because involvement of the construction team at an early stage in the development of the design should facilitate design of complex structures, mechanical services and other elements. The system would not appear to offer advantages for requirement (b) and a median rating has been given.

Ratings of 4 have been given for performance requirements (c) and (d) because competition between management contractors, initially, and work-package contractors subsequently, produce competition for building works. Because design and construction proceed in parallel, the project period is kept to a minimum.

The participation of the management contractor as a member of the 'team', rather than as an outsider, makes the system more satisfactory for exceptionally large or complex projects than the traditional system; hence the 4 rating for (e).

Price certainty at an early stage in the project's development is not possible because the cost of building is not known until tenders have been accepted for all work packages. A correspondingly low rating has been given to requirement (f). The client is normally provided with reasonably reliable estimates of the cost of the work packages by the consultant quantity surveyor as the design and construction develops.

A characteristic of these systems is parallel working. This makes it possible to vary the works until the work packages have been placed. Requirement (g) has been given a correspondingly high rating. The advantages of these systems increase with the size of the project and the extent to which time becomes the essence of the contract.

Package deal/ design-and-build

Performance requirements (a) and (c) have been given ratings of 4. The involvement of designers with constructors (builders/contractors) on a team basis from the inception stage of the project should produce the expertise to cope with any technical complexity the project may present. The result should be 'buildability' – an unattractive word describing a necessary characteristic of any construction project that is to succeed. Economy should be achieved because the team is concerned not just with producing a design but with building to a budget. The discipline of designing and building should ensure that, at the design stage, materials and components are selected which are economical and available. These remarks about economy apply also to time. Components or building systems can be designed into the proposed building, which will ensure that construction time is kept to a minimum. As the team has both design and construction organization and control under one roof it can arrange that drawings and specifications are available as and when they are required to ensure that the regular progress of the works is not disrupted. Design and construction progress concurrently, not consecutively, which minimizes total project time. Ratings of 4 may be less than generous for these performance requirements, as may 3 for requirement (b). A rating of 5 has been given to requirement (d).

Package deal systems are used for large and complex projects such as nuclear power plants and petro-chemical developments. For projects of exceptional size or complexity the system should, therefore, be appropriate provided the 'contractor' ensures that a member of the firm who has the managerial expertise is appointed to 'stand outside' the day-to-day activities and hold a balance between design and construction interests. A high, but not the highest, rating has been given to this system in this respect because it is likely that not all firms would have the level of managerial expertise necessary to undertake projects of exceptional size or complexity.

A rating of 4 has been given to requirement (f), price certainty, because the price is normally agreed on the basis of the client's requirements. Provided the requirements are not changed after the contractor has submitted his proposals the price should hold. From this it follows, however, that there is little facility for cost control of changes during the progress of the works. This is reflected by the rating of 1 for requirement (g).

Conclusions

When making comparisons it is essential to compare 'like with like'. For this reason it is difficult to make valid comparisons of the alternative systems. Each system has been developed to meet particular client needs. There is no universal system. If one seeks the system which best meets the client's performance requirements in broad terms, the ratings discussed above provide a guide for ranking.

Tests of the validity of awarding scores to the performance requirements suggests that the most reliable approach is to rating only, say, the three performance requirements which the client considers to be the most significant. If, for example, the client sought the system which would provide a building with maximum economy (c), with time of essence (d), and with price certainty at an early state in the project's design development (f), one might rate the systems as follows:

		Traditional	Management contracting	Design-and-build
(c)	Economy	3	4	4
(d)	Time	2	4	5
(f)	Price certainty	4	2	4
		9	10	13

Thus the design-and-build system appears to be the most appropriate procurement path. But if one takes as an example economy, time of essence and a facility to change the works during the progress of the works, one might score the systems as:

		Traditional	Management contracting	Design-and-build
(c)	Economy	3	4	4
(d)	Time	2	4	5
(g)	Change facility	5	5	1
		10	13	10

where the management contracting system appears to be the best option for the client.

To illustrate the method of rating, a less hypothetical project for a housing association, registered as a charity which provides homes for the elderly, may be used. The association requires an 'advanced care unit' to meet the needs of residents from its various homes who will undergo treatment as short-stay or out-patients. Operating theatres and specialist equipment will be required. The estimated cost of the unit is between £1m and £1.5m and it will be funded by the sale of investments and from a legacy. Outline planning approval has been given for the unit to be built in the spacious grounds of one of the association's homes which is listed as a building of architectural interest in a conservation area. An experienced member of the association's board of management will give his time, freely, to act as client's representative.

Which of the client's performance requirements should be given priority?

The association requires a building which will satisfy aesthetic standards associated with a listed building and which are consistent with a conservation area (requirement (b)). The association may also wish to retain the facility to vary the works during their progress as medical technology for the elderly develops (requirement (g)).

The association owns the site so it will not incur site purchase costs, nor will it incur interest charges on the cash required to purchase the site. Time is not a priority (requirement (d)).

Requirement (e), exceptional size and/or administrative complexity, is not relevant and the ratings indicate that a traditional approach should be the most appropriate for this project.

Having compared the relative advantages and disadvantages of the alternative procurement systems it is appropriate to consider the extent to which they are used in practice.

7 Incidence of use

The survey of clients' needs and expectations in the Appendix demonstrates that the majority of clients in the sample expected to be involved in the project during both the design and the construction stages of the project's life. All 'developer' clients were involved through their in-house project managers but, with the exception of the local authority clients, between 75 and 90 per cent of other clients expected to be involved in the project during both the design and the construction stages. The nature of their involvement varied significantly.

Clients' 'professional' representation

Taken as a whole, 54 per cent of the clients had within their own organizations a person (or persons) who acted as the focal point through which the corporate requirements passed to the building team. Such a person most frequently held the title 'project manager', 'project coordinator' or similar. The title 'client's representative' seldom occurred.

An analysis of the sample showed the point of contact between clients and the building teams in the various client groups (see Table 7.1, reproduced from the Appendix). The table shows that 60 per cent of the Group A ('occasional') clients employed in-house project managers, but this may be a misleading statistic because a disproportionate number of the clients in the sample are major commercial firms and public service bodies. A sample containing smaller projects for clients who commissioned building works infrequently

Table 7.1 Client contact with building team

Group	In-house project manager (%)	Consultant project manager (%)	Architect (%)
A: Occasional	60	8	32
B: Developers	98	2	–
C: Housing	25	–	75
D: Local authority	–	–	100
E: Health care	50	–	50

would almost certainly show greater employment of an architect as the leader of the team. With only one or two exceptions, clients who commission building works infrequently and whose works are typically less than £3m for each project, tended to employ an architect to design and manage the works in the traditional manner.

All but one of the developers (Group B) employed in-house project managers; a major firm of project managers provided management services for the client who did not.

The samples in Groups C, D and E were too small to be statistically representative but they are believed to give a reliable indication of the contact between the client and the building team. Housing associations and local authorities tended to employ architects either in-house or as consultants to act in the traditional manner.

Health authority projects tended to be larger and more complex and project managers were more in evidence. The majority of clients, approximately 80 per cent of the sample, decided on the contractual arrangement, often in consultation with the construction team.

Clients for smaller projects tended to rely on the architect and quantity surveyor to decide on the contractual arrangements to be used for procurement of their works. The clients' observations on their experiences of building projects, on their own failings and on the failings of others in the teams were recorded in the survey and are included in the Appendix.

Procurement systems

The RICS surveys of standard forms of contract in use provide a comprehensive guide to the incidence of use of the alternative procurement systems. The first survey was made in 1984 and subsequent surveys have been made biennially. The surveys use data provided by quantity surveying practices. The RICS has recognized that quantity surveyors' offices are not necessarily involved in all non-traditional forms of contract, from which it follows that the non-traditional systems may be more widely used than the following figures and tables would indicate. The surveys do not include speculative house building.

The illustrations and tables are prepared from the writer's interpretation of the data contained in the RICS reports. Figure 7.1 provides a basis for comparing the rise and fall in the use of the systems between 1984 and 1995. It shows the incidence of use of alternative systems expressed as percentages of the total value of work carried out in Great Britain in the years when the surveys were carried out.

Traditional system Until 1984 when the first RICS survey was conducted, the majority of building work, probably more than 80 per cent, was carried out using the traditional

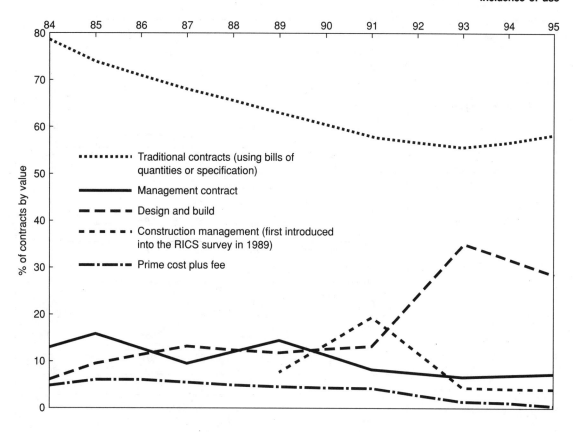

Fig. 7.1 Alternative methods of procurement (percentage by value of work)

system. Between 1984 and 1993 the use of the traditional system declined from 78 to 57 per cent. The slight increase in use of the system between 1993 and 1995 coincides with the increasing severity of the recession which commenced in the early 1990s.

Management contracting

Before the 1980s few clients procured buildings using management contracting forms of contract. Demand for management contracting increased from a very low base until 1985 when it represented 15 per cent of the value of work carried out. Demand appears to have declined to 9 per cent in 1987 and recovered to 14 per cent by 1989, but has again declined to 7 per cent in 1995.

The decline in demand commenced before the recession of the early 1990s, but the decrease in demand for this procurement system coincides with an increased in demand for the use of the construction management system.

Table 7.2 and Figure 7.2 demonstrate the massive decline in the number of projects in the 'less than £0.5m' size range. The number of projects in the other size ranges has, however (with a blip in the £3m–£10m size range), been reasonably steady. The blip marked the beginning of the decline in popularity of management contracts.

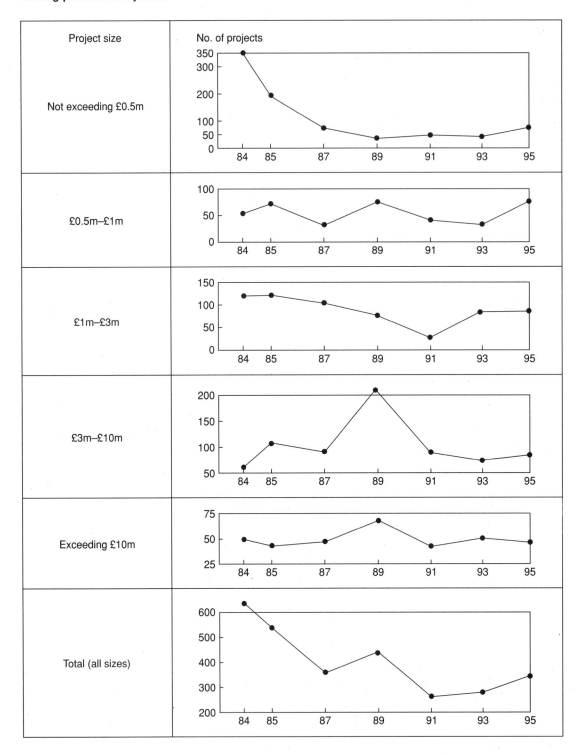

Fig. 7.2 Management contracts (by size and number)

Table 7.2 Management contracts (by size and number)

Year	Contract size (£m)/No. of contracts					
	<£0.5	£0.5–£1	£1–£3	£3–£10	£10+	Total
1984	350	50	125	63	50	638
1985	200	67	126	111	44	548
1987	69	28	110	97	48	352
1989	31	63	83	208	63	448
1991	50	40	40	90	40	260
1993	33	25	82	75	50	267
1995	55	75	89	82	48	349

Table 7.3 Construction management (by size and number)

Year	Contract size (£m)/No. of contracts					
	<£0.5	£0.5–£1	£1–£3	£3–£10	£10+	Total
1989	–	–	–	52	21	73
1991	10	–	20	–	20	50
1993	33	8	50	8	17	116
1995	219	48	55	62	14	398

An examination of Figures 7.1 and 7.2 demonstrates that the decline in number of projects and percentage of contracts by value have similar profiles.

Construction management

Construction management did not enter the RICS surveys until 1989. Before that year the construction management system was little used but there is no record of the incidence of use.

Figure 7.1 shows that from an 8 per cent of total value of work in 1989, construction management increased its market share to 19 per cent in two years. Its popularity was, however, short-lived and by 1993 construction management represented only 4 per cent total value.

Table 7.3 and Figure 7.3 show that between 1989 and 1995 the number of projects using construction management systems increased significantly in the smaller size ranges (between £0.5m and £3m), but despite this numerical increase the annual value of management contracting projects, as a percentage of the total value of projects, was constant between 1993 and 1995 at approximately 4 per cent of the total value.

Design-and-build

This grew from a base of 5 per cent of total value of work in 1984 to 12 per cent by 1987. For the next four years design-and-build output continued at

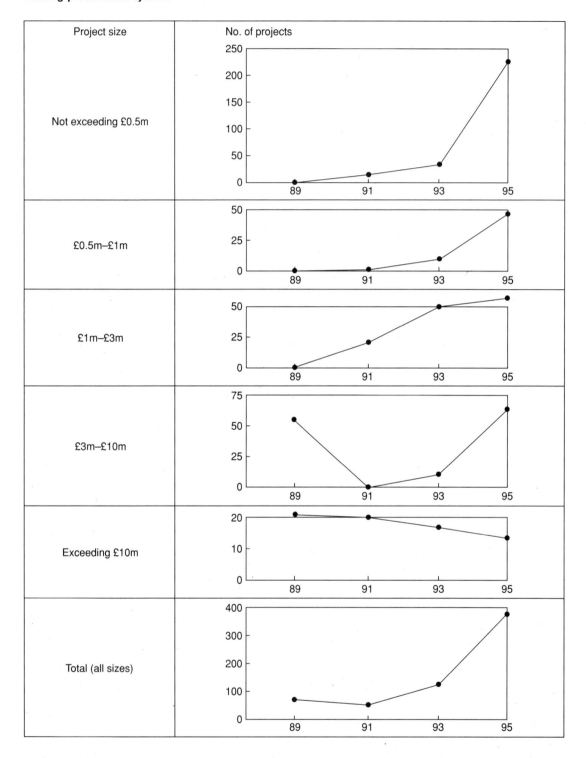

Fig. 7.3 Construction management (by size and number)

Table 7.4 Design-and-build (by contract size and number)

| Year | Contract size (£m)/No. of contracts | | | | | |
	<£0.5	£0.5–£1	£1–£3	£3–£10	£10+	Total
1984	544	169	106	38	0	857
1985	569	251	207	104	17	1148
1987	311	255	311	117	35	1029
1989	542	354	469	229	21	1615
1991	2110	400	460	110	50	3130
1993	1542	1033	1292	417	125	4409
1995	1267	897	1062	349	103	3678

approximately 12 per cent until, in 1991, the system increased in popularity and, in 1993, approximately 35 per cent of total value of work was carried out using one of the variations of design-and-build systems. The increase was gained from the traditional system's share of the market, but during the period 1993–1995 the traditional system appears to have regained much of the ground it had lost.

Table 7.4 and Figure 7.4 show that the profiles for all design-and-build project sizes are similar – a steady rise until 1993 followed by a slight decline.

Predictions in 1990 indicated that design-and-build procurement approaches might be used for 50 per cent of building work by the end of the century, but as the decade progressed that prediction appears to have been an overestimate.

Prime-cost plus fee   Figure 7.1 shows that this form of procurement has a small part to play but that its use is in decline.

Summary

This section has concentrated on the alternatives rather than the traditional system but this does not mean that the alternatives have supplanted the traditional.

NEDO surveys for the reports on building for industry and commerce found that, in 1982, 43 per cent of the industrial projects and, in 1986, 70 per cent of the commercial projects were carried out using traditional arrangements.

Only passing reference has been made to the use of the BPF system. The contribution of this system to the industry's attitudes and approaches to building procurement is acknowledged, but the incidence of use is negligible. Statistically, its contribution has been insignificant.

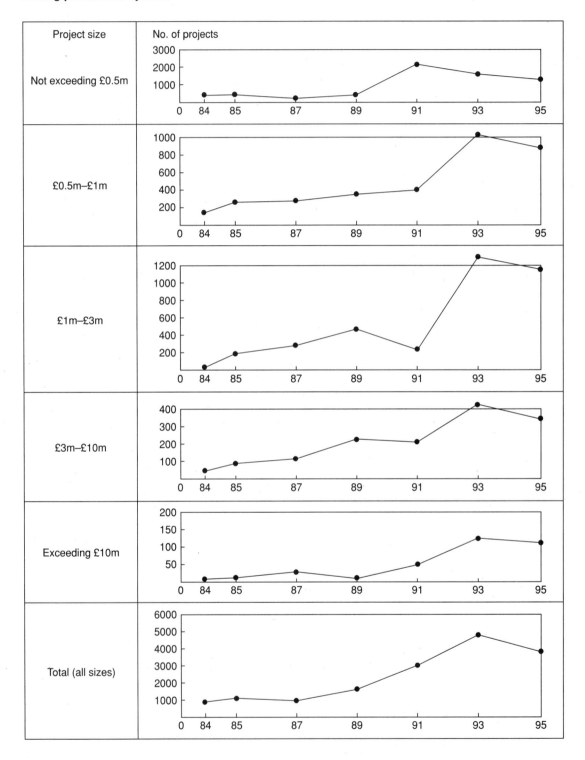

Fig. 7.4 Design-and-build (by contract size and number)

8 Procurement systems in Europe

Numerous observers from Britain have visited Europe to investigate aspects of building procurement in one or more countries. Their findings have varied considerably, depending on the opinions of the persons or organizations with whom they communicated. Participants in the construction industries in other countries are as subjective in their responses as their counterparts in the UK.

The following review draws on published texts, personal communications with observers and field studies over a period of years. It provides only an introduction to the procurement processes in France, Germany and Sweden. Italy is regarded as having more in common with British procurement arrangements than with other European countries. There are passing references, below, to systems in use in Belgium, Denmark, Netherlands, Spain and Switzerland.

France

The first-stage design, during which the client's needs are expressed as a 'grand conception', is traditionally the province of the Ecoles des Beaux Arts educated architect. The development of the design is carried out by engineers, technicians and administrative personnel in *bureaux d'études* (technical offices), which perform the functions undertaken by the various consultant engineers, quantity surveyors, etc., in the UK. The activities of the *bureaux* include project cost control and may also include town planning, cost benefit analyses and management and supervision of projects.

The construction manager operates under the title *maitre d'oeuvre* (master of works).

Comparable with the project manager's role is that of the *promoteur*, who most frequently plays a part in major commercial developments but is not unknown in other sectors of the French construction industry's activities.

Construction firms are similar to those in Britain in that they vary greatly in size and capability. Contracts for projects may be between client and a main contractor or between client and several specialist contractors. The latter, *lots séparés*, arrangement is more generally used.

In recent years there has been a significant increase in the use of design-and-build.

Contractual arrangements in Belgium and Spain are probably nearer to those in France than to other European countries, but Spain appears to be interested in British contractual arrangements.

Germany

All stages of design are undertaken by the architect/engineer who may be university or technical institute educated or, exceptionally, self-taught.

Construction works for the majority of projects are carried out by specialist contractors, each of whom has a contract with the client.

Construction management may be undertaken by specialist staff within the architect's office or by an independent construction manager or *bauleiter*, who is responsible for production and cost management. His tasks include preparation of the equivalent of bills of quantities as a tool for cost management. An alternative course is for the architect to appoint a management contractor (*bauträger*) to coordinate site activity.

In recent years the 'traditional' (British) contractual arrangement has gained ground. Reports vary as to the incidence of use of the various contractual arrangements. Main contractors are by no means unknown and are probably increasing in number.

Contractors frequently undertake design-and-build contracts, employing architects to design the project, usually on an *ad hoc* basis. Other contractual arrangements include the formation of *ad hoc* consortia and joint ventures. This is a common approach for major projects.

Independent project managers may act in much the same manner as in the UK.

Contractual arrangements in the Netherlands and in Switzerland are probably nearer to those in Germany than to other countries in Europe.

Sweden

Sweden pioneered the concept of the project manager (*byggleder*), appointed by the client to head and coordinate the building team and act as a single line of communication with the client. Many project management firms are well established and offer comprehensive services world wide.

Architects and/or engineers undertake the design of buildings and all structural and engineering services. The role of the *byggandskontrolant* approximates to that of construction manager or, perhaps, quantity surveyor. The role of the *kalkylator* is also similar to that of the quantity surveyor but the *kalkylator*'s role is not as sophisticated as that of his British counterpart. Specialist contractors entering into separate 'works contracts' with the client predominate but traditional (British) contracts are used regularly.

The other Scandinavian countries have similar contractual arrangements to those in Sweden but their markets are not as large and their industries are not as developed.

The overall scene in the European Union

To some extent the approaches by the countries referred to above appear to mirror national traits. The French with a bias (in British eyes) to élitism and social class distinctions tend to separate the 'art' from the 'craft'. The German tendency to relish technical expertise leads to stratified professional 'classes' with varying levels of social recognition. The Swedish lead in human resource management has led to Scandinavia recognizing the need to have building projects 'professionally' managed rather than managed by designers who had little or no training in management skills.

There is, then, a rag-bag of alternative systems for building procurement operating in Europe, with which most, if not all, of the British industry is familiar. There is ample evidence that in property development the United Kingdom is probably ahead of other countries in Europe. British property development firms are established in many major cities in Europe.

There is considerable evidence that there is little by way of standard procedures for the procurement of buildings in any of the countries, and certainly there is no one procedure that may be regarded as a standard in Europe.

Appendix: Findings of a survey on clients' needs and expectations

Clients of the construction industry range from those who commission build-ing works once or twice in their lifetimes and do not know what to expect, to those who are, in effect, 'professional' clients with regular projects, clearly defined needs and high expectations. To ascertain the nature of these needs and expectations a survey of fifty clients was carried out during October and November 1989. Subsequent spot checks and references to other reports sug-gest that the findings of this survey are valid at time of publication.

The clients in the sample have been grouped as follows:

- *Group A: Occasional*
  'Occasional' clients who build for their own use or occupation such as church authorities, public service utilities, industrialists, manufacturers, commercial undertakings, medical practitioners, etc. (52 per cent of the sample).

- *Group B: Developers*
  Those acquiring land and/or property and developing them to let on their own behalf or to sell to pension funds or similar investors. These are referred to below as the developers (18 per cent of the sample).

- *Group C: Housing*
  Housing associations, both local authority backed and private. The group includes associations providing homes for the elderly (8 per cent of the sample).

- *Group D: Local authority*
  Local authorities at district and county level (10 per cent of the sample).

- *Group E: Health care*
  Health care bodies, National Health Service and private sector (12 per cent of the sample).

Views were obtained from two members of staff of the, then, Property Ser-vices Agency and these are included in the text. The PSA has not been included in the statistical analysis.

Table A.1 Client contact with building team

Group	In-house project manager (%)	Consultant project manager (%)	Architect (%)
A: Occasional	60	8	32
B: Developers	98	2	–
C: Housing	25	–	75
D: Local authority	–	–	100
E: Health care	50	–	150

The survey provides a sample of client types with a disproportionate emphasis on clients who had commissioned more than ten projects in the past ten years and on clients undertaking larger projects. Nevertheless, it provides some indication of clients' needs and expectations.

Client contact with the building team

The questionnaire separates those persons who are employed full-time by the client as project managers and those who are engaged as consultant project managers. Taken as a whole, 54 per cent of the clients have within their own organizations at least one person who acts as the focal point through which the corporate requirements pass to the building team. Such a person most frequently holds the title 'project manager', 'project coordinator' or similar. The title 'clients' representative' seldom occurs.

An analysis of the sample indicates that the point of contact between clients and the building teams in the various client groups is shown in Table A.1.

The table shows that 60 per cent of the Group A ('occasional') clients employ in-house project managers, but this may be a misleading statistic because a disproportionate number of the clients in the sample are major commercial firms and public service bodies. A sample containing smaller projects for clients who commissioned building works infrequently would almost certainly show greater employment of an architect as the leader of the team. With only one or two exceptions, clients who commission building works infrequently and whose works are typically less than £3m for each project, tend to employ an architect to design and manage the works in the traditional manner.

All but one of the developers (Group B) employ in-house project managers; a major firm of project managers provides management services for the client who does not.

The samples in Groups C, D and E are too small to be statistically representative but they are believed to give a reliable indication of the contact between the client and the building team. Housing associations and local authorities tend to employ architects either in-house or as consultants to act

Table A.2 Client involvement in the project

Involvement	Group				
	A Occasional (%)	B Developer (%)	C Housing (%)	D Local authority (%)	E Health care (%)
● Only at initial design stage	8	–	25	40	17
● During the whole of the design stage	4	–	–	20	–
● During both design and construction stages	88	100	75	40	83

in the traditional manner. Health authority projects tend to be larger and more complex and project managers are more in evidence.

The majority of clients, approximately 80 per cent of the sample, decide on the contractual arrangement, often in consultation with the construction team. Clients for smaller projects tend to rely on the architect and quantity surveyor to decide on the contractual arrangements to be used for procurement of their works.

Client involvement

The majority of clients in the sample expect to be involved in the project during both the design and the construction stages of the project's life. Table A.2 shows, as a percentage of each client group, the extent to which the clients in the sample expect to be involved in running the project.

Contractual arrangements

Table A.3 shows, as a percentage of each client group, the extent to which clients have used various contractual arrangements during the ten-year period up to the survey. Developers (Group B) show the greatest propensity to use alternative contractual arrangements, local authorities the least. Considered as a whole, 100 per cent of clients have used the traditional system, 56 per cent

Table A.3 Use of contractual arrangements

| Contractual arrangement | Group | | | | |
	A Occasional	B Developer	C Housing	D Local authority	E Health care
Traditional	100	100	100	100	100
Project manager	59	100	33	20	50
Management contracting	50	100	–	–	33
Construction management	27	38	–	–	17
Design-and-build	59	75	33	20	83
British Property Federation system	–	13	–	–	–

project management, 46 per cent management contracting, 22 per cent construction management, 56 per cent design-and-build and 4 per cent the British Property Federation system.

Local authority clients refer to their council's standing orders as a reason why they tend to make little use of alternative contractual arrangements. The Property Services Agency has no such inhibitions and uses whichever arrangement it considers appropriate for the project under consideration.

For future projects, the majority of clients do not anticipate using different contractual arrangements but most do not have closed minds.

Several Group A clients (18 per cent) are considering the use of design-and-build and one intends to use *more* management contracts. One is considering using the British Property Federation system and another is developing its own form of contract.

The majority of developer clients (Group B) are already using most of the arrangements but 22 per cent of the sample are considering design-and-build, 11 per cent the British Property Federation system and 11 per cent construction management – the last-mentioned arrangement being mainly for exceptionally large projects.

Of the housing associations, local authorities and health authorities, 42 per cent are considering the use of design-and-build.

Clients' priorities

The questionnaire suggests that technical complexity, aesthetics/prestige, economy, time of essence, price certainty at an early stage, facility for variations, and exceptional size forms a list of *priorities* from which clients might

Table A.4 Clients' priorities

1	2	3	4	5	6	7	8	9	10	11
				Groups						
Priority	Ranking	A	B	C	D	E	Total	Ranking	Total	Ranking
Technical	1	–	–	–	–	4	4	4		
complexity	2	6	–	–	–	–	6	5		
	3	2	–	–	–	2	4	6	14	6
Aesthetics/	1	12	10	–	–	–	22	2		
prestige	2	4	2	–	–	2	8	4		
	3	10	–	2	2	–	14	= 3	44	4
Economy	1	12	4	2	2	4	24	1		
	2	10	4	2	6	4	26	1		
	3	6	4	2	2	–	14	= 3	64	= 1
Time of	1	12	4	–	–	2	18	4		
essence	2	10	6	2	2	–	20	2		
	3	14	4	2	4	2	26	1	64	= 1
Price	1	10	–	2	6	2	20	3		
certainty	2	12	–	2	–	4	18	3		
	3	12	4	–	–	2	18	2	56	3
Facility for	1	–	–	–	–	–	–	= 6		
variations	2	4	–	–	–	–	4	6		
	3	4	4	–	–	4	12	5	16	5
Exceptional	1	–	–	–	–	–	–	= 6		
size	2	–	–	–	–	–	–	7		
	3	2	–	–	–	–	2	7	2	7

select three that are the most relevant to their projects. The priorities are listed in Table A.4; the numbers are rounded percentages of the number of clients in the sample.

During interviews some clients remarked that the list of priorities made no provision for 'low maintenance cost/quality'. Some remarked that 'value for money' is their top priority. Value for money is considered to be insufficiently specific to be recorded as a priority but a record was made of low maintenance cost/quality when this was suggested as a priority. Provision has not been made in the table for this priority because it was not suggested to all who took part in the survey. There is no doubt that a significant number of clients regard low maintenance cost as a priority for their projects.

Columns 1 to 7 in Table A.4 are self-evident. The numbers in column 8 are the sums of those to their left and those in column 9 are the order of rank for first, second and third priorities. The numbers in column 10 are the sum of those in column 8 and those in column 11 are the order of rank for the priorities listed in column 1.

The table also shows that *economy* and *time* are priorities for most clients, with economy being marginally of more importance as first priority. Price certainty at an early stage in the development of the project's design is the next most important priority, followed by appearance (aesthetics/prestige). Several clients remarked that their priorities varied from project to project.

Clients' observations on project organization

Of the clients in the sample, 80 per cent believe that the organization of their projects could or should be better. Their comments are discussed below under seven headings. The comments which occurred most frequently are discussed first.

Architectural design and coordination

The most numerous comments (35 per cent) are concerned with the architect's performance. The principal complaint is concerned with the architect's inability to design within predetermined cost limits and, in one instance, failure to follow his brief. One client suggests that alterative designs should have been provided for his consideration.

Most clients regard the architect as the design leader and criticize the lack of teamwork between members of the design team. These failures are attributed to lack of professional experience and insufficient staff being provided by the consultants. A 'better understanding of the client's needs by the architect' is required.

Problems did not end with completion of the design stage. Indeed, lack of coordination and control of the works is a frequent cause of complaint. Complaining about this aspect, a client with experience of only one project comments about her architect that he was 'a great designer but lacking in management skills'. A 'regular' client points out that the designer is the essential link in the project and when he fails it is a serious matter. Another, that some architects fail at the commencement of the project to provide adequate information to the contractor and that there is a 'lack of mechanical and engineering coordination into designs'. The complaint about lack of control extends to control of costs.

A client who has built more than ten times during the previous ten years, and whose building works are in the £0.5 million to £1 million price range, has employed both architects and project managers as point of contact. He states that the organization has been better on projects managed by project managers.

Another small, infrequent client of the building industry, who is among the minority of those who consider that the organization of their projects could not be better, uses the services of a project manager when he has cause to build.

Communication and liaison

The next most frequent cause of comment (25 per cent) is poor communication. As one client puts it, 'between all members of the team at all stages and in all forms of communication, written, oral, etc.'.

Another client with previous experience in the petro-chemical industries compares his present experience unfavourably with those industries. In the building industry 'there is a lack of liaison between members of the team and lack of feedback'.

One client actually uses the words of the 1962 Emmerson Report with reference to the 'divorce of design from production' being the cause of so many of the building industry's problems.

Positive steps to improve communication are being taken by a developer client with considerable experience of using the British Property Federation system. The company is constantly refining its contractual arrangements with the aim of 'enforcing marriage between architect, structural engineer and contractor'. The 'refinement' moves more quickly when the building industry's workload is light and members of the team are concerned with keeping full order books.

Client failures

Many clients (25 per cent) in the sample are critical of their own performance. In some instances positive steps have been taken to put their houses in order. Perceived weaknesses are poor briefing and a tendency to commence site works before the design has been sufficiently developed. As one client puts it, 'more haste, less speed'. Another remarks that a certain project could have been less costly but building economy had been sacrificed for early completion.

The principal problem experienced by clients when they 'inflict their own wounds' is their failure to define their requirements in order to obviate variations at a later date. Lack of cooperation within the client body, particularly in the larger organization, may lead to the project manager being unable to act effectively as the focal point between corporate requirements and the building team which will realize them.

Contractors

Contractors are criticized by 10 per cent of the clients in the sample. One criticism is that contractors fail to coordinate sub-contractors' works. Their failure to complete the works in the contract period may lead to the client deducting liquidated damages. To the credit of contractors, a major industrialist is highly critical of his consultants, but comments that he is 'rarely let down by contractors'.

Claims and delays

The words 'delay' and 'claim' occur in 8 per cent of the clients' comments. Where the delays lead to successful application of the liquidated damages clause by the client, the contractor must be regarded as being at fault and reference has been made to such situations above.

Other delays, which lead to successful claims by the contractor, are caused by various factors, some of which, such as poor communications, have also been referred to above. A housing association client remarks that highly competitive tenders lead to 'claims and over-runs'. Claims appear to occur more frequently on traditional contracts.

Engineering services

Reference has been made above to the failure of the design team to satisfactorily incorporate services engineering installations into the design and to the failure of contractors to manage the sub-contractors concerned. The complexity and magnitude of engineering services, particularly on some major projects, is referred to by clients when discussing ways in which the organization of their projects have proved unsatisfactory.

Human factors

Indirect reference has been made above to the human factor when considering communication failures and lack of teamwork. More than 30 per cent of the clients comment on those aspects. In addition, other clients make particular reference to the extent to which 'people' are the 'variable factor' which determines the success or failure of their projects.

The short note of an interview with a major developer client encapsulates the views of many when it refers to the need for 'better coordination of information in the team and better communication. Good people are the key.'

Summary

Not surprisingly, the needs of clients in terms of contractual organization vary widely. The more experienced and knowledgeable the client, the more he tends to identify a single point of contact, a person to act as his representative and leave that person to manage the project. For most clients that person is not an architect. The first-time client for one of the smallest projects referred to her architect as 'a great designer but lacking in management skills'. One of the largest and most sophisticated property owners in Britain even referred enquiries in connection with the survey to the company's consultant project managers.

Increasingly, clients look to a manager rather than an architect to manage their projects. This applies to large clients such as the PSA, to developers and to many of the occasional clients with some experience of building. The exceptions are local authorities and, to a lesser extent, housing associations which are bound by 'standing orders'.

The majority of clients expect to be involved in running the project during both the design and construction stages. The extent to which they are involved, because work on site is frequently commenced before the design is completed, is difficult to ascertain. Whatever the reason for their involvement, the experience of many client leads them to expect involvement at both the design and the construction stages. They may not wish to have involvement over such a long period, but they expect it.

Clients who contributed to the survey

Arnold Project Services for Kumagi Gumi
B&Q
Barclays Bank
Basildon District Council
BP Oil UK
Brentwood Roman Catholic Diocese
British Airways Property Development Department
British Rail
Church View Surgery
Citycorp Investment
Cloth Kits
Cornwall County Council
County and District Properties
Crest Estates
Dartford Borough Council
Darlington Health Authority
Fitzwilliam College, Cambridge
Fleetway House Construction Management
Gatwick Airport
Grenada Studio Tours
Greycoat Group
Grosvenor Developments
Harrison Homes

Imry Merchants
Land Securities
London Docklands Development Corporation
Luton Football Club
Lysander Group
National Gallery Services
Norfolk Capital Hotels
Nuffield Hospitals
Plessey Property
Printers Charitable Corporation
Property Services Agency
Retirement Security
River Lodge Surgery
Sainsbury's Homebase
Saint Martin's Property
Saint Pancras Housing Association
South West Thames Health
Standard Chartered Bank
Sussex Housing Association for the Aged
Westminster Roman Catholic Diocesan Trustees
Willis Faber
Wimpey International
Windsor, Royal Borough of

I thank all others who advised or assisted but whose names have been inadvertently mislaid, and I apologize for any omissions.

Glossary

BOO (Build Own Operate)
An arrangement where a private client provides and operates a facility on behalf of a (usually) public client.

BOOT (Built Own Operate Transfer)
An arrangement where a private client provides and operates a facility on behalf of a (usually) public client for a fixed term. On completion of this term the facility is transferred to the client.

Collaboration contract
A variant of the negotiated approach where, having established a price for the project, the client and contractor agree a sum to be included in the builder's price for the management of the construction phase. Part of this to be paid to the client in return for secondment of a senior member of the client's organization to act as construction manager.

Competitive tender *see* Traditional contracting

Consortia
A consortium is the grouping together of three or more organizations, generally of differing skills, with the objective of carrying out a specific project.

Continuity tender
A continuity tender is similar to the serial tender. Contractors competitively tendering for a project are informed that, given satisfactory performance, they will be awarded a similar project to follow on from the completion of the first and that the price for this will be negotiated, possibly using the prices of the original bill.

Construction management (CM)
Construction management or CM is the term used in the USA to describe management contracting. (*See also* Professional construction management.)

Cost reimbursement *see* Fixed fee/prime cost contract

Design-and-build

Design-and-build or design-and-construct is where the contractor provides the design and construction under one contract.

DFBO (Design Fund Build Operate)

One of the systems whereby the private client can contribute to the provision of a public service.

Design-and-construct *see* Design-and-build

Fast-tracking

Fast-tracking is a means of reducing project time by the overlapping of design and construction. Each trade's work commences as its plans and specifications are substantially completed.

Fixed fee/prime cost contract

Under this arrangement the contractor carries out the work for the payment of a prime cost (defined) and a fixed fee calculated in relation to the estimated amount of the prime cost.

Fixed price contract

A fixed price contract may be a lump sum contract or a measurement contract based on fixed prices for units of specific work.

Joint venture

A joint venture is the pooling of the assets and liabilities of two or more firms for the purpose of accomplishing a specific goal and on the basis of sharing profits/losses.

Lump sum contract

With a lump sum contract, the contractor agrees to perform the work for one fixed price, regardless of the ultimate cost.

Management contracting

In management contracting the contractor works alongside the design and cost consultants, providing a construction management service on a number of professional bases. The management contractor does not undertake either design or direct construction work. The design requirements are met by letting each element of the construction to specialist sub-contractors.

Management fee *see* Management contracting

Negotiated contract

In a negotiated contract the client selects, at the outset, one main contractor with whom to negotiate. In essence the arrangement is the same as that for a two-stage tender.

Novation

In this approach the client employs consultants to design and specify the project in accordance with stated requirements. On the basis of the documentation prepared, a contractor is selected by competition. The client then novates (or transfers) his agreement with the consultants to the contractor, who then takes full responsibility for the project through to completion.

Package deal

A package deal follows the same lines as design-and-build, with the contractor providing the design and construction under one contract, but there is the implication that the building provided will be of a standardized or semi-standardized type.

Partnering

A concept where organizations agree to work together for a period of time, perhaps unspecified, on a basis of mutual trust and with common objectives thereby optimizing each partner's strengths.

Private finance initiative (PFI)

PFI is a means whereby the private sector can contribute to the provision of what has been regarded, traditionally, as a public service. The promoter designs, builds, finances and operates the facility on behalf of the (public) client. *See also* DFBO, BOO and BOOT.

Procurement

Procurement is the amalgam of activities undertaken by the client to obtain a building.

Professional construction management

PCM is a term used in the USA to describe an arrangement whereby the tasks of planning, design and construction are integrated by a project team comprising the owner, construction manager and the design organization.

Professional construction manager (PCM) or Construction manager

The PCM acts as a management contractor (UK) specializing in construction management within the professional construction management concept.

Project management

Project management is concerned with the overall planning and coordination of a project from inception to completion, aimed at meeting the client's requirements and ensuring completion on time, within cost and to required quality standards.

Separate contracts

With separate contracts the client's professional adviser lets contracts for the work with a number of separate contractors. This arrangement was commonplace prior to the emergence of the general contractor.

Serial tender

A serial tender is where a number of similar projects are awarded to a contractor, following a competitive tender on a master bill of quantities. This master bill forms a standing offer, open for the client to accept, for a number of contracts. Each contract is separate and the price for each calculated separately.

Target cost contract

This form of cost-reimbursable contract involves the fixing of a cost either for the complete project or in respect of certain elements only, e.g. labour, or materials, or plant. If the final cost deviates from the target, the saving or excess is divided between client and contractor in predetermined proportions.

Traditional contracting

The traditional form of contracting is where the client appoints an architect or other professional to produce the design, select the contractor and to supervise the work through to completion. The contractor is selected on some basis of competition.

Turnkey

A turnkey contract is one where the client has an agreement with one single administrative entity, who provides the design and construction under one contract, and frequently effects land acquisition, financing, leasing, etc.

Two-stage tender

With a two-stage tender three or four contractors with appropriate experience are separately involved in detailed discussions with the client's professional advisers regarding all aspects of the project. Price competition is introduced through an approximate or notional bill or schedule of rates. Further selection criteria are then used to determine which contractor carries out the job.

Abbreviations

ACA	Association of Consultant Architects
BEC	Building Employers Confederation
BPF	British Property Federation
CD 81	JCT Standard form of building contract with contractor's design, 1981 edition

CIOB	Chartered Institute of Building
ECC	Engineering and Construction Contract (the new name for the New Engineering Contract)
IFC 84	JCT Intermediate form of building contract, 1984 edition
JCT	Joint Contracts Tribunal
JCT 80	JCT Standard form of building contract, 1980 edition
MC 87	JCT Standard form of management contract
NEDO	National Economic Development Office
NEC	New Engineering Contract (*see* ECC)
PSA	Property Services Agency
RIBA	Royal Institute of British Architects
RICS	Royal Institution of Chartered Surveyors
RICS JO (QS)	RICS Junior Organization (Quantity Surveyors' Division)

References

HMSO (1964) *The Planning and Management of Contracts for Building and Civil Engineering Works*. Report of the (Banwell) Committee. HMSO.

Latham, M. (1994) *Constructing the Team*. HMSO.

NEDO (1975) *The Public Client and the Construction Industries*. HMSO.

NEDO (1985) *Thinking about Building*. HMSO.

NEDO (1988) *Faster Building for Commerce*. NEDO.

Bibliography

The following annotated bibliography is in chronological order with the most recent items coming first. It is based on material first published in the CIOB bi-monthly publication *Building Management Abstracts* and its successor *Construction Information Digest* from 1970 onwards.

1996

894
A.W. Siddiqui
NOVATION: AND ITS COMPARISON WITH COMMON FORMS OF BUILDING PROCUREMENT
Construction Paper 60. CIOB. 1996, 8pp.
The types of project for which novation is appropriate are identified and an assessment of its ability to satisfy the client in regard to time, cost, quality and performance.

893
HM Treasury: Private Finance Unit
PRIVATE FINANCE INITIATIVE: GUIDELINES FOR SMOOTHING THE PROCUREMENT PROCESS
1996 DoE 4pp.

892
FORM FAVOURITE
Procurement (Building supplement) 1996 December, pp. 22–3
The RICS latest survey of types of contracts in use demonstrate the popularity of construction management. Design and build represented 30.1 per cent, a fall of 5.6 per cent on the previous survey two years ago.

891
Shen, Liyin et al.
APPLICATION OF BOT SYSTEM FOR INFRASTRUCTURE PROJECTS IN CHINA
Journal of Construction Engineering and Management (ASCE) 1996 122 December, pp. 319–23.

890
C.M. Ruff et al.
OWNER–CONTRACTOR RELATIONSHIPS ON CONTAMINATED SITE REMEDIATION PROJECTS
Journal of Construction Engineering and Management (ASCE) 1996 122 December, pp. 348–53
Sixty completed remediation projects were studied to identify and document the effects of different project management structures and contracting strategies on project outcomes. Survey results indicated that changes in scope, budget overruns, delays, disputes and change orders are common on remediation projects. Flexible project management strategies such as turnkey and partnering arrangements, and flexible contracting schemes, such as cost plus fee, were found to be better suited to accommodate such changes. Turnkey and design/construct project structures had the best performance overall of the management structures reported. Mechanisms to promote cohering and team building contributed significantly to project success as defined by budget and schedule.

889
STATE FARM FINDS A BETTER WAY
Engineering News Record 1996 November 18, pp. 44–6
Details are given of the fast-track design–build project for a 254,000 ft^2 high-tech data processing centre. Its favourable comparison with a conventional project in terms of time and dispute avoidance is highlighted.

888
J. Macneil
FEE WISE MEN
Building 1996 November 1, pp. 40–2
The experience is reported of British Airways and Sainsbury in using construction management.

887

TOWARDS A CONCURRENT ENGINEERING MODEL FOR DESIGN AND BUILD PROJECTS
Structural Engineer 1996 74 November, pp. 388–91 (Discussion)
Among the issues discussed are the role of the client; construction as a manufacturing process; tendering; costs; and value engineering.

886

J. Smit
ADD SALESMAN
Procurement (Building Supplement) 1996 October, pp. 14–15
Wates Integra 2+2 procurement route is outlined. Its key selling points for the client are its combination of D&B guaranteed minimum price with front-end construction management.

885

R.L.K. Tiong
CSFs IN COMPETITIVE TENDERING AND NEGO-TIATION MODEL FOR BOT PROJECTS
Journal of Construction Engineering and Management (ASCE) 1996 122 September, pp. 205–11
It is shown that the financial and technical strength of the consortium is the most important critical success factor in a BOT tender. The competitive tendering and negotiation model for BOT promoters involved in tendering for BOT projects is presented. BOT promoters must give special and continued attention to the model in order to develop a superior proposal that will increase their chances of securing a profitable BOT contract.

884

D.H.T. Walker
WHAT SORT OF PERSON MAKES A GOOD PROJECT MANAGER?
Building Economist 1996 September, pp. 26–9.

883

D.K. Stager
ORGANIZING AND MANAGING A FINANCE–DESIGN–BUILD PROJECT IN TURKEY
Journal of Construction Engineering and Management (ASCE) 1996 122 September, pp. 199–204
The Izmir-Aydin project based on a fixed price, finance, design–build is described from the viewpoint of the problems that an international contract is likely to experience.

882

SHELL SHOCK
Building 1996 August 6, pp. 36–40, 42–3, 46

Three facets of design and build are explored: architect control in Foster and Partners first D&B project; architects on the main board of contractors; and problems of quality.

881

H.M. Bedelian
SUCCESSFUL MAJOR PROJECTS IN A CHANG-ING INDUSTRY
Proceedings ICE Civil Engineering 1996 114 August, pp. 117–23
The major structural change now affecting the UK construction industry is examined and its likely impact on the procurement of major projects is evaluated. A number of case studies are considered in an attempt to identify the ingredients leading to success.

880

J. Stock
D&B AND ITS ALTERNATIVES
Architects' Journal 1996 July 18, pp. 42–3
Three case studies are presented which illustrate the increasing diversity of procurement.

879

D. Trench
CONSTRUCTION MANAGEMENT: BORN IN THE USA
Contract Journal 1996 July 4, pp. 16–17
A view is given of the benefits and downside of construction management from both the US and the UK. It would seem to be gaining favour as design and build stagnates.

878

PROJECT MANAGEMENT: USING THE WEB TO MANAGE A JOB
Engineering News Record 1996 June 24, p. 17
Use of a Web site allows project management, contractor, designer and subcontractor to communicate via E-mail or forum; upload and download files on schedules, information requests, project logs, drawings, specifications and change orders. The site was also used to conduct the initial partnering session.

877

G.J. Tulacz
TOP 100: OWNER ACCEPTANCE OF ALTERN-ATIVE PROJECT DELIVERY SPURS CM AND DESIGN–BUILD WORK
Engineering News Record 1996 June 10, pp. 32–3, 35–6
A review made of the market for design–build and construction management in the US. Tabular details are given of the top 100 firms involved in D&B, CM for fee, and CM at risk.

876
PROJECT MANAGEMENT–A ROLE FOR THE ARCHITECT
RIBA Journal 1996 June, pp. 67–8, 71–2
A report aimed at re-establishing the architect as project manager. It deals with the essential nature of PM and the opportunities for lead designers, relationship with the client, the brief, education and qualification and promoting the architect as PM.

875
A. Webb
PROJECT MANAGEMENT: 40 YEARS YOUNG AND STILL LOOKING FOR A PHILOSOPHY: PART 2
Project Manager Today 1996 May, pp. 8–9
In tracing the development of project management attention is given to the new model for PM, bodies of knowledge and the conditions ensuring its future.

874
R. Newcombe
EMPOWERING THE CONSTRUCTION PROJECT TEAM
International Journal of Project Management 1996 14 April, pp. 75–80
Traditional procurement and construction management are compared in terms of the power bases and processes used by the project manager. It is postulated that a power gap exists between that given under the contract and that required to manage. Construction management would appear to be structured to bridge this power gap more effectively than traditional arrangements.

873
A.K. Munns and B.F. Bjeirmi
ROLE OF PROJECT MANAGEMENT IN ACHIEVING PROJECT SUCCESS
International Journal of Project Management 1996 14 April, pp. 81–7
The overlap that exists between projects and project management is highlighted. For project success it is suggested that there must be an improved appreciation of the role of PM within projects and that this role must be placed within the context of a wider project alongside other criteria and long-term expectations. The project manager must allow the client to contribute to both planning and production and the PM team's involvement extended into the utilization phase.

872
A. Webb
PROJECT MANAGEMENT: 40 YEARS YOUNG AND STILL LOOKING FOR A PHILOSOPHY: PART 1
Project Manager Today 1996 April, pp. 8–11.

871
P. Phippen
CHANGING TIMES FOR D&B
Architects' Journal 1996 April 4, pp. 38–40
Both an architect's and a client's view is given of design and build for social housing, including complex buildings designed for occupation by frail, elderly people.

870
N.F.O. Evbuoman and C.J. Anumba
TOWARDS A CONCURRENT ENGINEERING MODEL FOR DESIGN AND BUILD PROJECTS
Structural Engineer 1996 74 March, pp. 73–8
The new model applying the principles of concurrent engineering and Design Function Deployment to design and build projects is nationally enunciated. It is believed that this model could help to improve the business process in D&B projects in particular and also provide a basis for the development of a generic concurrent engineering model for general design and construction projects.

869
A.W. Fleming and M. Koppelman
EARNED VALUE PROJECT MANAGEMENT – RE-ENGINEERING THE PROCESS FOR THE PRIVATE SECTOR: PART 2
Project 1996 March, pp. 9–10
A vision is projected of what changes must happen to the earned value concept in order to make it a broad-based project management tool for use on all projects.

868
V.P. Rao and B. Egginton
PREREQUISITES FOR EFFECTIVE PROJECT IMPLEMENTATION: PART 2
Project 1996 February, pp. 10–12
Organization and cost control are briefly covered to complete the description of the overall project landscape. The need is stressed for the project manager to play a strong and proactive role within the organizational framework.

867w
P. Collard
TRANSPORTABILITY OF PROJECT MANAGEMENT SKILLS
Project 1996 February, pp. 22–4
The results of a study demonstrate the transportability of construction project management skills.

866
A.W. Fleming and M. Koppelman
EARNED VALUE PROJECT MANAGEMENT – THE CONCEPT AND ITS ORIGIN: PART 1

Project 1996 February, pp. 15–16
The benefits to be gained from the earned value
approach are identified.

865
A. Gibb and P.R. Brand
**VINTERS PLACE: PROCUREMENT, DESIGN
DEVELOPMENT AND CONSTRUCTION OF A
COMPLEX BUILDING FACADE WITH A TRA-
DITIONAL ARCHITECTURAL APPEARANCE**
Proceedings ICE: Structure and Buildings 1996 *116*
February, pp. 96–108
Particular attention is given to the management of
the pre-construction phase with emphasis on the
procurement process.

864
D. Chevin
WEDDED BLISS
Building 1996 February 9, pp. 36–7
The proactive value of partnering is demonstrated
by reference to the active experience of a steelwork
contractor.

863
M. McIntyre
**PARTNERING: CHANGING ATTITUDES IN
CONSTRUCTION**
Constructor 1996 February, pp. 54–6
The historical background is summarized of part-
nering, the benefits that its application to construc-
tion has created being identified.

862
T. Fleet
**PARTNERING IN THE CONSTRUCTION INDUS-
TRY 1: CONTRACTUAL ISSUES**
Construction Law 1996 6 January, pp. 175–7.

861
S. Porter
PARTNERING 2: SOME PRACTICAL MATTERS
Construction Law 1996 6 January, pp. 178–80
The likely problems to be encountered with part-
nering are identified together with the benefits that
can be obtained.

860
**DESIGN AND BUILD SETS THE TREND IN THE
UK**
Contract Journal 1996 January 11, p. 13
A summary of a report identifying the leading D&B
contractors together with their respective share of
the market.

859
Young Hoon Kwak and C.W. Ibbs
**FINANCIAL AND ORGANIZATIONAL IMPACTS
OF PROJECT MANAGEMENT**

International Symposium for the Organization and
Management of Construction: Shaping Theory and
Practice: 1996 2, pp. 252–63
A proposed project management process maturity
analysis methodology is summarized which can be
used to evaluate financial and organizational impacts
of PM to organizations. A benchmarking system is
also described for the quantitative measurement of
an organization's level of PM sophistication.

858
C. Elliot
**TOTAL RESOURCE ASSESSMENT BASED ON
EXTENSION OF TRADITIONAL PROCURE-
MENT SYSTEMS**
International Symposium for the Organization and
Management of Construction: Shaping Theory and
Practice 1996 2, pp. 352–9
An alternative system of resource assessment is pro-
posed which can be incorporated into existing pro-
curement systems by extending the use of BOQ to
encompass total resource assessment.

857
I.C. Jennings and R. Kenley
INTEGRATING COMPLEXITY
International Symposium for the Organization and
Management of Construction: Shaping Theory and
Practice 1996 2, pp. 339–51
The emergence is examined of integration systems
within the context of the industry's development. In
particular the role of integration for building project
organizations is discussed with project management
as an example.

856
P. Pernu
**TENDERING DOCUMENTS FOR DESIGN AND
CONSTRUCT COMPETITION**
International Symposium for the Organization and
Management of Construction; Shaping Theory and
Practice 1996 3, pp. 126–34.

855
J.L. Conlin et al.
**RELATIONSHIP BETWEEN CONSTRUCTION
PROCUREMENT STRATEGIES AND CON-
STRUCTION CONTRACT DISPUTES**
International Symposium for the Organization and
Management of Construction; Shaping Theory and
Practice 1996 2, pp. 360–71.

854
G.D. Holt et al.
**TENDERING PROCEDURES, CONTRACTUAL
ARRANGEMENTS AND LATHAM: THE CON-
TRACTOR'S VIEW**

Engineering, Construction and Architectural Management 1996 *3(1/2)*, pp. 97–115
The results are presented of a survey of UK contractors' opinion of the Latham procurement recommendations and of an alternative selection procedure. In general, contractors appear to be in tune with the ideas of the Latham review.

853
G.S. Birrell
FRENCH BUILDING PROCUREMENT APPROACHES: INPUT TO THEORY AND PRACTICE
International Symposium for the Organization and Management of Construction: Shaping Theory and Practice 1996 *2*, pp. 326–38.

852
S. Borke et al.
INTERNATIONAL CONSORTIA IN THE EUROPEAN CONSTRUCTION INDUSTRY
International Symposium for the Organization and Management of Construction: Shaping Theory and Practice 1996 *2*, pp. 712–21
A five-nation study of international consortia is presented with particular reference to public policy, strategic management, technology management, project management and employment and labour.

851
C. Allen
VALUE JUDGEMENT
New Civil Engineer 1996 November 7, pp. 18–19
It is argued that construction managers have become contract administrators to the detriment of the project. Real improvement in the production process is believed to tie in a different approach to procurement and one method advocated is an open book two-stage tendering process.

850
A. Pitney and C. Smith
PUBLIC TRANSPORT SYSTEMS: THE ALLOCATION OF RISKS IN CONSTRUCTION CONTRACTS
Construction Law Journal 1996 *12(4)*, pp. 240–58
Particular attention is given to risk in the context of BOT and BOOT projects.

849
D. Partington
PROJECT MANAGEMENT OF ORGANIZATIONAL CHANGE
International Journal of Project Management 1996 *14(1)*, pp. 13–21
The overall lack is considered of empirical studies of project management from the context of organizational

innovation. A potentially fruitful new direction for PM research is suggested.

848
J.E.L. Quartey
DEVELOPMENT PROJECTS THROUGH BUILD–OPERATE SCHEMES: THEIR ROLE AND PLACE IN DEVELOPING COUNTRIES
International Journal of Project Management 1996 *14(1)*, pp. 47–52.

847
I. Wirth
HOW GENERIC AND HOW INDUSTRY-SPECIFIC IS THE PROJECT MANAGEMENT PROFESSION?
International Journal of Project Management 1996 *14(1)*, pp. 7–11
Five industries, including construction, are compared in terms of typical project size and activities, project management uncertainties and project managers' qualifications. The results indicate the extent to which project management is transportable across different industry sectors.

846
J. Matthews
PRE-CONSTRUCTION PROJECT PARTNERING: DEVELOPING THE PROCESS
Engineering, Construction and Architectural Management 1996 *3(1/2)*, pp. 117–31
Semi-project partnering adopted by a top UK contractor as a means of improving relationships with sub-contractors is described.

1995

845
T. Baxendale and D. Logan
THE CLIENT AND CONSTRUCTION MANAGEMENT: THE ROLE OF THE CLIENT IN INITIATING INFORMATION SYSTEMS WITHIN THE CONSTRUCTION MANAGEMENT FORM OF PROCUREMENT
Construction Paper 47. CIOB. 1995, 7pp.
Attention is given to information flow and to the significance of the use of formal management information systems.

844
House Builders' Federation: Social Housing Unit
MORE THAN JUST A BUILDER: MAKING THE MOST OF HOUSE BUILDERS' DEVELOPMENT

SKILLS USING DEVELOPER LED DESIGN AND BUILD CONTRACTS
*c*1995, 24pp.
The advantages to housing associations of using developer led design and build contracts are identified.

843
D.F. Turner
DESIGN AND BUILD CONTRACT PRACTICE
Longman. 2nd edition 1995, 328pp.
The principles and operation of D&B contracts are examined in detail. An analysis is provided of the advantages and limitations of D&B, together with an exposition on the common forms of contract and on design responsibilities and liabilities. New chapters cover the JCT supplement for the BPF system, the GC/Works/1 and ICE contracts, and performance specified works.

842
Construction Round Table
THINKING ABOUT BUILDING
1995, 12pp.
A logical approach to building procurement is described. Seven steps to success are identified before more detailed guidance is given on selecting the procurement route, identifying priorities and selecting the right team.

841
B. Norton and G. D'Vaz
PROJECT MANAGEMENT
1995. Institute of Management Foundation, 56pp.
One of the series summarizing key management topics focusing on current theory and practice, and targeted at the practising manager. It provides an overview of project management incorporating an objective summary of current thinking. In addition there is a literature review, a listing of key organizations, authors and reference sources.

840
C. Walker and A.J. Smith
PRIVATIZED INFRASTRUCTURE: THE BUILD–OPERATE–TRANSFER APPROACH
Thomas Telford. 1995, 258pp.
The many issues associated with often complex BOT/BOOT relationships are addressed as are the means to overcome the complexities. Attention is given to funding, cost estimating, risk, legal framework and procurement option and the role of government. Five relevant case studies are included.

839
Construction Audit and Trowers & Hamlin
HAPM GUIDE TO DESIGN AND BUILD EMPLOYERS REQUIREMENTS AND JCT 81 AMENDMENTS

1995. HAPM Publications, 42pp.
The results are discussed of a survey of design-and-build documentation submitted by housing associations to HAPM as part of the audit process. They provide the basis for guidance on the preparation of the Employers Requirements, JCT amendments and associated documentation.

838
A. Potter
PLANNING TO BUILD? A PRACTICAL INTRODUCTION TO THE CONSTRUCTION PROCESS
Special Publication *113*. 1995. CIRIA, 88pp.
Aimed at clients the guide provides a step-by-step introduction to the activities needed to take a building project from initial idea to takeover of the completed work. It outlines the various procurement routes and those factors which influence choice.

837
D. Borrie
PROCUREMENT IN FRANCE: SOME INFORMATION FOR UK PROFESSIONALS CONSIDERING WORKING IN THE FRENCH CONSTRUCTION MARKET
Construction Paper 49. CIOB. 1995, 8pp.
A succinct review is made of the construction industry in France with particular attention being given to the various parties involved, planning and building regulations, procurement, liability and insurance, contracting and sub-contracting, tendering, and forms of contract.

836
R.B. Hellard
PROJECT PARTNERING: PRINCIPLE AND PRACTICE
Thomas Telford. 1995, 200pp.
Partnering is regarded as the essential philosophical framework for the application of the principles and practices of TQM. The essential elements of the partnering concept as applied to construction projects are discussed and supported by a series of case studies. Appendices include model forms and sample documents.

835
J. Bennett and S. Jayes
TRUSTING THE TEAM: THE BEST PRACTICE GUIDE TO PARTNERING IN CONSTRUCTION
University of Reading: Centre for Strategic Studies in Construction. 1995, 82pp.
The benefits and costs of partnering are discussed to illustrate the benefits it can provide. Specifics of project partnering and strategic partnering and how they might be implemented are discussed. Finally, contractual and legal issues are examined.

834
M. McIntyre (ed.)
PARTNERING: CHANGING ATTITUDES IN CONSTRUCTION
AGCA. 1995 (October), 163pp.
This is an essentially practical guide of US practice on how to 'partner'. Following an introductory section on definition and the benefits, guidance is given on how to start and setting up a workshop. Managing partnering in the project is considered next, before tips on partnering for the small project are given. How to spread the gospel outside the company is covered and to complete the volume there are some case studies in partnering which have been award winners.

833
Efficiency Unit: Cabinet Office
CONSTRUCTION PROCUREMENT BY GOVERNMENT
1995. HMSO, 87pp.
Based on a review aimed at improving efficiency and making Government a 'best practice client'. A series of recommendations are made in relation to best practice; organizing for success; risk management; and working with industry.

832
P. Mitchell et al.
PROJECT MANAGEMENT
BIFM News 1995 November, pp. 4–11
A series of articles is presented providing an overview of project management. It includes the following contributions managing project management; what is project management?; project management – the big brick; fast-track project management; project management: collaboration and support.

831
PARTNERING: ALL TOGETHER NOW
Building Services 1995 17 November, pp. 31–4
The process of partnering, its various permutations and how it can assist integrated design and construction are discussed. Some indications are given of the likely drawbacks.

830
G.D. Holt
APPLICATION OF AN ALTERNATIVE CONTRACTOR SELECTION MODEL
Building Research and Information 1995 23(5) October/November, pp. 255–64
Initial results are presented from the application of the model to real-life examples.

829
D. Mosey
PROCUREMENT OF NHS CAPITAL PROJECTS: 2

Construction Law 1995 6 October/November, pp. 131–4
The implications of the Private Finance Initiative for the application of the construction investment manual are considered. Particular attention is given to the place of design build finance and operate schemes.

828
R.A. Mohsini et al.
PROCUREMENT: A COMPARATIVE ANALYSIS OF CONSTRUCTION MANAGEMENT AND TRADITIONAL BUILDING PROCESSES
Building Research and Information 1995 23(5) October/November, pp. 285–90
A comparative study is presented of the two procurement processes as employed in Singapore.

827
J. Caunce
HYBRID PRETENDERS THREATEN D&B IMAGE
Construction Manager 1995 1 October, p. 21
The dangers to contractors are highlighted where clients operate a hybrid design-and-build contract and where the contractor becomes responsible for variations, caused by unknown factors.

826
G.D. Holt and K.F. Potts
DEVELOPING AN EFFECTIVE METHODOLOGY FOR CONTRACTOR SELECTION
Project 1995 October, pp. 9, 11.

825
A. Schneider
PROJECT MANAGEMENT IN INTERNATIONAL TEAMS: INSTRUMENTS FOR IMPROVING COOPERATION
International Journal of Project Management 1995 13 September, pp. 247–51.

824
Low Sui Pheng
LAO TZU'S TAO TE CHING AND ITS RELEVANCE TO PROJECT LEADERSHIP IN CONSTRUCTION
International Journal of Project Management 1995 13 September, pp. 295–302
It is argued that project managers could benefit from a study of the ancient Chinese book of philosophy if they wish to complete projects to time, cost, quality and environmental specifications.

823
C.M. Tam
FEATURES OF POWER INDUSTRIES IN SOUTH EAST ASIA. STUDY OF BUILD-OPERATE TRANSFER POWER PROJECTS IN CHINA
International Journal of Project Management 1995 13 September, pp. 303–11.

822

M. Betts and P. Lansley

INTERNATIONAL JOURNAL OF PROJECT MANAGEMENT: A REVIEW OF THE LAST 10 YEARS

International Journal of Project Management 1995 *13* September, pp. 207–17.

821

D. Woodward

USE OF SENSITIVITY ANALYSIS IN BUILD-OWN-OPERATE-TRANSFER PROJECT EVALUATION

International Journal of Project Management 1995 *13* September, pp. 239–46.

820

F.M. Ewbanks and G.A. Bruno

PARTNERING: THE CONSTRUCTION MANAGE-MENT OF THE FUTURE

American Professional Constructor 1995 *19* September, pp. 11–17

Based on a desk study the basis of partnering is described, reference being made to VE and constructability reviews. Consideration is then given to the mechanics of partnering and to a five-step approach to implementation. Several case studies are presented to illustrate the benefits.

819

R.L.K. Tiong

COMPETITIVE ADVANTAGE OF EQUITY IN BOT TENDER

Journal of Construction Engineering and Management (ASCE) 1995 *121* September, pp. 282–9

It is shown that a high level of equity is necessary in a BOT tender if it is specified in the request for proposal, the competition is keen, and financing for the project is uncertain. The threshold equity level proposed by the promoters must be high – typically between 20 and 30 per cent – for them to be short-listed and to proceed to the final round of negotiation when the selection will be made.

818

R.L.K. Tiong

IMPACT OF FINANCIAL PACKAGE VERSUS TECHNICAL SOLUTION IN A BOT TENDER

Journal of Construction Engineering and Management (ASCE) 1995 *121* September, pp. 304–11

The impact is examined of a financial package when assessed against the technical design during the selection process. It is concluded that the ability to provide an attractive financial package is critical under the conditions when (1) the project is technically certain; (2) the tolls to be charged are of government's main concern; (3) competition is keen; and (4) the project viability and financing are uncertain. However,

promoters must not underestimate the importance of an innovative technical solution as it could make an attractive financial package possible.

817

DBF&O: OPPORTUNITY OR BOOBY TRAP?

Building Services 1995 September, pp. 34–5

The development is discussed of DBF&O (Design Build Finance and Operate) schemes which are largely facilitated by the PFI. Areas of risk are identified.

816

C. Stoker

DESIGN AND BUILD: CHOOSING THE RIGHT CONTRACT

Building Services 1995 September, pp. 31–3

Consideration is given to those forms of contract which lend themselves to design-and-build. How to obtain the best from the design-and-build approach is briefly discussed.

815

L. Davis

DESIGN AND BUILD: HAPPY MARRIAGE OR UNHOLY UNION?

Building Services 1995 September, pp. 29–30

The relative merits and limitations of design-and-build are summarized. Some attention is given to other options, including novation.

814

J.P. Connolly

CHOOSING APPROPRIATE CONSTRUCTION CONTRACTING METHOD

Journal of Construction Engineering and Management (ASCE) 1995 *121* September, p. 330 (Discussion).

813

A. Griffith and J.D. Headley

DEVELOPING AN EFFECTIVE APPROACH TO THE PROCUREMENT AND MANAGEMENT OF SMALL BUILDING WORKS WITHIN LARGE CLIENT ORGANIZATIONS

Construction Management and Economics 1995 *13* July, pp. 279–89

It is shown that efficient and effective approaches to small works procurement and management focus on understanding the core business, total small works workload, and the requirements of the individual small works themselves.

812

DESIGN AND BUILD 95

Contract Journal 1995 July 2, pp. 18–25

A ranking list is provided of the top 75 contractors. This is broken down into novated D&B (36 per cent); traditional (35 per cent); and develop and construction (29 per cent).

811
Construction Round Table
THINKING ABOUT BUILDING
Building 1995 July 7, pp. 63–74
A guide for clients which deals in turn with planning the business, procurement path, identifying priorities, selecting the construction team, and start-up.

810
DESIGN AND BUILD
Building (Supplement) 1995 July 7, p. 18
The series of articles presented cover the increasing trend of clients novating the design team to the contractor, Higgs & Hills approach to developing long-term partnerships, and guidance for housing associations in letting D&B contracts.

809
A. McLellan
BUILDING AFFAIR
New Builder 1995 June 23, pp. 23–6, 28–9, 32–40, 42–4
A series of articles is presented which reviews the current market for design and build, evaluates current preoccupations and describes some major projects. Finally, a tabulated list of D&B contractors is given.

808
J. Bradenburger
MANAGING BRIEFING AND DESIGN
Architects' Journal 1995 *201* June 1, pp. 39–40
The case for architects as project managers is argued, reference being made to the duties and skills required.

807
B. Scott
COMPETITIVE ADVANTAGE THROUGH ALLIANCING
Engineering, Construction and Architectural Management 1995 *2* June, pp. 83–92
The approach adopted by BP Exploration Europe in facilitating closer relationships between client and contractors is described. It involves the pooling of skills, expertise and resources to find creative solutions to achieving individual business goals, and underpinning this are alliancing contractual arrangements. These are designed to align the business objectives, to promote efficiency, to ensure the sharing of risks and to link rewards finally and clearly to the outcome of the project.

806
R. Tiong
RISKS AND GUARANTEES IN BOT TENDER
Journal of Construction Engineering and Management (ASCE) 1995 *121* June, pp. 183–8
Consideration is given to the risks to be retained by the promoter and the guarantees to be offered to the government in the selection process of a BOT tender. It is critical for the promoter to understand that the ability to retain risks and offer guarantees does provide the competitive advantage in being awarded the concession.

805
K. Charmer
PROJECT MANAGEMENT IN THE HEALTH CARE SPHERE: PART 2
Project 1995 June, pp. 11–13
The views are summarized of health care managers in the introduction of new NHS procedures for capital investment and for seeking private finance.

804
K. Charmer
CHANGES IN PROJECT MANAGEMENT OF HEALTH CARE PROJECTS
Project 1995 May, pp. 11–12
The basis of change is considered before attention is given to the capital investment manual as it relates to the 'outline' and 'full' business cases.

803
M. Roe
LEGAL ASPECTS OF PROJECT MANAGEMENT
Project 1995 May, pp. 6–8
Statutory duties and liabilities of a project manager are reviewed. Reference is also made to the qualities required of a PM as detailed in the Latham Report.

802
A. McLellan
TAKE YOUR PARTNERS
New Builder 1995 May 12, pp. 16–19
The current state of acceptance of the partnering concept in the UK is briefly reviewed. How it works in practice is discussed in relation to contractor's SDC relationship with Rover.

801
R.S. Mills
GUARANTEED MAXIMUM PRICE CONTRACTS
Construction Law 1995 *6* April/May, pp. 28–31
The options offered by GMP contracts are reviewed.

800
PROJECT MANAGEMENT BODY OF KNOWLEDGE
International Journal of Project Management 1995 *13* April, pp. 67–140
The issue is given over to an examination of European, North American and Australian initiatives in developing a formal project management body

of knowledge (BOK). The papers include: 'Criteria for a project management BOK' – R.M. Wideman; 'Establishing some basic PM BOK concepts' – W.E. Allen; 'Leadership and the PM BOK' – D.I. Cleland; 'Development of PM BOK documents: the US Project Management Institute's approach, 1983–94' – W.R. Duncan; 'APM PM BOK: the European view' – B.E. Willis; 'Addendum: PM capability test' – R. Pharro; 'Dutch PM BOK policy' – H. Watta; 'Australian competency standards' – A. Snetton; 'Towards a defense extension in the PM BOK' – F.L. Ayer and W. Bahmaler; 'Exploiting established sources for cost effective training' – A. Tsakanas; 'Upgrading skills using the US Project Management Institute BOK' – D. Ono.

799
G. Morrison
PARTNERS IN QUALITY
Chartered Builder 1995 April, pp. 9–11
The partnering concept as practised by the Morrison Construction Group is discussed, with some of the benefits to be attained by the builder being indicated.

798
P. Lansley and M. Betts
ROOTS OF A NEW DISCIPLINE: THE CASE OF CONSTRUCTION MANAGEMENT AND PROJECT MANAGEMENT
In: 'Construction / Building Education and Research beyond 2000' Proceedings of the CIB W89 Symposium, held in Orlando, Florida, USA, 5–7 April 1995, pp. 267–73
The development is considered of a performance base of knowledge to be found in the published literature of construction management and project management. It is suggested that they are both developing in an essentially empirical and non-theoretical manner.

797
A. Bolton
ROLE REVERSAL
New Civil Engineer 1995 March 23, p. 25
The ability for civil engineers to act as project managers is demonstrated by reference to the success of Procon, run by three civil engineers and a QS.

796
DESIGN AND BUILD
New Builder 1995 March 15, pp. 25, 27–8, 30, 33–4, 36, 38–40
A series of articles is presented including details on how the Ministry of Defence is now a major user of D&B, and what project management brings to this method of procurement.

795
R.A. Waterhouse
IMPLEMENTING PROJECT MANAGEMENT – IS THE CLIENT THE PROBLEM?

Chartered Builder 1995 March, pp. 21–3
It is suggested that a lack of understanding by clients of the role of the project manager is hampering its wider adoption.

794
A. Akintoye and E. Fitzgerald
DESIGN AND BUILD: A SURVEY OF ARCHITECTS' VIEWS
Engineering Construction and Architectural Management 1995 2 March, pp. 27–44
It was found that although 20 per cent of architects' private sector workload (8 per cent of public sector) is derived from D&B, architects perceive this procurement approach as sacrificing quality and design innovation. Where clients insist on a choice of D&B architects prefer the use of either novation D&B or develop and construct.

793
N.S. Ferguson et al.
EMPIRICAL STUDY OF TENDERING PRACTICE OF DUTCH MUNICIPALITIES FOR THE PROCUREMENT OF CIVIL ENGINEERING CONTRACTS
International Journal of Project Management 1995 13(3), pp. 156–61
The study reported demonstrates that some form of contractor selection was preferred and that the reputation of the contractor was the most important criterion in selection, and that negotiated contracts delivered a higher quality of work.

1994

792
B. Alexander
CHANGES IN PROCUREMENT PRACTICES: APPLYING THE EXPERIENCE OF PRIVATIZED ORGANIZATIONS IN THE PRIVATE AND PUBLIC SECTORS
Construction Round Table. 1994, 14pp.
The changes in procurement practices are examined of four organizations who have changed their status from public authority to private company. The practices adopted have provided a means of reducing costs whilst ensuring that project deliverables are enhanced in quality and timeliness.

791
National Joint Consultative Committee
CONSTRUCTION MANAGEMENT: SELECTION AND APPOINTMENT OF CONSTRUCTION

MANAGER AND TRADE CONTRACTORS (GUIDANCE NOTE 8)
RIBA Publications. 1994, 8pp.

790
National Joint Consultative Committee for Building
CODE OF PROCEDURE FOR SINGLE STAGE SELECTIVE TENDERING
RIBA Publications. 1994, 12pp.

789
National Joint Consultative Committee for Building
CODE OF PROCEDURE FOR TWO STAGE SELECTIVE TENDERING
RIBA Publications. 1994, 12pp.

788
M.N. Dawood et al.
DBID – ANALOGY BASED DSS FOR BIDDING IN CONSTRUCTION
Journal of Construction Engineering and Management (ASCE) 1994 *120(4)* December, pp. 894–7
The use is highlighted of expert system technology in developing a decision support system for bidding strategies and the importance of seeking the view of construction managers before selecting a bidding tool.

787
J. Smit
RESOLVING DIFFERENCES
New Builder 1994 December 9/16, pp. 22–3
The problems in relationships between architects and contractors in design and build projects are examined and some means for their resolution are discussed.

786
A. Souger et al.
PROCESS MODEL FOR PUBLIC SECTOR DESIGN BUILD PLANNING
Journal of Construction Engineering and Management (ASCE) 1994 *120(4)* December, pp. 857–74
The model described includes identifying (1) sequential, concurrent, and hierarchical management activities; (2) management decisions required throughout the process; and (3) relationships between activities and decisions required to plan the project. The five phases of design–build planning presented in the model include identifying facilities for design–build, performing proposal evaluation, and conducting contract administration.

785
R.J. Perreault
PROJECT MANAGER COMPETENCIES OF MECHANICAL CONTRACTORS
American Professional Constructor 1994 *18* December, pp. 12–19

Specific competencies have been derived for the major competencies identified, namely, communication, claims, cost control, schedule control, general management, document control, contracts, design and technology.

784
G. Naoum
CRITICAL ANALYSIS OF TIME AND COST OF MANAGEMENT AND TRADITIONAL CONTRACTS
Journal of Construction Engineering and Management (ASCE) 1994 *120(4)* December, pp. 687–705
Ten factors were identified to measure project performance: (1) preconstruction time; (2) construction time; (3) total time; (4) speed of construction; (5) unit cost of building; (6) time overrun; (7) cost overrun; (8) time; (9) cost; (10) quality. A theoretical framework was used to assist in comparing project performance in a case study sample of 39 management contracts and 30 traditional contracts. It was concluded that in neither the management nor the traditional systems lies the solution to all the problems facing the construction industry. To achieve project success, the parties need to match the various organizational forms to the client's characteristics, criteria, and priorities with respect to time, cost and quality. The statistical analysis suggests that management contracting performs significantly better in some respects than traditional contracting, in particular, when time was the essence of the contract and when the project was highly complex. However, the research did not provide enough evidence to support the view that management contracting can reduce the overall building cost, or that the system can increase the standard of quality.

783
VIEW FROM THE OTHER SIDE
New Builder 1994 December 2, pp. 18–19
The performance of the top 25 design-and-build consultants is reviewed and the prospects assessed.

782
DESIGN AND BUILD
New Builder 1994 December 9/16, pp. 28–32, 34
Tabulated data are provided on consultants working in design-and-build.

781
A. Webb
PROJECT ORGANIZATION STRUCTURES – 3
Project Manager Today 1994 November/December, pp. 16–17
Attention is given to the situation where the project manager has total responsibility.

780
B. Scott
COMPETITIVE ADVANTAGE THROUGH ALLIANCING
Proceedings of the ECI Conference: European Construction retaining the competitive edge. Lisbon. November 1994, pp. 145–52.

779
R.K. Loraine
PROJECT SPECIFIC PARTNERING
Engineering Construction and Architectural Management 1994 *1* September, pp. 5–16
The development is reviewed of partnering since 1985. It is pointed out that the real growth of partnering in the US has been on a project by project basis mainly in the public sector and it is argued that this arrangement has the greatest potential. In conclusion recent examples of partnering in the US are used to formulate proposals for developing partnering arrangements in the UK public sector.

778
K. Pannenbacker
PROJECT MANAGEMENT IN MAINLAND EUROPE
EPM Conference: 'Effective Project Management'. London. September 1994, 20pp.
Reference is made through a series of viewfoils to the operation of a German practice.

777
R. Dow
TURNING POINT
New Builder 1994 August 5/12, pp. 10–12
The potential for design-and-build is summarized with tabular data being provided on the major contractors.

776
DESIGN AND BUILD
Contract Journal 1994 July 28, pp. 16–35
The review identifies the major contractors in the field and provides tabulated data on performance. Other considerations cover specific projects and quality control. Details are also given of the various contractors offering D&B, their locations, markets, work profile and performance.

775
G. Ridout
CONSORT PITCH
Building 1994 August 5, pp. 30–3
Attention is given to the concept of partnering with contributions from a housebuilder, a QS, a client and a contractor.

774
M. Pettipher
EQUAL OPPORTUNITIES
New Civil Engineer 1994 July 28, pp. 14–15
The concept of partnering is evaluated with reference to Anglian Water/Morrison Construction Group.

773
J. Deal
COORDINATION NOT CHAOS – A CONTRACTOR'S VIEW
Building Services 1994 August, pp. 14–16
Attention is given to the benefits of nomination and partnering.

772
L. Davis
PARTNERING: UNION BENEFITS
Building Economist (UK) 1994 July, p. 7
Response by the industry to the concept of partnering is reviewed.

771
DESIGN AND BUILD
(Building Supplement) 1994 July 8, 13pp.
A series of articles is presented dealing with novation, the Japanese approach to procurement, partnering, problems with D&B contracts and actual projects.

770
J. Reason
MATCHING PROJECT MANAGEMENT SKILLS TO PROJECT REQUIREMENTS – A SYSTEM FOR PROJECT MANAGERS USING THE BODY OF KNOWLEDGE
Project 1994 July, pp. 24–5.

769
J. Scriven
BANKING PERSPECTIVE ON CONSTRUCTION RISKS IN BOT SCHEMES
International Construction Law Review 1994 *11* July, pp. 313–29
Following an outline of the principles of BOT schemes, the approach to risk analysis of banks lending to these schemes is described in the light of experience of schemes to date. A more detailed discussion of the allocation of risk is then undertaken with reference to parties involved and the manner of risk sharing.

768
DESIGN & BUILD
New Builder 1994 June 10, pp. 25–62

A special report analysing changes in the market and considering the architect's response, its application in France and its potential in Germany. A feature is included on IT Design & Build and two case studies are presented. A listing of D&B contractors is given.

767
R. McManamy
DESIGN-BUILD GOES BACK TO THE FUTURE
Engineering News Record 1994 June 6, pp. 26–8
Market forces in the US leading to a greater use by clients of D&B are examined. The scope of D&B within the various construction sectors is analysed.

766
I. Ndekugri and A. Turner
BUILDING PROCUREMENT BY DESIGN AND BUILD APPROACH
J. of Construction Engineering & Management 1994 *120* June, pp. 243–56
The results are presented of a survey of UK contractors, designers, and building clients regarding design and build issues. These issues include the circumstances in which the approach would be suitable, the project organizations commonly employed on design-and-build projects, the difficulties commonly encountered by practitioners and the attitudes of the construction professionals to the procurement route.

765
K. Makinson
COORDINATION, NOT CHAOS: AN ARCHITECT'S VIEW
Building Services 1994 June, pp. 16–18
The problems caused by the large number of consultants and specialists employed on a typical contract are considered. Reference is made to the current enthusiasm for design-and-build, and construction management and some thoughts expressed on where these best apply.

764
I.B. Anderson
IS THE CONSTRUCTION INDUSTRY TOO DIFFICULT TO BUY FROM? A SIMPLE GUIDE TO BUILDING PROCUREMENT
Project 1994 June, pp. 9–11.

763
L. Cohen
PORTABILITY OF PROJECT MANAGEMENT SKILLS
Project 1994 May, pp. 9–10.

762
S. Wearne
PREPARING FOR PRIVATIZED PROJECT MANAGEMENT
International Journal of Project Management 1994 *12* May, pp. 118–20
It is shown how training can help changes of attitude, values and authority needed for state organizations to be effective in conditions of privatization and competition.

761
DESIGN AND BUILD'S SUBTLE SHIFT
New Builder 1994 April 8, pp. 14–15
A review of D&B shows that it grew by more than 8 per cent in 1992 to £5500m. Although there was no change in 1993 it is estimated that it will increase by 4 per cent in 1994 and by 1988 it will have grown 16 per cent to £6636m.

760
A.P.C. Chan and P.T.I. Lam
CONSTRUCTION MANAGEMENT: A NEW ROLE TO BUILDING CONTRACTOR
In: 'Changing role of contractors in Asia Pacific Rim'. Proceedings of the first international conference held in Hong Kong on 9–10 May 1994, pp. 145–62
A comparison is made between CM and the traditional procurement route, reference being made to organizational structure, duties and responsibilities of the parties, and communication.

759
S.W. Stein
BUILD-OPERATE-TRANSFER (BOT) – A RE-EVALUATION
International Construction Law Review 1994 *11* April, pp. 101–13
The evaluation of BOT as a means of procurement considers its background, expectations and problems in relation to finance and contract structure. Finally, some conclusions are drawn in regard to its efficacy for financing infrastructure in developing countries.

758
P.D. Rwelamila
GROUP DYNAMICS AND CONSTRUCTION PROJECT MANAGER
Construction Engineering & Management (ASCE) 1994 *120* March, pp. 3–10
Some of the classic theories on human group behaviour are reviewed and related to construction project management. It is argued that group dynamics have significant impact on project performance. Overall effectiveness and efficiency of the project depend on the coordinated efforts of individuals working together on- and off-site in groups within the whole

project management system. Communication is presented as the basis of construction project group dynamics, allowing the interactions that are necessary in carrying out project activities. Two-way communication, feedback, and 'checking for meaning' are means of facilitating mutual understanding between project team members, and between various groups. Finally, the purpose of project groups or teams is examined.

757
C.M. Gordon
CHOOSING APPROPRIATE CONSTRUCTION METHOD
Construction Engineering & Management (ASCE) 1994 *120* March, pp. 196–210
The compatibility is examined of various construction contracting methods with certain types of owners and projects. Contracting methods consist of four parts: scope, organization, contract, and award. A client must create and appropriate contracting method for each project. It was determined that there are six main organizations around which the contracting variations are created: general contractor, construction manager, multiple primes, design-build, turnkey, and build-operate transfer.

756
A. Akintoye
DESIGN AND BUILD: A SURVEY OF CONSTRUCTION CONTRACTORS' VIEWS
Construction Management & Economics 1994 *12* March, pp. 155–63
The results of a survey suggest that novating D&B is not favoured by contractors. Contractors prefer consultants to provide concept design and specification and support the develop and construct technique. Design and manage, and its variants, are not attractive to clients and resented by contractors.

755
P.J. Murphy
PRICING STRATEGY FOR TARGET INCENTIVE CONTRACTS
Building Economist 1994 March, pp. 5–8
A model is described for clarifying the sensitivity of effects on project recovery to the uses of a bonus system in a target contract. It demonstrates that a contract containing fixed and variable components which may advantage the contractor at the client's expense can be mutually advantageous to both parties by the use of an appropriate incentive system.

754
V.K. Dorris
PROJECT PARTNERING: THE ARCHITECT'S PERSPECTIVE
Constructor 1994 March, pp. 20–2

The value is considered of partnering to designers and examples are given of where it has worked to the advantage of all parties.

753
R. Curl
IF THE BOOT FITS
Building Market Report 1994 February, pp. 8–9
The working of BOOT schemes in the UK is examined and guidance is given on how to minimize the risk for contractors.

752
M. McIntyre
PARTNERING SUCCESS STORIES – WINNERS IN THEIR OWN RIGHT
Constructor 1994 January, pp. 68, 70–2.

751
R.M. Drogemuller and J. Smith
INTEGRATING THE BUILDING PROCUREMENT PROCESS USING KNOWLEDGE BASED TECHNOLOGY
International Journal of Construction Information Technology 1994 *2(1)*, pp. 57–67.

750
R.M. Drogemuller and J. Smith
INTEGRATING THE BUILDING PROCUREMENT PROCESS USING KNOWLEDGE BASED TECHNOLOGY
In: 'Management of information technology for construction', K. Mathur (ed.), pp. 495–507
The system described has been developed around the design and construction of detached houses. It allows access to the geometric and spatial parameters of the building, can derive cost data and perform the final analysis. There is also an option scheduling the information to an external CPM programme.

749
A.P.C. Chan
MANAGERIAL RESPONSIBILITY OF PROJECT MANAGERS
Australian IOB Papers 1993/94 *(5)*, pp. 109–19
It is shown that the profile of the responsibilities of project managers was generally consistent. Most time was spent on coordinating and controlling, and less time on planning and organizing, and least time on motivation. However, relative involvement in these functions varied with the personal and project variables.

1993

748
W.H. Choquette
PARTNERING: A TEAMWORK APPROACH

Proc. CMAA 1993 National Construction Management Conference, CM: Strategies for rebuilding America, 5pp.
The principles and benefits of partnering are considered briefly.

747
T.J. Driscoll
DELIVERY METHODS FOR CONSTRUCTION PROJECTS
Proc. CMAA 1993 National Construction Management Conference, CM: Strategies for rebuilding America, 27pp.
Attention is given in turn to the traditional approach, design–build, CM and negotiated contracts.

746
J. Franks
DESIGN AND BUILD APPROACH TO PROCUREMENT
Construction Paper 27 CIOB. 1993, 11pp.
An overview is made of the design-and-build form of procurement formulated by its phenomenal growth since the 1980s. Attention is given to its origins, the reasons underlying its adoption, advantages/disadvantages for the client, types of client employing D&B, contractors offering the services, attitudes towards its use, market trends and its suitability for specific projects.

745
K. Allinson
WILD CARD OF DESIGN. A PERSPECTIVE ON ARCHITECTURE IN A PROJECT MANAGEMENT ENVIRONMENT
Butterworth. 1993, 436pp.
In two parts, the first reviews the nature and development of project management against a background of architectural professionalism, the use of PM as a formal discipline, and the extension of the project method to many aspects of commercial life. Part two examines in detail the fundamentals of PM, noting the differentiation between two disparate perspectives – that of the client and that of project agencies.

744
J.D. Irish
CM AT RISK: THE OWNER'S BEST BANG FOR THE BUCK
Proc. CMAA 1993 National Construction Management Conference, CM: Strategies for rebuilding America, 6pp.
Some personal thoughts are expressed on the scope and meaning of CM.

743
C. Kluenker
CM ROLES AND SERVICES

Proc. CMAA 1993 National Construction Management Conference, CM: Strategies for rebuilding America, 27pp.
The role and duties of those providing CM are summarized under the headings: pre-design; design; bid award; construction; and post-construction.

742
Construction Management Association of America
CM CERTIFICATION PROGRAM MANUAL – DRAFT
Proc. CMAA 1993 National Construction Management Conference, CM: Strategies for rebuilding America, 24pp.
The manual is designed to assist understanding of the CM Certification Programme. It incorporates general programme information; CM certification requirements; CM body of knowledge; CM certification process; and conferral and maintenance of certification.

741
N. Thompson
BUILDING THE NEW ROLE MODELS
Construction News 1993 December 2, p. 14
The shortcomings of the industry are identified and the case made for more respect and integration between design and construction if effective procurement is to be achieved.

740
J. Pain
DESIGN AND BUILD COMPARED WITH TRADITIONAL CONTRACTS
Architects Journal 1993 November 23, pp. 34–5
The benefits of design-and-build are summarized and compared to those found when using the traditional approach to procurement.

739
G.L. Church
NOTHING SUCCEEDS LIKE SUCCESS
Chartered Quantity Surveyor 1993 November, p. 10
The concept is discussed of using success forecasting as a pre-contract tool in regard to design-and-build.

738
R. Slavid
SHOULD ARCHITECTS BECOME CONSTRUCTION MANAGERS?
Architects Journal 1993 November 17, p. 18
A brief report is given of a round table IAAS meeting which considered whether construction management and the design process were compatible.

737
R. Turnbull
IMPLICATIONS FOR INTERNATIONAL CONTRACTORS

European Construction Institute, 5th Conference: 'Construction Europe: construction clients and construction in a changing world'. Florence, Italy. 18–19 November 1993, pp. 69–76
The development of BOOT projects and how they are changing the markets are discussed.

736
R.D. Hindle and P.D. Rwelamlla
CHANGE IN BUILDING PROCUREMENT SYSTEMS AND ITS EFFECT ON QUALITY IN BUILDING CONSTRUCTION
Proceedings of the Association of Researchers in Construction Management (ARCOM), 9th annual conference: 'Advances in Construction Management Research'. Oxford. September 1993, pp. 62–72.

735
J. Lewis and D.W. Cheetham
HISTORICAL ROOTS OF CURRENT PROBLEMS IN BUILDING PROCUREMENT
Proceedings of the Association of Researchers in Construction Management (ARCOM), 9th annual conference: 'Advances in Construction Management Research'. Oxford. September 1993, pp. 50–61
The current problems stemming from the separation of design and construction are examined in terms of the environment which existed in the development of traditional methods between the late eighteenth century and the early twentieth century.

734
PARTNERING ON A TROUBLED PROJECT
Constructor 1993 75 October, pp. 45–6
It is argued that partnering can be introduced on troubled projects with success. Some guidelines on how this can be achieved are presented.

733
R.K. Lorain and O. Bannmark
MRICA HYDRO-ELECTRIC PROJECT – A STUDY IN PARTNERING
Proc. ICE Water Maritime and Energy 1993 1 September, pp. 133–40
The key elements of cooperation are identified and their impact discussed on the negotiation of contracts and completion of the works.

732
D. Stevens
PARTNERING AND VALUE MANAGEMENT
Building Economist 1993 September, pp. 5–7
The basic concepts of partnering and the benefits that it can bring are summarized. Attention is given to the use of group workshops in problem evaluation and resolution which are the overlapping of partnering, value management and strategic planning.

731
J.B. Dorter
CONSTRUCTION AND PROJECT MANAGEMENT – AUSTRALIAN EXPECTATION AND EXPERIENCE
International Construction Law Review 1993 10 October, pp. 435–42
Following a comparison of management and traditional contracting, attention is then given to contractual relationships, advantages and disadvantages, contracts and dispute resolution.

730
B. Somers
SPACE RACE – MANAGING DESIGN AND BUILD
Chartered Builder 1993 October, pp. 10–11
The importance is discussed of designer-site communication links on the Farnborough Aerospace Centre in ensuring each phase of the project was completed on time.

729
G.W. Jones
CONSTRUCTION AND PROJECT MANAGEMENT – THE STRUCTURE AND ITS IMPACT ON PROJECT PARTICIPANTS. USA – THE EXPERIENCE AND TRENDS
International Construction Law Review 1993 10 October, pp. 425–34
Attention is given to construction management with particular emphasis on insurances, variations, disputes and liability.

728
S. Nelson
STUDY OF THE USE OF DESIGN-BUILD CONTRACTS BY HOUSING ASSOCIATIONS
Housing Review 1993 42 July/August, pp. 69–70

727
ROLES OF A PROJECT MANAGER
Architecture 1993 84 July, pp. 115–17
The skills are identified of a project manager and matched with the experience and inclinations of the typical architect. Suggestions intended to overcome the mismatch are made, including recruitment and investment in training.

726
R. Lush
PROCUREMENT – CHOOSING THE APPROPRIATE SYSTEM. PART 3
Construction Law 1993 4 August/September, pp. 335–8
Attention is given to the client's role and responsibilities defining performance and payment systems.

725
V. Powell-Smith
SINGLE STAGE DESIGN & BUILD
Contract Journal 1993 August 19, p. 17
The salient points are described of the single stage design-and-build variant of the GC/Works 1/Edition 3 form of contract.

726
D. Chevin
VARIETY PERFORMERS
Building 1993 August 6, pp. 36–7
Attention is given to potential for project managers operating outside building sites.

724
J. Franks
MAKING THE MOST OF DESIGN AND BUILD
Chartered Quantity Surveyor 1993 July/August, pp. 18–21
The current state of design-and-build is reviewed with data being provided on the extent of its use in the range of projects to which it is applied.

723
M. Frillet
MANAGEMENT CONTRACTING: A CIVIL LAW APPROACH BASED ON THE FRENCH EXAMPLE
International Construction Law Review 1993 10 July, pp. 337–47.

722
T. Kreifeb
CONSTRUCTION OR PROJECT MANAGEMENT IN GERMANY – THE STRUCTURE AND ITS IMPACT ON PROJECT PARTICIPANTS – AN OVERVIEW
International Construction Law Review 1993 10 July, pp. 326–36.

721
E. Jones
CONSTRUCTION MANAGEMENT AND PROJECT MANAGEMENT – THE DIFFERENCES IN STRUCTURE AND ITS IMPACT ON PROJECT PARTICIPANTS
International Construction Law Review 1993 10 July, pp. 348–65.

720
R.H. Turner
CONSTRUCTION MANAGEMENT – ARABIAN GULF REGION
International Construction Law Review 1993 10 July, pp. 301–25
A comprehensive review is made of the systems in operation in the Arabian Gulf, both in legal and commercial terms, as they affect the construction industry.

719
K. Takayanagi
CONSTRUCTION OR PROJECT MANAGEMENT – THE STRUCTURE AND IMPACT ON PROJECT PARTICIPANTS
International Construction Law Review 1993 10 July, pp. 294–300
Japanese contractual arrangements and practices in relation to construction/project management are summarized.

718
D. Nunn
D&B 93
Contract Journal 1993 July 29, pp. 14–16, 18–27
The current state of the design-and-build market is surveyed, with some views expressed by clients and a ranking list of D&B contractors based on 1993 figures provided. Finally, there are details of the performance of individual contractors, their markets and a breakdown of work with novated design, designed in-house, and work design and manage.

717
D. Chevin (ed.)
DESIGN & BUILD. THE PROFILE OF CONTEMPORARY DESIGN & BUILD
Building Supplement 1993 July, 29pp.
Articles included cover the results of a client's survey, limiting client risk, architect-led procurement and novation.

716
J. Wright
PITFALLS OF DESIGN AND BUILD
Construction News 1993 July 1, p. 14
Some areas of potential risk to contractors in design and build contracts are discussed.

715
S. Woodward and T. Butcher
NHS PROJECT MANAGEMENT AGREEMENT
Construction Law 1993 4 June/July, pp. 288–92
The agreement emphasizes the services to be provided and addresses and accommodates the structures, procedures and interests which exist within the NHC. The major points of the Agreement are described and discussed.

714
R. Lush
PROCUREMENT – CHOOSING THE APPROPRIATE SYSTEM (PART 2)
Construction Law 1993 4 June/July, pp. 301–3
Attention is given to management contracting and guaranteed maximum price.

713

D. Mosey

NHS PROCUREMENT – IS THERE AN ALTERN-ATIVE TO JCT80? (PART TWO)

Construction Law 1993 4 June/July, pp. 304–6

Attention is given to management contracting and construction management and how they might be accommodated within Capricode.

712

DESIGN AND BUILD

New Builder 1993 June 11, pp. 19–22, 25–9, 31–2, 34, 36, 39–40, 42–4

A series of articles is presented demonstrating the application of design-and-build. There is a tabular listing of firms offering the service with details of turnover, areas of operation and types of work.

711

DESIGN AND BUILD. LIABILITY PITFALLS FOR CONSULTANTS

Building Engineer 1993 April, pp. 22–3

Guidance is given on liability issues as they relate to consultants, contractors and clients under the design–build approach.

710

D. Mosey

NHS PROCUREMENT – IS THERE AN ALTERN-ATIVE TO JCT80–1

Construction Law 1993 4 April/May, pp. 255–8

Alternative approaches to construction procurement and how these can be applied by NHS authorities and trusts are considered.

709

P. Cowley

ELECTRICAL & MECHANICAL SERVICES ON DESIGN AND BUILD PROJECTS. CONTROL-LING THE VALUABLES

Surveying Technician 1993 April, p. 16.

708

A.B. Vickery

CONSTRUCTION MANAGEMENT: INTRACT-ABLE PROBLEM?

Construction Law Journal 1993 9(2), pp. 87–95

The theoretical advantages and disadvantages are discussed of construction management, particular attention being given to the conceptual problems faced by draftsmen in translating the apparent advantages to contractors into workable contractual provisions in regard to the coordination of trade contractors, apportionment of blame for delay and disruption and the application of sanctions thereof.

707

R.A. Waterhouse

PROJECT MANAGEMENT – BUZZ WORD OR PROFESSIONAL DISCIPLINE?

Construction Law Journal 1993 9(2), pp. 96–100

The different forms of project management and their roots are reviewed.

706

B. Danks

ROLE OF THE PROJECT MANAGER

Proc. IBC Legal Studies and Services Conf. 'Effective Project Management for Construction Projects'. London, 18 March 1992, 7pp.

A summary paper covering the emergence and growth, workload and future of the project manager.

705

PARTNERING – RETURNING COMMON SENSE TO THE CONSTRUCTION JOB SITE

Constructor (US) 1993 March, p. 20.

704

R. Lush

PROCUREMENT – CHOOSING THE APPROPRI-ATE SYSTEM

Construction Law 1993 3 February/March, pp. 213–16

An appropriate approach to procurement selection is given.

703

DESIGN AND BUILD SPECIAL

Construction News 1993 February 25, pp. 15–17

A series of short contributions is given illustrating the application and benefits of design-and-build. The results of a survey suggest that design-and-build is growing in popularity, is less prone to disputes, and can be used on any size of job.

702

M. Ryan and G. Rounce

NEW APPROACH TO DESIGN AND BUILD

Project 1993 5 January, pp. 15–18

The basis is described of a design-led design and build approach, attention being given to its advantages and limitations.

701

C. Bound and N. Morrison

CONTRACTS IN USE

Chartered Quantity Surveyor 1993 15 January, pp. 16–17

The survey notes a striking decline in lump sum contracts countered by an increase in design-and-build, together with dramatic acceptance of Construction Management.

700
A. Tan
PARTNERING – THE NEW WAY OF ENDING CONSTRUCTION CONFLICTS IN MALAYSIA
Building Technology and Management 1992/1993 *19*, pp. 77–9.

699
W.D. O'Sullivan
USE OF SYSTEM METHODS IN THE SELECTION OF A PROCUREMENT PATH
Building Technology and Management 1992/1993 *19*, pp. 35–41.

1992

698
K. Hutchinson and T. Putt
USE OF DESIGN/BUILD PROCUREMENT METHODS BY HOUSING ASSOCIATIONS
RICS. 1992, 18pp.
A study is presented of the effects of procurement methods of new approaches to the funding of housing associations and their implications for housing quality and maintenance costs.

697
RICS
CONTRACTS IN USE: A SURVEY OF BUILDING CONTRACTS IN USE DURING 1991
1992, 9pp.
The survey demonstrates a marked decline in lump sum contracts countered by a substantial growth in design and build. Construction management, although used in only a small number of projects, appears to have captured nearly 20 per cent of the total value.

696
M.A. Cairney
DESIGN AND BUILD – THE ROLE OF A PROJECT MANAGER
Proc. 'Architectural Management' 1992. E&F N Spon, pp. 160–8.

695
I. Macpherson
SATISFYING THE CLIENT'S NEEDS
Proc. IBC Legal Studies & Services Conf. 'Effective Project Management for Construction Projects'. London, 1992, 9pp.
Attention is given to the roles and responsibilities of the project manager, decision-making aids, procure-

ment route, services to the client, reporting techniques and post construction support.

694
CODE OF PRACTICE FOR PROJECT MANAGEMENT FOR CONSTRUCTION AND DEVELOPMENT
CIOB. 1992, 171pp.
The definitive guide which allows a detailed understanding of the processes involved and the techniques employed. The structure of the Code mirrors the project management process itself. Each chapter deals with a specific phase of project management and is supported by specimen forms, checklists and examples of typical documentation. The key issues are considered under the headings of feasibility, strategy, pre-construction, construction, fitting out, commissioning, completion and handover, and occupation. At Part 2 the Project Management Agreement and Conditions of Engagement issued by the RICS is reproduced and the Code is completed by a typical Project Handbook at Part 3.

693
W.P. Hughes
AN ANALYSIS OF TRADITIONAL GENERAL CONTRACTING
1992. CIOB. Construction Paper No. 12, 8pp.
Following a consideration of the use of general contracting, attention is then given to the basic characteristics of traditional general contracting and the associated risks.

692
D. Burton
PROJECT MANAGEMENT IN PRACTICE
Proceedings of a conference organized by the School of Business and Industrial Management on effective project management, 1992, 21pp.
In providing a checklist of key issues, attention is given to assembling the brief, assembling consultants, practical management, optimum procurement route, and control systems and reporting.

691
G. Reiss
PROJECT MANAGEMENT DEMYSTIFIED: TODAY'S TOOLS AND TECHNIQUES
1992. E&F N Spon, 213pp.
Covers the role of the project manager, project management concepts and philosophy, implementation of a project management approach, project planning, network diagrams, resource planning and site optimization, cost control, work behaviour structures, programme monitoring and control, motivation, building the project team, project tools and software, selection criteria.

690
R.F. Cushman and K. Sperling Taub (eds)
DESIGN BUILD CONTRACTING HANDBOOK
John Wiley & Sons. 1992, 424pp.
Related to US practice a series of contributions is presented on design–build issues. They include single-point responsibility, application to technologically advanced projects, organization, bonding, insurances, contract award and eligibility, environmental issues, allocation of risk between designer and builder, protecting the owner, designer-builder and sub-contractor with contract clauses, and performance guarantees.

689
R.M. Kliem and I.S. Ludin
THE PEOPLE SIDE OF PROJECT MANAGEMENT
Gower. 1992, 190pp.
The management relationships with clients, sponsors and members of the project team themselves are considered. Interactions among them and the impact of these interactions on scheduling, budgeting, change management, monitoring and other project activities are discussed. In doing so the psychological and political problems and their solutions are examined.

688
Royal Institute of British Architects
STANDARD FORM OF AGREEMENT FOR THE APPOINTMENT OF AN ARCHITECT: DESIGN AND BUILD: CONTRACTOR CLIENT VERSION
RIBA. 1992, 8pp.

687
Royal Institute of British Architects
STANDARD FORM OF AGREEMENT FOR THE APPOINTMENT OF AN ARCHITECT: DESIGN AND BUILD: EMPLOYER CLIENT VERSION
RIBA. 1992, 8pp.

686
P. Waterhouse
SPOT THE DIFFERENCE
Chartered Quantity Surveyor 1992 *14* December/January, pp. 21–2
The definition of project management is discussed and the role identified.

685
G. Reiss
GREAT PROJECTS OF THE PAST. A VICTORIAN LESSON IN PROJECT MANAGEMENT
Project Manager Today 1992 November/December, pp. 12–15
An examination is made of the construction of the Crystal Palace.

684
A. Pike
CONSTRUCTION MANAGEMENT AND THE JCT CONTRACTS
International Construction Law Review October 1992 *9(4)*, pp. 476–504
The contractual background is outlined to construction management and other forms of procurement and to the employer's existing choices under the JCT conditions. Particular attention is given to the provisions of the JCT Management Contract.

683
P. Fenn
MANAGING THE CONTRACTUAL RELATIONSHIPS: PRIVATIZATION AND PROJECT MANAGEMENT
Proceedings of the Association of Researchers in Construction Management (ARCOM), 8th annual conference, September 1992, Isle of Man, pp. 81–7
It is suggested that privatization of professional services by substituting contractual for hierarchical relationships adds to the endemic conflict and disputes associated with construction.

682
D. Chevin
MULTIPLE CHOICE
Building 1992 *257* August 14, pp. 24–7, 29, 34, 38, 42–6
A series of articles is presented covering mainly the practical applications of design and build.

681
L. Rogers
MANAGING FINE WITHOUT YOU
Architects Journal 1992 *196* July 11, p. 10
The salient points of the report 'Architects as Project Managers' are discussed.

680
G. Haley
CURRENT ISSUES FACING BOOT PROJECTS IN UK AND OVERSEAS
Project 1992 *5* July, pp. 21–3, 34
Attention is given to bidding costs, industrial policy, industrial targeting, financing, risk allocation and a choice of partners.

679
J. Price
DESIGN AND BUILD CONTRACTING: PROCURING THE DESIGN
BEC Contract Bulletin 1992 *5* July, pp. 3–6
The contractual rules are considered which govern the sub-letting of design. Key aspects are highlighted

of the conditions of engagement on which such designers are employed and comments made on the practice of novation of the architect's conditions of engagement from the employer to the contractor.

678
A. Hemsley
COST IMPLICATIONS OF DESIGN AND BUILD
Paper to IBC Seminar on Design and Build Contracting held in London on 15 July 1992, 34pp.
The elements of design-and-build contracts discussed are the types available, the appropriateness of the arrangement, the brief, choosing between negotiation and tendering, controlling cost and quality and client changes. The last section considers the economic advantages of design-and-build.

677
O. Luder
ROLE AND RESPONSIBILITIES OF THE CLIENT WHEN USING DESIGN AND BUILD TYPE CONTRACTS
Paper to IBC Seminar on Design and Build Contracting held in London on 15 July 1992, 16pp.

676
T. O'Sullivan
GETTING THE BEST FROM THE SYSTEM
Paper to IBC Seminar on Design and Build Contracting held in London on 15 July 1992, 13pp.
The features of design-and-build discussed are establishing the client's requirements, bidding and variations.

675
J. Franks
DESIGN AND BUILD TENDERING – DO WE NEED A CODE OF PRACTICE?
Chartered Builder 1992 4 June, pp. 8–10
The case is argued for a design-and-build code of tendering which might include an agreement that the number of tenderers be kept to a minimum of three; that for major projects a two-stage arrangement be employed and that payment be made to all tenderers as a contribution to design costs.

674
J.H. Pack
KNOWLEDGE ACQUISITION METHODOLOGY FOR A DESIGN/BUILD CONSTRUCTION EXPERT SYSTEM
American Professional Constructor 1992 16 July, pp. 13–20.

673
S. Kirby
DESIGN AND BUILD: INSURANCE REQUIREMENTS
BEC Contract Bulletin 1992 5 July, pp. 6–8.

672
R.L.K. Tiong et al.
CRITICAL SUCCESS FACTORS IN WINNING BOT CONTRACTS
ASCE Journal of Construction Engineering and Management 1992 118 June, pp. 217–18
The build-operate-transfer (BOT) concept represents a step forward in meeting the needs of developing countries for more capital investments in infrastructure and industrial construction. However, for a private-sector consortium bidding for a BOT concession, the road to winning a major BOT contract is not easy. The consortium must be willing to take calculated risks and at the same time be adaptable to changing demands and circumstances in the host country. This paper describes the importance and characteristics of six critical success factors (CSF) that are vital for project sponsors in their endeavours to win lucrative BOT contracts. These factors are: entrepreneurship, picking the right project, a strong team of stakeholders, an imaginative technical solution, a competitive financial proposal, and the inclusion of special features in the bid.

671
J.H. Pack et al.
SELECTION OF DESIGN/BUILD PROPOSAL USING FUZZY-LOGIC SYSTEM
ASCE Journal of Construction Engineering and Management 1992 118 June, pp. 303–17
Design/build procurement approaches have been proposed as alternatives to the traditional design/bid/build method. The successful selection process for choosing a design/build proposal is based on a high degree of technical factors and low construction cost. However, the objectives of maximizing the degree of the technical factors and minimizing the cost are in conflict and the evaluation of the technical factors and cost is associated with the uncertainty. In this study, a multicriterion decision-making methodology using a fuzzy-logic system is provided to assist decision makers in selecting the winning design/build proposal that best satisfies the requirement of technical factors and the cost reduction. An example application of the proposed evaluation methodology to an actual project is provided.

670
R. Catt
OPEN FORUM
Chartered Quantity Surveyor 1992 14 June, p. 20
The principles of the open forum management approach to procurement are outlined. The system is claimed to save 10–15 per cent of the cost of development projects.

669

Z. Herbsman and R. Ellis

MULTI-PARAMETER BIDDING SYSTEM – INNOVATION IN CONTRACT ADMINISTRATION

ASCE Journal of Construction Engineering and Management 1992 *118* March, pp. 142–50

The vast majority of construction contracts are procured using the low-bid system. In the low-bid system price is the sole basis for determining the successful bidder. This traditional approach has certain drawbacks. In recent years, several innovative modifications to the low-bid system have been tried. A more comprehensive approach to bid award criteria is wanted. A presentation of a multiparameter bid award system would include various owner-selected parameters, such as cost, time and quality. Quantification of these parameters and bidder evaluation methodology are included. Finally, a discussion of the advantages and disadvantages of a multiparameter bid award criteria system is presented.

668

D. Woodward et al.

RISK MANAGEMENT OF BOOT PROJECTS

Project 1992 *11* March, pp. 10–12.

667

J.S. Russell et al.

CONTRACTOR PREQUALIFICATION DATA FOR CONSTRUCTION OWNERS

Construction Management & Economics 1992 *10* March, pp. 117–35

Data are presented regarding the perceived impact of various decision factors on contractor pre-qualification analysis techniques. Results of this analysis can aid employers in reviewing their procedures.

666

T. Beresford and P. Kelland

DESIGN AND BUILD. WHAT'S ALLOWED

New Builder 1992 February 27, p. 22

The benefits of capital allowances to design-and-build contracts are assessed.

665

R. Church and K. Potts

TRENDS IN DESIGN AND BUILD CONTRACTING

Chartered Quantity Surveyor (Bulletin) 1992 *14* February, pp. ii–iii

Results are presented into certain aspects of design-and-build, such as turnover, contract form used, cost comparison, etc.

664

S. Drayton and K. Potts

DESIGN AND BUILD IN CIVIL ENGINEERING

Civil Engineering Surveyor 1992 *17* February, pp. 4–5

The pitfalls and advantages of design–build for civil engineering are considered. Typical amendments are suggested to the 6th edition of the ICE Conditions where a design–build project is envisaged.

663

T. McMahan

CONSTRUCTION MANAGERS AND THE PROVISION OF SAFETY SERVICES: SCOPE OF THE CM'S DUTY

CM Advisor 1992 January/February, pp. 5–8.

662

J. Whitelaw

PROGRAM CONTROL

New Builder 1992 January 30, pp. 22–3

An outline is given of programme management – an extended form of project management – as practised by Heery International.

661

G. Ridout

EAST WEST TRADE ROUTE

Building 1992 *257* January 10, pp. 42–3

An interview with Akio Yamamoto who has recently completed a study into the difficulties facing Japanese clients and project managers in the UK. To overcome many of the problems a hybrid project management approach is proposed.

660

P.K. Goulding

PROJECT MANAGEMENT IN EUROPE

Structural Survey 1992 *11(1)*, pp. 10–14

Some broad comparisons are made with practice in the UK.

1991

659

D. French

ON TARGET: A DESIGN AND MANAGE TARGET COST PROCUREMENT SYSTEM

1991. Thomas Telford, 155pp.

The target cost design-and-manage contract described advocates teamwork between the client, systems designer and manufacturer to develop the most appropriate solution to a project. The methodology hinges around contractors submitting a basic fee for the prime costs, together with a sliding fee for cost savings and overspending within a pre-set band. Any savings are shared between employer and contractor and vice versa if an overspend occurs.

658
D.E.L. Janssens
DESIGN–BUILD EXPLAINED
1991, Macmillan, 216pp.
A very practical line is taken to this description of design–build which is approached in turn from the viewpoint of the client, and the contractor.

657
CODE OF PROCEDURE FOR THE SELECTION OF A MANAGEMENT CONTRACTOR AND WORK CONTRACTORS
1991. RIBA Publications, 12pp.

656
S.G. Naoum
PROCUREMENT AND PROJECT PERFORM-ANCE: A COMPARISON OF MANAGEMENT AND TRADITIONAL CONTRACTING
CIOB, 1991 (Occasional Paper No. 45), 37pp.
A comparison is made of management and traditional contracts based on research which sought to establish whether the means of procurement influenced project performance, whilst recognizing that the characteristics of the client, designer and the project may also play a significant part in shaping success.

655
B. Curtis et al.
ROLES, RESPONSIBILITIES AND RISKS IN MANAGEMENT CONTRACTING
CIRIA, 1991 (Special publication 81), 88pp.
The concepts and practice of management contracting (MC) are examined and the relative merits of construction management (CM) are debated. The difficulties sometimes encountered in putting MC into practice are investigated with particular reference to learning new roles and accepting different responsibilities. The effect of JCT87 is covered and allied management systems – purporting to offer enhanced benefits – are compared with MC in terms of effectiveness and suitability for different projects and clients.

654
W.P. Hughes
ANALYSIS OF CONSTRUCTION MANAGE-MENT CONTRACTS
CIOB, 1991 (Technical Information Service Paper 135), 6pp.
The construction management (CM) approach to procurement is discussed with particular reference to its field of use, the basic characteristics of CM contracts and the apportionment of risk. It is concluded that CM is a better approach than management contracting to creating a project team which is conducive to teamwork and to the more effective fulfilment of client objectives.

653
A.A. Kwakye
FAST TRACK CONSTRUCTION
CIOB, 1991 (Occasional Paper 46), 36pp.
Following a brief review of traditional modes of procurement attention is focused on fast-tracking and its application. The characteristics, benefits, risks and costs of the technique are considered in detail before some of the problems limiting its application are identified. The final part of the report discusses its application and the types of organization best suited for its adoption.

652
D. Livingstone and C. Pouncey
IMPACT OF THE EC's PUBLIC PROCUREMENT DIRECTIVES ON THE NEGOTIATION OF CON-STRUCTION CONTRACTS
Proceedings of Legal Studies and Services Conference Choosing the right procurement method; Which contract is the best for whom and why. December 1991, 18pp.

651
C. Gilmour
WHY USE DESIGN AND BUILD?
Proceedings of Legal Studies and Services Conference: Choosing the right procurement method; Which contract is the best for whom and why. December 1991, 15pp.
Aspects of design-and-build briefly considered include its strengths and weaknesses, clients' involvement and cost implications.

650
T. Blackler
MANAGEMENT CONTRACTOR V CONSTRUC-TION MANAGER
Proceedings of Legal Studies and Services Conference: Choosing the right procurement method; Which contract is the best for whom and why. December 1991, 49pp.
Some of the major points arising from reports prepared by Reading University and Southampton University are compared. Attention is then given to legal problems unique to management systems such as default of a works contractor, programming, delays by trade contractors. Other issues considered are set-off, insolvency and latent defects. Extracts from relevant cases are included as an appendix.

649
C. Manzoni
TRADITIONAL FORMS OF CONTRACTING

Proceedings of Legal Studies and Services Conference: Choosing the right procurement method; Which contract is the best for whom and why. December 1991, 23pp.

An assessment is made of the relative merits of the JCT80, JFC84, Minor Works Agreement, Prime Cost with Fixed Fees, JCT81, JCT87 and measured term contracts.

648

M. Walker

MANAGEMENT CONTRACTING

Proceedings of Legal Studies and Services Conference: Choosing the right procurement method; Which contract is the best for whom and why. December 1991, 23pp.

A comparative assessment is made of management contracting, attention being given to relationships with the professional team, obligations and responsibilities, risk and future prospects.

647

P. Capper

DESIGN RESPONSIBILITIES UNDER THE VARIOUS CONTRACTUAL OPTIONS

Proceedings of Legal Studies and Services Conference: Choosing the right procurement method; which contract is the best for whom and why. December 1991, 20pp.

646

C. Forrest

CONSTRUCTION MANAGEMENT

Proceedings of Legal Studies and Services Conference: Choosing the right procurement method; Which contract is the best for whom and why. December 1991, 22pp.

The principles and organization and contractual relationship of CM are outlined. Criteria to employ in the selection of CM are identified and some details given relating to contract administration, design management, cost management and time and quality management.

645

M. January

BRITISH PROPERTY FEDERATION SYSTEM – A CRITICAL REVIEW OF THE BPF MANUAL

Building Economist 1991 *30* December, pp. 16–18.

644

S.C. McCarthy and R.L.K. Tiong

FINANCIAL AND CONTRACTUAL ASPECTS OF BUILD–OPERATE–TRANSFER PROJECTS

Int. Journal of Project Management 1991 *9* November, pp. 222–7

The financial aspects discussed cover raising finance, assistance needed from host government, use of existing

facilities, retention of title, and construction cost overrun. The methods of forming the concession and the construction and operation agreements, and the role of the *maitre d'oeuvre* are also discussed.

643

C. Leong

ACCOUNTABILITY AND PROJECT MANAGEMENT: A CONVERGENCE OF OBJECTIVES

Int. Journal of Project Management 1991 *9* November, pp. 240–9

The value is considered of accommodating an accountability framework for construction project management.

642

D.G. Woodward

MODEL CONCESSION AGREEMENT AND FINANCING ISSUES

Project 1991 *4* November, pp. 23–6

Consideration is given to the use of turnkey contracts and their relationship with the BOOT concept; the analysis of comparison of a number of concession agreements; the underlying principles of BOOT financing; and risk analysis of BOOT projects.

641

D.J.O. Ferry

CONTRACTUAL SYSTEMS FOR THE DESIGN AND CONSTRUCTION OF CIVIL ENGINEERING WORK IN THE UK COMPARED WITH THOSE IN OTHER EUROPEAN COUNTRIES

ICE Proc. 1991 *90(1)* October, pp. 1113–15 (Discussion).

640

R.M. Denny

DESIGN AND BUILD – THE BPF SYSTEM – BUILDING TOWARDS 2001

Property Journal 1991 *16* October, pp. 21–2

It is argued that the principles of the BPF system for design-and-build have been adopted and modified and that they coincide with recommendations for 'design and manage' in the NCG report 'Building towards 2001'.

639

A.A. Kwakye

FAST TRACKING CONSTRUCTION PROCUREMENT

Chartered Builder 1991 *3* October, pp. 15–17

The cost, risks and benefits of fast-tracking are outlined.

638

Y. Rosenfeld and D. Geltner

COST-PLUS AND INCENTIVE CONTRACTING: SOME FALSE BENEFITS AND INHERENT DRAWBACKS

Construction Management & Economics 1991 9 September, pp. 481–92
Two problem areas are described which are associated with cost-plus and incentive contracts, viz. the financial costs of an earlier construction start through the use of 'fast-tracked' design-build cycle, and the counter productive effects of the adverse selection of competing firms that most occur.

637
S.J.A. Tolson
BUILDING PROCUREMENT – AN END IN ITSELF OR A MEANS TO AN END?
Arbitration 1991 57 August, pp. 198–204
This overview considers the trend towards management contracts and fast-tracking concluding that there is much to be gained by improving the management of projects and giving less concern to risk allocation and the form of contract used.

636
D. Gowan and J. Bolton
US CONSTRUCTION TECHNIQUES – HELP OR HINDRANCE?
Building Research & Information 1991 19 July/August, pp. 212–13
Corporate insolvencies in the UK resulting from cash flow problems appear to be independent of contractual arrangement. Lessons are available from US experience where a less confrontational approach is adopted by contractors and employers. Particular attention is given to the benefits of CM.

635
R. Saxon
DESIGN AND BUILD: 3. WHAT DO WE DO NEXT?
Architects Journal 1991 194 July 17, pp. 52–3
Future trends for procurement are examined.

634
D. Chappell
DESIGN AND BUILD: 2. FACING THE FACTS
Architects Journal 1991 194 July 10, pp. 57–60
Consideration is given to contracts, liability and warranties.

633
D. Hutchinson and J. Spencely
DESIGN AND BUILD: 1. VIEWS FROM THE PEWS
Architects Journal 1991 194 July 3, pp. 51–3
Two opposing views of design-and-build by architects are presented.

632
G. Rounce
FAST TRACK – THE DESIGNER'S RISK?

Project 1991 4 June, pp. 20–3
The risk elements for the design team in fast-track projects are discussed.

631
CM CONTINUES GAIN IN SHARE OF CONSTRUCTION
CM Advisor 1991 10 June, pp. 1, 3
Key facts from two reviews are presented which demonstrate CM's share of construction primarily in the US but also in foreign markets.

630
D&B LISTINGS
New Builder 1991 June 6, pp. 34, 38, 40–4
A list is given of contractors offering design-and-build services, indicating turnover, in-house facilities, areas of work, and types of work.

629
J. Whitelaw
DESIGN AND BUILD: POPULAR CHOICE
New Builder 1991 June 6, pp. 20–1
The reasons for the growing popularity of design-and-build are traced.

628
P. Fidler
DESIGN AND BUILD: CLASSIC PROBLEMS
New Builder 1991 June 6, pp. 22–3
The merits and limitations of design-and-build are assessed.

627
D. Trench
DESIGN AND CONSTRUCTION PROCUREMENT OF GRAND BUILDINGS USING THE BPF SYSTEM
Property Journal 1991 16 June, pp. 12–14
Redevelopment of Grand Buildings in Trafalgar Square using the BPF system is outlined, reference being made to client's requirements, tendering, VE and cost savings, contractor design, shell and core construction and fitting out.

626
M.J. Bresnen
CONSTRUCTION CONTRACTING IN THEORY AND PRACTICE. A CASE STUDY
Construction Management & Economics 1991 9 June, pp. 247–63
Evidence is presented from a case study of the management contract to demonstrate how the motives or aims that each party to the contract brings to the relationship and the ability they have to influence successfully the decision and actions taken, can have a substantial effect on the course of events. It is

concluded that any assessment of the efficacy of delivery systems should take into account the factors likely to influence the operation of these systems in practice.

625
C.W. Ibbs
INNOVATIVE CONTRACT INCENTIVE FEATURES FOR CONSTRUCTION
Construction Management & Economics 1991 9 April, pp. 157–69
The strategic choices are outlined which are available for designing and administering incentivized construction contracts. The project conditions that facilitate use of particular features and some of the pitfalls associated with each are also discussed.

624
G. Ridout
TARGET PRACTICE
Building 1991 256 April 19, pp. 43–5
Brief details are given of the target cost design-and-manage systems operated by David Trench.

623
R.A. Waterhouse
BUZZ WORD OR PROFESSIONAL DISCIPLINE?
Project 1991 April, pp. 23–5
An evaluation is made of the concept of project management.

622
D.G. Woodward et al.
HANDS UP IF YOU KNOW WHAT A BOOT IS
Project 1991 April, pp. 28–30
The development and current status of BOOT (build-own-operate-transfer) contracts are reviewed.

621
R. Mohsini and C.H. Davidson
BUILDING PROCUREMENT – KEY TO IMPROVED PERFORMANCE
Building Research & Information 1991 19 March/April, 106pp.
Consideration is given to alternative procurement in terms of the owner's strategies and how they affect his chance of obtaining best value for money.

620
A. Bhoyrue
PROFILE – BILL MARTIN: WIMPEY CM IN THE PUBLIC EYE
Contract Journal 1991 March 21, p. 14.

619
L. Whitting
WORLDWIDE SPREAD FOR AMEC DESIGN AND MANAGE

Construction News 1991 March 14, p. 31
AMEC's approach of offering design and build packages based on lump sum guaranteed price is discussed.

618
D. Ferry
CONSTRUCTION PROCUREMENT IN THE EC
Structural Engineer 1991 69 March, pp. 98–9
A summary of practice in UK, France, Spain, Germany and Italy is given.

617
J.J. Tighe
BENEFITS OF FAST TRACKING ARE A MYTH
Project Management 1991 9 February, pp. 49–51
The negative impacts that fast-tracking has on both the design and construction of a project are examined. It is argued that fast-tracking is remedial rather than a desirable alternative and that with proper planning fast-tracking is unnecessary.

616
A. Mills
HOW EFFECTIVE IS PUBLIC TENDERING?
Chartered Builder (Australia) 1991 February, 20pp.
A survey is reported of the factors affecting the tendering and procurement process. It was found that the performance of projects procured by open tender was unacceptably poor. It is suggested that a balance between reasonable competition and the reasonable cost of competition is represented by about four tenderers.

615
M.M. Cusack
Proceedings of the First National RICS Research Conference held 10–11 January 1991 at the Barbican Centre
CONSTRUCTION MANAGEMENT – THE WAY FORWARD
In: 'Investment, procurement and performance in construction', pp. 242–55.

614
T. Cornick
Proceedings of the First National RICS Research Conference held 10–11 January 1991 at the Barbican Centre
CONSTRUCTION MANAGEMENT – DELIVERY AND DISCIPLINE
In: 'Investment, procurement and performance in construction', pp. 236–41.

613
A. Yates
Proceedings of the First National RICS Research Conference held 10–11 January 1991 at the Barbican Centre

PROCUREMENT AND CONSTRUCTION MANAGEMENT

In: 'Investment, procurement and performance in construction', pp. 219–35

The current pressures exerted on procurement decisions are examined, with particular attention being given to the factors influencing decisions and their implications.

612
D. Ferry
Proceedings of the conference held on 24–25 January 1991 at Heathrow, organized by the Institution of Civil Engineers

ORGANIZATION OF PROCUREMENT

In: 'Civil engineering project procedure in the EC', pp. 17–28
Discussion pp. 29–31
Following an outline of the components of procurement, differences in UK and European practice are identified before some detail is given of procedures in the UK, France, Spain, Germany and Italy.

1990

611
Fussell et al.

QUALIFIER – 2: KNOWLEDGE BASED SYSTEM FOR CONTRACTOR PREQUALIFICATION

J. Construction Engineering & Management (ASCE) 1990 *116*, pp. 157–71.

610

CONSTRUCTION MANAGEMENT GUIDE

1990. US Dept of Commerce, 64pp.
Guidance is given to CMs performing construction management services for GSA. It describes GSA's project delivery process intended to shorten and facilitate the learning curve for CM staff. The CM's role and other parties involved in planning and executing major construction projects in project delivery is also defined.

609
A. Turner

BUILDING PROCUREMENT

Macmillan Education, 1990, 179pp.
The basics of the building process are set out, together with the principal participants and how they practice, general conventions and rules of building contracts and conditions of engagement. Procurement assessment criteria, procurement arrangement options, procurement route and form of contract are considered.

Twelve case studies are presented to illustrate the progressive nature of procurement.

608

GROWING STATUS OF PROJECT MANAGEMENT

New Builder 1990 December 6, pp. 18–19
A survey has established that the status of project managers is second only to architects and that any professional background is appropriate. Other data obtained relate to size of contract, skills required and the role of the client.

607

BUILDING IN VALUE – THE PROJECT MANAGER'S VIEWPOINT

Building Economist 1990 *29* December, pp. 31–4
The concept of building in value from the project manager's viewpoint is discussed with reference to specific projects.

606
S. Middleboe

BEST WAYS TO MANAGE BUILDINGS

New Builder 1990 November, 22, p. 6
The results of a survey show the relative merits for a range of procurement systems in relation to a number of criteria. Overall, construction management appears to be the most favourable.

605
J.M. Allen

BALANCE OF RISK AND REWARD

Construction News 1990 November 15, p. 18
The case for management contracting is presented by the Chairman of Laing Management Contracting.

604

DESIGN AND BUILD

Construction News 1990 November 1, pp. 22–30
A series of articles is presented covering current growth, CAD, the contractor's role, Wimpey and Laing approach and client response.

603

PROCURING BY NUMBERS

Building Supplement: Homes 1990 October 12, pp. 14–17, 20–2
Compares nine methods of procurement for housing, including design-and-build; develop and construct; lump sum contracts; standard contracts and package deals.

602
N. Parkyn

DESIGN AND BUILD

Building 1990 *255* October 12, pp. 45–8
A comparison of two major design-and-build contracts and two architect-led established the

advantages of the former. The views of architects involved in design-and-build are also presented.

601

J. Pain

DESIGN AND BUILD CONTRACTS. WHAT ARE THEY AND DO THEY WORK?

Estates Gazette 1990 October 6, pp. 20–2

Explains the difference between design-and-build contracts and traditional contracts, pointing out the advantages of the former and when it should be used.

600

D. Bucknall

TAKING THE LEADING ROLE

Chartered Quantity Surveyor 1990 *13* October, pp. 9–11

A brief account is given of the project management of the Birmingham International Convention Centre.

599

G.G. Kallo

DECISION MAKING IN PROJECT MANAGE-MENT

Civil Engineering Surveyor 1991 *16* September, p. 31.

598

I. Davies

ON TARGET DOWN UNDER

Chartered Quantity Surveyor 1991 *14* September, pp. 22–3

The target sum method of procurement is now gaining acceptance in Australia.

597

S.G. Naoum

Proceedings of the international symposium held 10–13 September 1990 in Zagreb, Yugoslavia, organized by the CIB

MANAGEMENT CONTRACTING – REVIEW AND ANALYSIS

In: 'International symposium on Procurement Systems', 9pp. (Publication 132).

596

M.P. Nicholson

Proceedings of the international symposium held 10–13 September 1990 in Zagreb, Yugoslavia, organized by the CIB

COMPARATIVE STUDY OF PROCUREMENT METHODS FOR DESIGN WORK, WITH PAR-TICULAR REFERENCE TO DESIGN AND BUILD CONTRACTS

In: 'International symposium on Procurement Systems', 9pp. (Publication 132).

595

N. Hamilton

Proceedings of the international symposium held 10–13 September 1990 in Zagreb, Yugoslavia, organized by the CIB

REVIEW OF UK PROJECT PROCUREMENT METHODS

In: 'International symposium on Procurement Systems', 9pp. CIB, 1990 (Publication 132).

594

D.W. Cheetham and D. Jaggar

Proceedings of the international symposium held 10–13 September 1990 in Zagreb, Yugoslavia, organized by the CIB

PROCUREMENT SYSTEMS – WHICH WAY FOR-WARD?

In: 'International symposium on Procurement Systems', 10pp. (Publication 132)

It is suggested that the pattern for the future might be based on schematic design, schedule of employers requirements and performance specifications developed from British 'design-and-build' and the French 'La consullation performancielle'.

593

R.A. Waterhouse

WHAT IS PROJECT MANAGEMENT ANYWAY? BUZZ WORD OR PROFESSIONAL DISCIPLINE?

Hong Kong Engineer 1990 August, pp. 43–6

Discusses the role of a project manager.

592

J. de Vulden

RIGHTS OF PACKAGE

Hospital Development 1990 *(7)* August, pp. 21, 23

The experience is reported of NE Thames RHA of design-and-build.

591

A. Merna and N.J. Smith

PROJECT MANAGERS AND THE USE OF TURN-KEY CONTRACTS

Int. Journal of Project Management 1990 *(8)* August, pp. 183–9

The suitability is considered of turnkey contracts for multi-discipline projects. The form of turnkey contract is examined, together with the contract documentation and style of project management.

590

B. Hamilton

PROJECT MANAGEMENT. DESIGN DIRECTION

New Builder 1990 July 19, p. 25

The principles of managing the design and procurement phases are considered.

589
B. Hamilton
PROJECT MANAGEMENT: OUTLINING CON-
CEPTS
New Builder 1990 July 5, p. 18.

588
DESIGN AND BUILD SURVEY
Contract Journal 1990 355 June 28, pp. 14–16, 18, 20,
22, 24–8, 30, 32–4, 36, 39, 41, 43–9
A series of articles exploring the extent and mode of
operation of design–build is presented. Major attention is given to brief details of firms offering the
service, together with a 'skill statement'. A ranking
list based on turnover is also included.

587
B. Hamilton
PROJECT MANAGEMENT. RELATIONSHIP
CHOICES
New Builder 1990 June 28, pp. 18–19
The key features are identified of management con-
tracting, construction management, design and man-
agement contracting and project management.

586
B. Hamilton
PROJECT MANAGEMENT – KEY TO CHARAC-
TERISTICS
New Builder 1990 June 21, pp. 26–7
Organizational options are examined.

585
J.D. Allen
TEAMWORK THE KEY TO MANAGEMENT
CONTRACTING
Construction News 1990 June 14, pp. 34–5
An interview with John McKenna, head of Taylor
Woodrow's management contracting company.

584
1989 CM COST SURVEY RELEASED
CM Advisor 1990 May/June, pp. 3, 7
The results are summarized of a survey of construction management (CM) costs which focuses on general company data, direct and indirect cost data and
individual project data.

583
A. Pring
WHOSE DESIGN IS IT ANYWAY?
Contract Journal 1990 May 10, pp. 14–15
The significance is described of design management
in terms of the architect builder relationship and with
regard to current forms of project management.

582
G. Ridout
MANAGEMENT ON TRIAL
Building 1990 255 March 23, pp. 26–9
An evaluation is made of management contracting
in anticipation of the Reading University report.
Contributions are made by Chris Spackman, Ann
Minogue, John Huxtable and Geoff Trickey.

581
A.M. Barnett
LEGAL AND PROFESSIONAL LIABILITY OF
PROJECT MANAGERS AT COMMON LAW
Paper to CIB 90 Conference, Building Economics and
Construction Management, March 1990, Sydney. Vol-
ume 4, pp. 68–79
The Barnett classification system for the various type
of project manager is outlined before consideration
is given to their respective legal equivalents and the
potential heads of legal liability.

580
K.J. Campbell
PROJECT MANAGEMENT AND THE LAW –
ALLIES OR ADVERSARIES?
Paper to CIB 90 Conference, Building Economics and
Construction Management, March 1990, Sydney. Vol-
ume 4, pp. 127–33
The influence of the law on project management is
discussed with particular reference to the structure of
contract documentation and the imperatives generated
by new management techniques. Allocation of risk is
considered in the context of project documentation.

579
S. Gunnarson and Y. Hammarlund
PROJECT MANAGEMENT PROGRAMME – OPMP
Paper to CIB 90 Conference, Building Economics and
Construction Management, March 1990, Sydney. Vol-
ume 4, pp. 228–37
A project management syllabus applicable to all types
of project is described.

578
D. Hobson
FINANCIAL MANAGEMENT OF MANAGEMENT
CONTRACTING IN UK
Paper to CIB 90 Conference, Building Economics and
Construction Management, March 1990, Sydney.
Volume 4, pp. 243–54.

577
S.G. Naoum and D.A. Langford
INVESTIGATION INTO THE PERFORMANCE
OF MANAGEMENT CONTRACTS AND THE
TRADITIONAL METHOD OF PROCUREMENT

Paper to CIB 90 Conference, Building Economics and Construction Management, March 1990, Sydney. Volume 4, pp. 351–60.

576

R.A. Mohsini and A.F. Botros

PASCON: AN EXPERT SYSTEM TO EVALUATE ALTERNATE PROJECT PROCUREMENT PROCESSES

Paper to CIB 90 Conference, Building Economics and Construction Management, March 1990, Sydney. Volume 2, pp. 525–37.

575

G. Shaoxi

REFORM IN CONSTRUCTION PROJECT MANAGEMENT IN CHINA

Proc. of Hong Kong Polytechnic and Tsinghua University Symposium on Construction Project Management in China & Hong Kong, 9–10 January 1990. Hong Kong, pp. A2.1–A2.13

A brief review is made of the present state of project management in China and the objectives of reform in this field.

574

J. Ratcliffe

PROJECT MANAGEMENT – BALANCING TIME, COST AND QUALITY

Proc. of Hong Kong Polytechnic and Tsinghua University Symposium on Construction Project Management in China & Hong Kong, 9–10 January 1990. Hong Kong, pp. A4.1–A4.17.

573

T.I. Lam

PRIVATIZATION OF INFRASTRUCTURE CONSTRUCTION: AN INVESTIGATION OF BUILD-OPERATE-TRANSFER SCHEME IN HONG KONG

Proc. of Hong Kong Polytechnic and Tsinghua University Symposium on Construction Project Management in Hong Kong, 9–10 January 1990. Hong Kong, pp. C1.1–C1.8.

572

A. Walker

CONSTRUCTION PROJECT MANAGEMENT IN CHINA AND HONG KONG – SIMILARITIES AND DIFFERENCES

Proc. of Hong Kong Polytechnic and Tsinghua University Symposium on Construction Project Management in China and Hong Kong, 9–10 January 1990. Hong Kong, 19pp.

The differences in the two systems are illustrated by highlighting the diversity and complexity of the objectives of clients and the appropriateness or otherwise of the organizational structures.

1989

571

D.W. Cheetham et al.

CONTRACTUAL PROCEDURES FOR BUILDING

Liverpool: CIB Int. Workshop, 1989, 317pp.

Proceedings of a workshop held in Liverpool, April 1989. A series of papers is included covering procurement, standard forms of contract, expert systems and interpretation of contracts; tender documents; subcontracting; West German industry; sub-contractor/contractor relationships in Sweden and Denmark; risk; liability and insurance; refurbishment and client control; cash flow; organisational analysis of projects; management control information for architects.

570

A.M. Barnett

MANY GUISES OF A PROJECT MANAGER

Australian Institute of Building Papers 1988/89 3, pp. 119–34

The various types of project manager in the land and property development industry are classified and aligned with their legal equivalents. The importance is stressed of establishing, early in the project, the type of project manager involved.

569

RICS

PROJECT MANAGEMENT AGREEMENT AND CONDITIONS OF ENGAGEMENT

1989, 12pp.

568

RICS

PROJECT MANAGEMENT AGREEMENT AND CONDITIONS OF ENGAGEMENT. GUIDANCE NOTE

1989, 8pp.

567

A. Griffith

DESIGN–BUILD PROCUREMENT AND BUILD ABILITY

CIOB Technical Information Service Paper No. 112, 1989, 8pp.

The design–build method of procurement is considered in the context in the industry's increasing expectation of innovative and improved method.

Potential benefits and problems of application are considered and the likely implications for clients, contracts and the professions are addressed.

566
B. Dodworth
DESIGN AND BUILD
Contracts Management 1989 November, pp. 19–20
The advantages of design and build are summarized.

565
R.M. Denny
BUILDING AND CONTRACT MANAGEMENT
Contracts Management 1989 November, pp. 15–18
The BPF system of procurement is described.

564
R. Fellows
RISK IN MANAGEMENT CONTRACTING
Chartered Builder 1989 *1* November/December, pp. 32–4.

563
D. Marks
COMMUNITY LAW ON THE PROCUREMENT OF PUBLIC WORKS AND ITS APPLICATION IN THE UK
International Construction Law Review 1989 *6* October, pp. 424–4.

562
P.B. Booth and T.W. Crow
PROJECT MANAGEMENT – SHOULD IT BE THE QUANTITY SURVEYOR?
Building Economist 1989 *28* September, pp. 11–15
Following a short analysis of the role and quality of the project manager the role of the QS as quantity surveyor and as project manager is considered.

561
M. Evamy
ST OLAF REVIVED BY WALLIS
Contract Journal 1989 *350* August 17, pp. 10–11
It is claimed that use of BPF contract on a refurbishment job made a significant contribution to its success.

560

PROJECT MANAGEMENT
Chartered Surveyor Weekly 1989 August 17, pp. 27–9, 31–3, 35–6
A series of articles is presented covering basic reviews as seen through they eyes of PMI; liability of the project manager, PM courses; an agreement between PM and client formed by the RICS; case studies on recent jobs and some of the key personalities.

559
J.S. Russell
CONTRACTOR PRE-QUALIFICATION DATA FOR CONSTRUCTION MANAGERS
CM Advisor 1989 *7* July, pp. 6–7
The results are summarized of a survey of the impact various factors have on construction managers' decision-making process regarding contractor pre-qualification.

558
Rashid Mohsini and C.H. Davidson
BUILDING PROCUREMENT – KEY TO IMPROVED PERFORMANCE
Proc. CIB Int Workshop on Contractual Procedures, 6–7 April 1989, Liverpool, pp. 83–96
Alternative forms of procurement are considered in terms of the owner's strategies and how they affect his chances of obtaining best value for money. It is suggested that the stated objectives of procurement have shifted from a search for cooperation within an 'aggregated market' approach, to an attempt at balancing bargaining powers within an 'open market' approach.

557
R. Swanston
UNITED KINGDOM PROCUREMENT PROCEDURES
Proc. CIB Int Workshop on Contractual Procedures, 6–7 April 1989, Liverpool, pp. 23–36
Attention is given to procurement options, differences in the various systems and selection of the procurement system.

556
P. Harris
MANAGEMENT CONTRACTING: AN INSIDER'S VIEW
Architect, Builder, Contractor & Developer 1989 March, pp. 24, 26–7
An interview with John McKenna, MC of Taylor Woodrow Management Contracting concerning developments in the way the contractual arrangement is operated.

555

DESIGN AND BUILD SURVEY
Contract Journal 1989 *348* March 2, pp. 24–6, 28–30, 32, 34–7
The survey is based on the responses of 56 contractors, identifies under each organization the level of design–build activity, its financial contribution and recent clients.

554
J. Gosney
RISE AND RISE OF DESIGN AND BUILD

Contract Journal 1989 *348* March 2, pp. 18–20
The increasing rise is discussed of design–build, the views of a number of practitioners being included to demonstrate the basis of its success.

553
P. Harris
MANAGEMENT CONTRACTING: AN INSIDER'S VIEW A B C & D 1989 March, pp. 22–4, 26–7
An interview with John McKenna, MD of Taylor Woodrow Management Contracting on the way the system of procurement is operated within the firm.

1988

552
Dearle and Henderson
MANAGEMENT CONTRACTING: A PRACTISE MANUAL
1988. Spon, 113pp.
A text for quantity surveyors which deals in turn with management contracting and the QS; selection procedures and documentation; and financial management. Appendices provide sample contracts, forms and documents.

551
CIOB
PROJECT MANAGEMENT IN BUILDING
1988 3rd edition, 32pp.
Project management as practised in both the UK and abroad is examined before the objectives of project management and the role and duties of the project manager are described. The second part deals with education for project management, a framework being provided against which the syllabus of any individual course may be compared.

550
CIOB
CODE OF ESTIMATING PRACTICE: SUPPLEMENT 2. DESIGN AND BUILD
1988, pp. 40.

549
S. Hornby
FINANCE REQUIRED FOR WORKING CAPITAL IN MANAGEMENT CONTRACTING
RICS Occasional Paper, 1988, 16pp.
A comparison is made of the financing of ten firms providing management contracting with ten general contractors. It is shown that less finance is required for management contracting but that there are signifi-

cantly lower profit margins. Returns on capital employed were found to be similar.

548
D. Hobson
MANAGEMENT CONTRACTING – A STEP IN THE RIGHT DIRECTION?
RICS Occasional Paper 1988, 2nd edition, 25pp.
In addition to providing an overview, consideration is given to the role of the QS can play.

547
H. Dawson
DESIGN AND BUILD. A CLIENT'S VIEWPOINT
Chartered Quantity Surveyor 1988 *11* November, pp. 29–30.

546
P. Graham
MANAGEMENT CONTRACTS. DREAM OF FEES
Chartered Quantity Surveyor 1988 *11* October, pp. 24–25
Fee levels for quantity surveyors working on management contracts are discussed.

545
I. Davies
INDUSTRIAL AND COMMERCIAL BUILDING
Building Technology & Management 1988 *26* August/September, p. 20
The approach is described of IDC to in-house design and project management, without or with construction management.

544
M. Barnes
PROJECT MANAGEMENT TODAY IV. ORGANIZING TO ACHIEVE
Civil Engineering Surveyor 1988 *13* May, pp. 23–5
The responsibilities of the project manager are identified before consideration is given to various forms of procurement including target cost, cost reimbursable, design-and-build and management contracting.

543
Gardiner & Theobald
CHOOSING A FAST TRACK PRESCRIPTION
Building 1988 *253* April 29, p. 30
Some of the major limitations of management contracting are discussed. Of particular note is the increased reluctance of trade contractors to accept the additional risks without consequent enhanced financial rewards and the trend towards 'double prelims'.

542
M. Bar-Hillel
SWEET SUCCESS WITH TARGET COST

CS Weekly 1988 April 21, p. 25
A design and building variant – target cost – as developed by Cyril Sweet & Partners is outlined.

541
R.M. Skitmore and D.E. Marsden
WHICH PROCUREMENT SYSTEM? TOWARDS A UNIVERSAL PROCUREMENT SELECTION TECHNIQUE
Construction Management & Economics 1988 6 Spring, pp. 71–89
Two approaches are described which aid the selection of the most appropriate procurement arrangements. The first is a multi-attribute technique based on the NEDO procurement path decision chart and the other approach is by means of discriminate analysis.

540
PROJECT CASE BOOK: RAF BRAMPTON
Contract Journal 1988 March 31, pp. 12–14
The construction of headquarters buildings for RAF Support Command HQ is described. Management by Conder on a design-and-build basis, the fast-track approach adopted allowed completion within 21 months. Particular attention is given to the design challenge, procurement, planning and running the job.

539
S. Marshal and R. Morledge
RISKING DESIGN & BUILD
Chartered Quantity Surveyor 1988 10 March, pp. 25–6
The risk elements associated with design-and-build are discussed with reference to *Bolam v Friern Hospital Management Committee* and *Greaves v Baynham Meikle & Partners*.

538
M. Spring
HEALTHY RUSH OF BLOOD
Building 1988 253 March 18, pp. 43–7
The construction is described of the N. London Blood Transfusion Centre which was a fast-track management contract based on flexible layouts and prefabricated components.

537
K. Stansfield
MANAGEMENT CONTRACTING ON MAJOR PUBLIC SECTOR PROJECTS
Construction 1988 (63) February, pp. 29–30
Taylor Woodrow's approach to management contracting is described.

536
F.H. Archer and D.W.M. Knight
HONG KONG & SHANGHAI BANKING CORPORATION HEADQUARTERS CONSTRUCTION

ICE Proceedings. 1988 84 Part 1. February, pp. 43–65
An outline is given of the construction sequence with particular reference to the constraints imposed, the problems encountered and the solutions devised to complete on schedule, a fast-track, high-quality project. Examples are given of the proven flexibility of management contracting. New construction methods and materials are described, together with the adoption of traditional temporary works.

535
P. Reina
DESIGN & BUILD TAKES SHELTER
Contract Journal 1988 February 25, pp. 16–17
Professional indemnity insurance difficulties within the design–build contractors are assessed.

534
J.D. Allen
DESIGN & CONSTRUCT CAN OFFER CLIENTS A GUARANTEED PRICE
Construction News 1988 February 4, p. 20
An interview with the Chief Executive of the IDC Group which discussed how design-and-construct can offer a lump sum or GMP when only 15 per cent of the design work has been completed.

1987

533
A.A. Montague
RESPONSIBILITIES OF A CONTRACTOR UNDER A DESIGN AND BUILD CONTRACT: THE DRAFTING OF THE CONTRACT FOR THE DOCKLANDS LIGHT RAILWAY
Proc. Liability of Contractors Conference 1984. Longman, 1987, pp. 46–56.

532
J.J. Goudsmit
LEGAL LIABILITY IN CONTRACT STRUCTURES
Proc. Liability of Contractors Conference 1984. Longman, 1987, pp. 17–33
The implications are discussed of various contract structures for the liability of the contractor. Reference is made to contractor's compliance with instructions, his duty to warn, failure of equipment, inviting alternative tenders, limitations on liability, delay, turnkey contracts, design, variations, nominated subcontractors and choice of materials.

531
M. Furmston
LIABILITY OF CONTRACTORS: PRINCIPLES AND LIABILITY IN CONTRACT AND TORT

Proc. Liability of Contractors Conference 1984, Longman, 1987, pp. 10–16.

530
Royal Institution of Chartered Surveyors
PROJECT MANAGEMENT IN PROPERTY DEVELOPMENT
1987, 19pp.
A promotional booklet extolling the virtues of quantity surveyors as project managers.

529
S. Rowlinson
DESIGN–BUILD – ITS DEVELOPMENT AND PRESENT STATUS
CIOB Occasional Paper No. 36, 1987, 16pp.
The development is briefly examined of design–build contracting, of the industry's perception of it and of its organizational forms and attributes. An assessment is made of the performance of design–build projects based on over 40 detailed case studies.

528
C.J. Willis and A. Ashworth
PRACTICE AND PROCEDURE FOR THE QUANTITY SURVEYOR
1987, 9th edition. Collins, 249pp.
The major revisions cover the changes affecting private practice and there is a new chapter on the QS's work in a construction firm. The growing importance of computers is acknowledged and there is a new chapter on project management.

527
L.C.N. Fan
EQUITY JOINT VENTURES IN THE CONSTRUCTION INDUSTRY IN CHINA
CIOB, Occasional Paper No. 37, 1987, 17pp.
Following an outline of the construction industry in China attention is given to the formation and termination of equity joint ventures. This is followed by a case study illustrating the setting up of a services company. Appendices list the Chinese legislation relating to joint ventures.

526
S. Rowlinson
EXPERT SYSTEM DEVELOPMENT PROBLEMS IN PRACTICE
Proc. Application of Artificial Intelligence Techniques to Civil & Structural Engineering Conference, 1987, pp. 7–13
The development is described for an expert system to advise on procurement strategy.

525
I.N.D. Wallace
TURNKEY CONTRACTS

Proc. Liability of Contractors Conference 1984, Longman, 1987, pp. 34–9.

524
D.F. Turner
DESIGN & BUILD CONTRACT PRACTICE
1987, Longman, 264pp.
The basis of design–build and the type of client and work for which it is suited are discussed. Procedures to be followed are described and attention drawn to the requirements of each party and their consultants. In particular, consideration is given to design responsibilities, possible liabilities and financial arrangements. The text is linked to the JCT contract with contractor's design, the BPF/ACA system and obtaining design through nominated sub-contractors.

523
CIRIA
PRACTICAL ADVICE FOR THE CLIENT INTENDING TO BUILD
Special Publication 48, 1987, 12pp.

522
A.C. Sidwell and V. Ireland
INTERNATIONAL COMPARISON OF CONSTRUCTION MANAGEMENT
Australian Institute of Building Papers 1987 2, pp. 3–11
The forms of construction management practised in Australia, US and UK, including agency and direct construction management, are defined and contrasted.

521
S. Rowlinson
COMPARISON OF CONTRACTING SYSTEMS FOR INDUSTRIAL BUILDINGS
Managing Construction Worldwide. Volume 1. Systems for managing construction, 1987, Spon/CIOB/CIB, pp. 55–65
A comparison is made of design–build and traditional methods of procurement.

520
K.K. Bertli and Z. Herbsman
CONSTRUCTION MANAGEMENT – IS IT REALLY THE WAY TO GO?
Managing Construction Worldwide. Volume 1. Systems for managing construction, 1987, Spon/CIOB/CIB, pp. 4–15
A comparative analysis is made of the construction management approach (US) to procurement to illustrate its advantages and limitations.

519
S.G. Naoum and D.A. Langford
MANAGEMENT CONTRACTING

Managing Construction Worldwide. Volume 1. Systems for managing construction, 1987, Spon/CIOB/CIB, pp. 42–54
The relationship is evaluated between project success and building procurement method in industrial and commercial projects. A comparison is made between management contracting and the traditional method of procurement.

518
O.D. Wilson et al.
COMPETITIVE TENDERING: THE IDEAL NUMBER OF TENDERS
Managing Construction Worldwide. Volume 1. Systems for managing construction, 1987, Spon/CIOB/CIB, pp. 175–86
The effect is examined of the number of bidders on the outcome of the tendering process.

517
C.E. Haltenhoff
CONSTRUCTION MANAGEMENT PERFORMANCE UNDER DUAL SERVICES AGREEMENTS
ASCE Journal of Construction Engineering & Management 1987 *113* December, pp. 640–7
The standard documents of the American Institute of Architects and the Associated General Contractors of America for construction management projects imply processes and operational procedures that have become customary if not standard since publication in 1975. Adjustments must be made to accommodate the particular form and variation of construction management specifically required by the contract. However, construction management firms have a tendency to customize processes and procedures for their own convenience. This is especially true on projects where a firm is contractually assigned other service responsibilities such as design, contracting, or construction. When a CM process and its procedures exactly match the intent of the project delivery system, owners are positioned to gain from the use of the system. When convenience intervenes, the system cannot function effectively, and the owner may experience negative results. This paper argues that convenient customizing of the CM process and its procedures, especially customizing that mitigates the checks and balances specifically built into the construction management system and implied by established CM practice, represents a detrimental divergence from the fundamental reasons CM is selected for use by owners on their projects.

516
M. Branton and T. Butler
FIRM FOUNDATION FOR PROJECT MANAGEMENT
International Journal of Project Management 1987 *5* November, pp. 221–9

The basic principles of project management are reviewed.

515
A. Catto
NEW CONTRACTS FOR OLD PROBLEMS
Building Today 1987 *194* November 5, pp. 22–4
A review of the current situation in management contracting and project management, supplemented by personal observation. Reference is made to the imminent JCT form and the civil engineering form designed by Martin Barnes for the 'whole range of construction work'.

514
B. Meecham
FULL TIME SCORE FROM WATFORD
National Builder 1987 *68* October, pp. 330–1
The fast-track construction, by Dow-Mac design and build, of Watford's new football stand is outlined.

513
S.G. Naoum and D. Langford
MANAGEMENT CONTRACTING – THE CLIENT'S VIEW
ASCE Journal of Construction Engineering Management 1987 *113(3)* September, pp. 369–85
The development of and the market for management contracting in the UK is summarized. The results are reported of interviews with construction clients who are asked to compare management contracting with the traditional method of project procurement.

512
MANAGEMENT CONTRACTING – ON THE BRITISH TELECOM BUILDING
Construction 1987 (61) September, pp. 52–5
Aspects discussed include design brief, contract selection, organization and responsibilities, and costs and control procedures.

511
A. Westbrook
MANAGEMENT CONTRACTING – THE CLIENT'S EVALUATION
Building Technology & Management 1987 *25* August/September, p. 17.

510
P. Gregory
MANAGEMENT CONTRACTING – THE RECKONING
Building Technology & Management 1987 *25* August/September, pp. 18–22
Consideration is given to the way the cost of a management contract is constituted and the comparison of that figure with perceived cost of the project at inception.

509
J. McKenna
MANAGEMENT CONTRACTING – DEFINING THE SYSTEM
Building Technology & Management 1987 25 August/September, pp. 23–5.

508
R. Knowles
MANAGEMENT CONTRACTING – LAW AND CONTRACT
Building Technology & Management 1987 25 August/September, pp. 26–7, 30.

507
T. Scott
ARE CONTRACTORS MORE EFFICIENT AT BILL PRODUCTION?
Chartered Quantity Surveyor 1987 9 August, p. 15
Experience within a design-and-build organization is reported.

506
CLIENT PARTICIPATION. MANAGEMENT BY DESIGN
Architects Journal 1987 186 August 19 and 26, pp. 68–71
IBM's project management approach to its procurement of buildings is outlined.

505
R. Swan
DESIGN & BUILD
Contract Journal 1987 July 30, pp. 12–13
A review of the place and importance of design-and-build.

504
M. Kemp
APPLICATION OF QUALITY ASSURANCE IN A PROJECT MANAGEMENT PRACTICE
Chartered Quantity Surveyor 1987 9 June, pp. 25–6.

503
WHAT PRICE PROJECT MANAGEMENT?
Chartered Quantity Surveyor 1987 9 June, p. 28
The problems are discussed of professional indemnity insurances for project management companies.

502
C. Sayer and J. Sutton
BPF SYSTEM
Chartered Quantity Surveyor 1987 9 June, pp. 30–1
Experience is reported which was gained on a refurbishment project.

501
B. Martin
ALLOCATING THE RISK

Building 1987 252 June 12, p. 25
The risks likely to be assumed by a management contractor are discussed. It is suggested that future construction management arrangements should focus more on opportunities for improving management and less on assigning risks.

500
P. Reina
CHANGING THE RULES
Contract Journal 1987 May 21, pp. 14–15
Some personal views are expressed on the relative merits of management contracting and construction management.

499
S. MacVicar
SMALL BEGINNINGS
Contract Journal 1987 May 7, p. 16
Portrait of Genesis Design & Construct, a subsidiary of Sir Robert McAlpine & Sons.

498
CASE STUDY. MAKING THE GRADE AT BEVIS MARKS HOUSE
Building Technology & Management 1987 25 April/May, pp. 14–19
Fast-track construction of the seven-storey building let under a management contract is described, particular attention being given to project organization, production and quality control, and financial control.

497
T. Ostler
BUILDING A REPUTATION
Building Design 1987 April 17, pp. 14–16
A profile of J.T. Design Build based in Bristol.

496
A.S. White and M. Barnes
ROLES AND RESPONSIBILITIES UNDER THE BPF SYSTEM
Structural Engineer 1987 65A March, pp. 90–4.

495
QUALIFICATION AND SELECTION OF CONSTRUCTION MANAGERS WITH SUGGESTED GUIDELINES FOR SELECTION PROCESS
ASCE Journal of Construction Engineering & Management 1987 113(1) March, pp. 51–89
CM is a unique alternative system of contracting that competes with the general contracting and design–build contracting systems as a means of delivering projects. The CM system breaks down into several forms that have separate variations. CM services are provided by construction managers using different

practitioner formats. In essence, CM services comprise a menu from which a form and its variation are selected. For these reasons, clients often have difficulty understanding the service available and determining the combination of services that best suits their requirements when engaging a construction manager. The guidelines presented are in fundamental form in order to accommodate both first-time users of CM services and repeat users seeking additional CM information.

494
C.S. Tyler
CONSTRUCTION MANAGEMENT CONTRACT AND THE ROLE OF THE ENGINEER
Structural Engineer 1987 *65A* March, pp. 96–8.

493
J. Robinson
COMPARISON OF TENDERING PROCEDURES AND CONTRACTUAL ARRANGEMENTS
Project Management 1987 *5* February, pp. 19–24
The results are compared of the traditional procurement stages of a multistage industrial development and a package deal. Time over-runs and cost increases were much greater with the former.

492
R. Slavid
RESERVATIONS, BUT HEALTHY GROWTH IN DESIGN AND BUILDING
Construction News 1987 February 19, pp. 13–14
An analysis is made of the market, advantages and limitations of design–build based on a survey of contractors, designers, QSs and clients.

491
J. Bennett
CONSTRUCTION MANAGEMENT AND THE CHARTERED QUANTITY SURVEYOR
1986, Surveyors Press, 48pp.
Following a review of the state of construction management practice, attention is given to the advice which quantity surveyors might give to clients wishing to adopt the approach to procurement. Finally, practical steps to be taken by the PQS wishing to offer a construction management service are indicated.

490
P.W.G. Morris
PROJECT MANAGEMENT: A VIEW FROM OXFORD
International Journal of Construction Management & Technology 1986 *1(1)*, pp. 36–52
Work on project success and failure is reviewed and factors associated with success are identified.

489
I.N.D. Wallace
CONSTRUCTION AND CONTRACTS: PRINCIPLES AND POLICIES IN TORT AND CONTRACT
1986, Sweet & Maxwell, 696pp.
An extensive coverage of contractual issues under the main headings of new developments in the law; contractors' claims and owners' damages; certificates and their effect; guarantees and bonds; nominated sub-contractors; choice of contracting arrangements; comparative law; JCT standard forms; and Singapore SIA contract.

1986

488
R.T.P. McLaughlln and D.K. Doran
CONTRACTOR RELATIONSHIP
IABSE. 1986, 11pp.
The main types of contractual arrangement are summarized, with the designer–contractor interface being identified. This is supported by four case studies covering project management, turnkey, design and build and management contracting. Finally, liability is considered briefly.

487
J.W. Birnie
ECONOMIC EFFICIENCY OF CONSTRUCTION
Building Technology & Management 1986 *24* December, pp. 12–13
It is shown how traditional procurement kept unit costs of construction low.

486
A. Morris
INSPIRATION FOR QS DIVERSIFICATION
Chartered Quantity Surveyor 1986 *9* November, pp. 23–5
The construction management (CM) approach to procurement in the US is described.

485
PROJECT MANAGEMENT
Chartered Surveyor Weekly 1986 *17* November 27, pp. 893–4, 897, 900, 903, 908, 911
A series of articles is presented including
The men on the spot explain, by G. Parker
Who makes a building happen? by J. Thornton
The building surveyor as project manager, by M. Ridley
Picking the man for the job, by H. Evans
American way is best, by R. Catt

The multi-disciplinary man, by J. Fitton
Tenant benefits from early involvement in a project,
by G. Parker.

484
L.D. Phillips
CM CERTIFICATION AND REGISTRATION
Proceedings ASCE Convention on Construction Management, Boston, Mass. October 27, 1986, pp. 89–101
The present legal status of the CM system is reviewed from the perspective of a survey of 50 US states. A look is taken at the efforts to professionalize the construction manager's role in the industry.

483
L.S. Rigg
EDUCATIONAL PROGRAMMES SUPPORTING THE CM SYSTEM
Proceedings ASCE Convention on Construction Management, Boston, Mass. October 27, 1986, pp. 62–73
The differences are established between the educational requirements of a contracting-oriented programme and a CM-oriented programme with respect to the management tools and the philosophy of using those tools.

482
W.C. Kwasny
QUALITY IN THE CM CONSTRUCTED PROJECT
Proceedings ASCE Convention on Construction Management, Boston, Mass. October 27, 1986, pp. 74–80
It is shown that the services of a testing laboratory are an essential requirement of the CM quality management system.

481
F. Muller
CM's EXPOSURE TO LIABILITY
Proceedings ASCE Convention on Construction Management, Boston, Mass. October 27, 1986, pp. 117–33
Attention is given to contractual relationships and standard of care.

480
C.E. Haltenhoff
FORMS AND VARIATIONS OF THE CM SYSTEM
Proceedings ASCE Convention on Construction Management, Boston, Mass. October 27, 1986, pp. 1–15
In the CM system, the independent contractor relationship inherent in general contracting and in design-build, is altered by substituting a fiduciary/agent construction manager. The construction manager is responsible for all aspects of project delivery, the owner becoming, in effect, his own contractor, retain-

ing or assigning the various risks. The various forms of CM are described from a contract perspective.

479
C. Kluenker
BROAD SPECTRUM OF CM SERVICES
Proceedings ASCE Convention on Construction Management, Boston, Mass. October 27, 1986, pp. 16–50
Basic CM tools viz computer systems; documents and techniques; people and the organization; and CM industry associations, are discussed. Reference is made to contract risks, budgets, programmes, payments, meetings and bidding documents. Job descriptions are given for project manager and CM coordinator.

478
P.S. Scott and W.E. Showalter
HISTORY OF CONSTRUCTION MANAGEMENT
Proceedings ASCE Convention on Construction Management, Boston, Mass. October 27, 1986, pp. 51–61
The highlights are traced of the development of CM.

477
C.E. Haltenhoff
CM MULTIPLE CONTRACTING COST MODEL
Proceedings ASCE Convention on Construction Management, Boston, Mass. October 27, 1986, pp. 81–8
The economic advantages are demonstrated of CM when a multiple contracting format is utilized, which are based on actual data collected during the bidding of such contracts.

476
F. Roberts
MORE POWER TO THE ESTIMATOR'S ELBOW
Construction Computing 1986 (15) October, pp. 14–15
Lesser Design & Build's experience with Techsonix computer systems for taking off, bill generation, estimates and schedules to final accounts is summarized.

475
BPF CONTRACT: THE PROFESSIONALS' VERDICT
Construction News 1986 October 23, pp. 28–9
A round-table discussion is reported on the BPF system.

474
C. Wist
DESIGN/BUILD METHODS MATURE
Architecture 1986 October, pp. 107–9.

473
L. Parnell
PROJECT MANAGEMENT: WHO IS RESPONSIBLE?

Chartered Surveyor Weekly 1986 *16* September 25, pp. 90–1
Liability in project management is discussed.

472
S.M. Rowlinson and R. Newcombe
INFLUENCE OF PROCUREMENT FORM ON PROJECT PERFORMANCE
Proc. CIB 10th Triennal Congress. Washington. September 1986 Volume 8, pp. 3592–9
A comparison is made primarily between design–build and traditional.

471
D.W. Birchall and M.C. Bottjer
MANAGEMENT CONTRACTING. THE VIEWS OF GENERAL CONTRACTORS
Building Technology & Management 1986 *24* August/September, pp. 40–3, 49
The results are reported of a survey of medium-sized contractors to establish their intentions regarding management contracting, how they were organized to cope and how they viewed its future.

470
J.G. Perry and R.W. Hayes
RISK MANAGEMENT FOR PROJECT MANAGERS
Building Technology & Management 1986 *24* August/September, pp. 8–11
The various stages of risk management are considered, prior to an analysis of the ways it can be used throughout a project.

469
F. Mastrandrea
LIABILITY OF THE CONSTRUCTION PROJECT MANAGER
Construction Management & Economics 1986 *4* Autumn, pp. 105–34
A framework is developed of areas of potential civil liability of the consultant project manager. The basic principles of contract, agency and torts of negligence are explored and analogies for project management drawn. The developed principles are tested against several decisions in the USA.

468
R. Knowles
PROJECT MANAGER: LEGAL POSITION
Chartered Quantity Surveyor 1986 *8* August, p. 6
The areas of the law are considered which are relevant to the project manager's responsibilities.

467
J. Franks
CONTRACT WITHOUT COMBAT

Building 1986 *261* August 15, pp. 37–40
The application is described of the BPF system to an office refurbishment.

466
R. Ormerod et al.
PROJECT MANAGEMENT REVIEW PART 2
Construction Computing 1986 *(14)* July, pp. 25–37.

465
R. Knowles
PROJECT MANAGER: THE LEGAL POSITION, PART 1
Chartered Quantity Surveyor 1986 *8* July, p. 11
The legal responsibilities are considered with reference to relevant case law.

464
M.E. Schneider
TURNKEY CONTRACTS, CONCEPT, LIABILITIES, CLAIMS
International Construction Law Review 1986 *3* July, pp. 338–59.

463
E.A. Schwartz
DISPUTES BETWEEN JOINT VENTURERS: A CASE STUDY
International Construction Law Review 1986 *3* July, pp. 360–74
Following a discussion of the background to the dispute, certain aspects of the arbitration procedure are reviewed. In conclusion the most interesting aspects of the award are examined.

462
R. Hayes
WHO CARRIES THE RISK?
Building Technology & Management 1986 *24* June, pp. 42–5
The risk elements of management contracting are considered.

461
G. Vickers
PRACTICE EDUCATION. PROJECT MANAGEMENT
Architects Journal 1986 *183* June 25, pp. 75–6.

460
A. Hunter
PROJECT MANAGEMENT: DEFINING THE TERMS
Chartered Quantity Surveyor 1986 *8* June, pp. 20–1
Some misconceptions in relation to project management, construction management and management contracting are dispelled.

459

J.D. Allen

CONSTRUCTION MANAGEMENT KEEPS BROADGATE ON FAST TRACK

Construction News 1986 April 3, pp. 22–5

The management contracting approach is providing a fast-track operation. Some of the management issues are discussed.

458

J.G. Perry

DEALING WITH RISK IN CONTRACTS

Building Technology & Management 1986 24 April, pp. 23–6

The relationship between type of contract viz. lump sum, and measurement, target cost, and cost reimbursable and risk is discussed.

457

M. Taylor

PRACTICE CONTRACTS. TENDERING

Architects Journal 1986 183 April 23, pp. 61–2

The code for design and build and advice on joint venture tendering issued by the NJCC are reviewed.

456

M.R. Morris

CONSTRUCTION MANAGEMENT. US INSPIRATION FOR QS DIVERSIFICATION

Paper to RICS Annual Conference, March 1986, 14pp.

Construction management services in the USA provide management of cost, time and quality, with direct responsibility to the client. Its advantages are discussed.

455

D. Brooks

DOES PUBLIC ACCOUNTABILITY ACHIEVE VALUE FOR MONEY

Building Technology & Management 1986 24 March, pp. 11–14

The relative merits are compared of the various means of procurement.

454

N. Morrison

CONTRACT NEWS

Chartered Quantity Surveyor 1986 8 January, pp. 14–15

The results are presented of a survey as to the use of various forms of contract in 1984. Some data are presented on the forms of procurement employed related to size of project.

453

POLITICAL OBSTACLE COURSE TESTS PROJECT MANAGEMENT AND TURNKEY

Contract Journal 1986 329 January 16, pp. 14–16

The success of the Docklands Light Railway project is claimed to result from the appointment of a project management team to handle the contract and the letting of the contract on a turnkey basis. Main points of the contract provisions are summarized.

1985

452

D. Hobson

MANAGEMENT CONTRACTING. A STEP IN THE RIGHT DIRECTION

1985. Surveyors Publications, 30pp.

Consideration is given to the benefits of management contracting and to the role of the QS.

451

G.D.G. Cottam

MANAGEMENT CONTRACTING AND PACKAGE DEALS

Proc. Supervision of Construction Symposium. ICE. London. 7–8 June 1984.

1985, Telford, pp. 51–8; Discussion, pp. 79–88.

450

National Joint Consultative Committee

CODE OF PROCEDURE FOR SELECTIVE TENDERING FOR DESIGN AND BUILD

1985. RIBA Publications, 11pp.

449

National Joint Consultative Committee

JOINT VENTURE TENDERING FOR CONTRACTS IN THE UK

1985. RIBA Publications, 4pp.

448

Construction Industry Research and Information Association

CLIENTS' GUIDE TO COST REIMBURSABLE CONTRACTS IN BUILDING

1985, 12pp.

447

I. Pennington

GUIDE TO THE BPF SYSTEM AND CONTRACT

1985. CIOB, 36pp.

A commentary on the BPF manual is followed by details of the BPF/ACA form of building agreement.

446

P.A. Thompson

CONTRACTUAL ASPECTS OF INFRASTRUCTURE RENOVATION

Conference paper. 1985, 8pp.
The major forms of procurement are outlined.

445
G. Gosney
MANAGEMENT PROJECTIONS
Building 1985 *269* December 6, pp. 38–39
A profile of Project Management International.

444
P. Bil
CHEOPS MANAGEMENT PROJECTIONS
Building 1985 *269* December 13, pp. 36–7
A profile of Cheops project management services
offered by a quantity surveying practice.

443
R. Hayes
RISKS OF MANAGEMENT CONTRACTING
Chartered Quantity Surveyor 1985 *8* December,
pp. 197–8.

442
B. Waters
**SCHAL INTERNATIONAL MANAGEMENT PRO-
JECTIONS**
Building 1985 *269* December 20–27, pp. 18–19
A profile of the project management consultancy.

441
H. Nahapiet and J. Nahapiet
**COMPARISON OF CONTRACTUAL ARRANGE-
MENTS FOR BUILDING PROJECTS**
Construction Management and Economics 1985 *3(3)*
Winter, pp. 217–31
Contracts are considered from an organizational perspective, comparing the major forms of contracts
available for building projects and examining the
factors influencing their selection. The analysis is
based on the findings of a study of ten building
projects, six in the USA and four in the UK, together
with the results of a survey of those prominent in
the industry. A comparison of five different contractual arrangements indicates that they establish different patterns of responsibilities and relationships
between clients and the various parties involved in
building projects. In so doing, they are regarded as
offering clients differing combinations of expertise,
risk, flexibility and costs. For the projects studied,
three factors were found to be related to contract
selection: the characteristics of clients, particularly
their experience and expertise in construction, the
level of performance required by clients and the
construction complexity of projects. These findings,
together with previous research, suggest that it is
unlikely that there is one 'best' form of contract of
building projects. Rather, the appropriate contrac-

tual arrangement varies according to the particular
set of project circumstances, especially the type of
client, his time and cost requirements and the characteristics of the project.

440
J.S. McArthur
SHARPENING THE CLAUSES
Chartered Quantity Surveyor 1985 *8* November,
pp. 146–8
The reasons are considered why the Scottish
separate-trades contracting system is now in disuse,
being replaced by the all-trade contract.

439
**MANAGEMENT CONTRACTING CREATES
NEW VICTIMS OF UNFAIR TERMS**
Contract Journal 1985 *327* October 17, p. 13
The growth of onerous contract conditions, par-
ticularly in regard to management contracting, is
discussed.

438
G. Bushell
**ALTERNATIVE MANAGEMENT IN NORTH-
AMPTON**
Chartered Quantity Surveyor 1985 *8* September,
pp. 50–1
A separate trades approach to the construction of a
factory extension is described.

437
N. Fisher
**PROJECT MANAGEMENT EDUCATION IN THE
1990s**
Building Technology & Management 1985 *23* Sep-
tember, pp. 10–12
The Project Management Master's course at Reading
University is described.

436
J. Ratcliffe
PROJECT MANAGEMENT
Estates Gazette 1985 *275* August 17, pp. 620–2: August
24, pp. 707–9; August 31, pp. 791–3; September 7,
pp. 862, 864–5; September 14, pp. 1000–1
The role of the project manager is established under
the headings of total project management; funding;
procurement; marketing; and the future.

435
R. Judson
**DUCTWORKERS SHOULD LOVE MANAGE-
MENT CONTRACTS**
Building Services 1985 *7* July, p. 55
The advantages of management contracting to
ductwork contractors are identified.

434
D. Birchall and R. Newcombe
DEVELOPING THE SKILLS
Chartered Quantity Surveyor 1985 7 July, pp. 472–3
The qualities required of the project manager are discussed.

433
D. Dibb-Fuller
DESIGN AND BUILD USING COMPUTERS
Construction Computing 1985 July (10), pp. 37–9
Experience of Conder in using the CADAM system is reported.

432
D.H.T. Walker
PROJECT MANAGEMENT IN PERSPECTIVE
Construction Computing 1985 (11) Autumn, pp. 14–16
Information systems are identified for project management at the feasibility, design and construction stages.

431
C. Kluenker
CONSTRUCTION MANAGEMENT. EXPLODING SOME MYTHS
American Professional Constructor 1985 9 June, pp. 2–4
Construction management is defined on the bringing of construction expertise to the project team during all phases of project delivery, beginning with conceptual design.

430
B. Owens
CONSTRUCTION: A CLIENT'S VIEWPOINT
Building Economist 1985 24 June, pp. 17–20
The role and responsibility of the project manager are discussed, particular reference being made to value management and life-cycle costing.

429
D. Summers
BPF SYSTEM
Building Economist 1985 24 June, pp. 2–9
The salient points of the system are examined, its implications for quantity surveyors being summarized.

428
D. Birchall and R. Newcombe
LEARNING FROM EXPERIENCE
Chartered Quantity Surveyor 1985 7 June, pp. 436–7
Results are presented of a survey of the problem areas facing project managers.

427
J.D. Allen
BROADGATE MOVING ON FAST TRACK
Construction News 1985 June 27, p. 14
The client's reasons for appointing a construction manager for a property development project are outlined. Disenchantment with the JCT forms and bills of quantity appear to be two.

426
J. Bale
TRAINING FOR A NEW AGE
Building 1985 268 May 24, pp. 38–9
The demands that management contracting places on training both in higher education and on-the-job are discussed.

425
J. Osborne
CITY IN THE MAKING
Building 1985 268 May 3, pp. 36–41
Brief details are given of a fast-track office development – London Bridge City – let on a construction management (management contracting) contract.

424
M. Bar-Hillel
MASTER OF ALL TRADES?
Chartered Surveyor Weekly 1985 11 April 11, pp. 115–16
The case is made for the QS as project manager.

423
G. Hardwick
CONTROL AND IN-HOUSE EXPERTISE SELL: IDC DESIGN AND CONSTRUCT
Contract Journal 1985 324 April 11, pp. 20–1
A portrait of IDC and the success of its Guaranteed Maximum Price Contract.

422
MANAGEMENT MEASURES UP
Building 1985 268 March 1, pp. 30–1
The salient points are presented of a survey into the use of management contracting and the response by architects, clients and QSs. The top 16 management contractors are listed.

421
CASE STUDY – NO NEED FOR SUPER MANAGERS
Construction Computing 1985 (8) January, pp. 22–4
Computer use is outlined for a design-and-manage project by Kyle Stewart involving a site workforce of 200 from a complete range of sub-contractors.

1984

420
J.A. Armitt
JOINT VENTURES FORMATION AND OPERATION
Proceedings ICE Conference 'Management of Construction Projects' London. November 1984. Thomas Telford, pp. 61–71; Discussion, pp. 95–102.

419
F.R. Donovan
TURNKEY PROJECTS
Proceedings ICE Conference 'Management of Construction Projects' London. November 1984. Thomas Telford, pp. 45–59; Discussion, pp. 95–102
The essential elements of a turnkey project are outlined.

418
J.R. Elton
MANAGEMENT CONTRACTING
Proceedings ICE Conference 'Management of Construction Projects' London. November 1984. Thomas Telford, pp. 73–83; Discussion, pp. 95–102
The essential elements of management contracting are described.

417
B. Waters
CENTRE OF DEBATE
Building 1984 *267* November 16, pp. 37–46
The operational performance of the PSA management contract for the construction of the International Conference Centre is one aspect discussed. Another is the Artemis computer-based programming and progressing system.

416
E. Haltenhoff
INNOVATIVE CONTRACTING A TREND
American Professional Constructor 1984 *8* Winter, pp. 6–10
The four variant forms of construction management as practiced in the US are described.

415
R. Knowles
MORE ON THE BPF AGREEMENT
Chartered Quantity Surveyor 1984 *7* September, p. 51
Attention is given to additional drawings; named sub-contractors and suppliers; commencement and delay; final certificate and release of retention; termination; fluctuations; and arbitration.

414
J. Rawlinson
PROJECT MANAGEMENT – A QUANTITY SURVEYING VIEWPOINT
Building Economist 1984 *24* September, pp. 17–21.

413
A. Walker and W.P. Hughes
PRIVATE INDUSTRIAL PROJECT MANAGEMENT: A SYSTEMS-BASED CASE STUDY
Construction Management and Economics 1984 *2* Autumn, pp. 93–109
The technique of linear responsibility analysis is used for a retrospective case study of a private industrial development consisting of an extension to existing buildings to provide a warehouse, services block and packing line. The organizational structure adopted on the project is analyses using concepts from systems theory which are included in Walker's theoretical model of the structure of building project organizations. This model proposes that the process of building provision can be viewed as systems and sub-systems which are differentiated from each other at decision points. Further to this, the sub-systems can be viewed as the interaction of managing system and operating system. Using Walker's model, a systematic analysis of the relationships between the contributors gives a quantitative assessment of the efficacy of the organizational structure used. The causes of the client's dissatisfaction with the outcome of the project were lack of integration and complexity of the managing system. However, there was a high level of satisfaction with the completed project and this is reflected by the way in which the organizational structure corresponded to the model's propositions.

412
R. Owens
CAMBRIDGE COST CUTTER
Architects Journal 1984 *180* August 15, p. 18
A local authority has let a concrete-framed office block to a develop-and-construct builder. It has produced significant savings by introducing a competitive element into the structural design.

411
V. Ireland
VIRTUALLY MEANINGLESS DISTINCTIONS BETWEEN NOMINALLY DIFFERENT PROCUREMENT METHODS
Proc 4th Int. Symposium on Organization and Management of Construction. Waterloo. Canada. July 1984, pp. 203–11
The procurement methods of lump sum, provisional quantities and reimbursement, package deal, construction management and project management are

considered in terms of cost determining contractor selection; specialists roles; process structure and contract conditions.

410

S.M. Rowlinson and R. Newcombe

COMPARISON OF PROCUREMENT FORMS FOR INDUSTRIAL BUILDINGS IN THE UK

Proc. 4th Int. Symposium on Organization and Management and Construction. Waterloo, Canada, July 1984, pp. 247–56

A framework is set out within which the client and contractor conceptions of project performance can be assessed. The assessment takes place within the context of the forms of procurement currently available.

409

A.C. Sidwell

MEASUREMENT OF SUCCESS OF VARIOUS ORGANIZATIONAL FORMS FOR CONSTRUCTION PROJECTS

Proc. 4th Int. Symposium on Organization and Management of Construction. Waterloo, Canada, July 1984, pp. 283–9

The problems are discussed of evaluating project success, and the performance of various organizational forms is examined in terms of cost time and quality.

408

I.N.D. Wallace

CONTRACTS FOR INDUSTRIAL PLANT PROJECTS

International Construction Law Review 1984 1 July, pp. 322–55

Attention is given to methods of procurement including turnkey, separate contracts, joint ventures and project management and methods of payment.

407

M.W. Chin

ASSESSMENT OF ALTERNATIVE MANAGEMENT APPROACHES TO CONSTRUCTION PROJECTS IN THE WEST INDIES

Paper to CIB W–65 4th International Symposium on Organization and Management of Construction. Waterloo, Canada. July 1984, Vol. 4, pp. 1343–50

The paper reviews the current alternative management approaches to construction projects in the West Indies and discusses the problems and prospects of the various delivery systems in relation to a number of projects in the West Indies. Particular attention is given to the professional construction management (PCM) approach which has been emerging in the West Indies in recent years as a viable alternative to the traditional approach for the successful completion of construction projects. Some of the potential legal problems of using such an approach are highlighted.

The paper concludes with an assessment of the advantages and disadvantages of the various delivery systems in the light of the results of ten case studies undertaken in Trinidad and Tobago.

406

S.G. Naoum and D.A. Langford

MANAGEMENT CONTRACTING – A REVIEW OF THE SYSTEM

Proc. 4th Int. Symposium on Organization and Management of Construction. Waterloo, Canada, July 1984, Volume 3, pp. 1001–13.

405

J. Andrews

CONSTRUCTION PROJECT MANAGEMENT IN JOINT VENTURE IN DEVELOPING COUNTRIES

Proc. 4th Int. Symposium on Organization and Management of Construction. Waterloo, Canada, July 1984, Volume 3, pp. 687–96

Following a restatement of reservations concerning joint ventures, attention is drawn to the growing and ill-advised use of joint ventures in developing countries. Finally, some key aspects of management and organization are outlined.

404

M.R. Baker and R.W. Cockfield

INTERNATIONAL TURNKEY PROJECTS – THE RISKS AND METHODS OF IMPACT REDUCTION

Proc. 4th Int. Symposium on Organization and Management of Construction. Waterloo, Canada, July 1984, pp. 17–29.

403

C.E.E. Haltenhoff

CM (CONSTRUCTION MANAGEMENT): THE STATE OF THE ART

Proc. 4th Int. Symposium on Organization and Management of Construction. Waterloo, Canada, July 1984, pp. 179–91.

402

E.O.O. Sawacha and D.A. Langford

PROJECT MANAGEMENT AND THE PUBLIC SECTOR CLIENT – FOUR CASE STUDIES

Proc. 4th Int. Symposium on Organization and Management of Construction. Waterloo, Canada, July 1984, pp. 273–82

The use is investigated of project management for four public sector clients.

401

K.D. Waagenaar

TOTAL MANAGEMENT – AN ADVANCED APPROACH TO PROJECT MANAGEMENT

Proc. 4th Int. Symposium on Organization and Management of Construction, Waterloo, Canada, July 1984, pp. 310–19.

400
O. Oberti
PROJECT MANAGEMENT BY PROFESSIONALS: CORRECT PROCEDURES AND PITFALLS
Proc. 4th Int. Symposium on Organization and Management of Construction. Waterloo, Canada, July 1984, pp. 235–45
The value of the professional as a project manager is discussed. An outline of the fundamentals of the approach and procedures required for successful project management is combined with an insight into the key ingredients of the contractual arrangements.

399
H.R. Thomas et al.
GUIDELINES FOR THE DEVELOPMENT OF AUTHORITY STRUCTURES FOR HEAVY INDUSTRIAL CONSTRUCTION PROJECTS
Proc. 4th Int. Symposium on Organization and Management of Construction. Waterloo, Canada, July 1984, pp. 87–98
The organizational forms of project management are described and principles presented that relate project characteristics to the best items of a project management structure. Guiding principles in the establishment and responsibility and the location of the project manager within the hierarchy of the organization are also outlined.

398
R.K. Stocks and S.P. Male
INVESTIGATION INTO THE CLIENT'S PERCEPTIONS OF CONTRACTUAL FORMS AND PROCEDURES: THE INSTIGATION OF GOOD PRACTICE
Proc. 4th Int. Symposium on Organization and Management of Construction. Waterloo, Canada, July 1984, pp. 291–8
Contractual arrangements are considered in terms of the value to the client, it being concluded that they are over-emphasized. More attention should be given to organizational procedures, including communication, coordination, reporting procedures and inter-personal relationships.

397
S. Goth
CONSTRUCTION MANAGEMENT AND CONTROL OVER THE CONSTRUCTION LABOUR PROCESS
Proceedings 1983 Bartlett International Summer School, Geneva, 1984, pp. 4.3–4.7
The ramifications of management contracting for industrial relations and safety are considered.

396
G.E. Ninos and S.H. Wearne
RESPONSIBILITIES FOR PROJECT CONTROL DURING CONSTRUCTION. A GUIDE TO THE PROMOTERS AND CUSTOMERS OF BUILDING AND CIVIL ENGINEERING PROJECTS ON ORGANIZING THE CONTROL OF COST, QUALITY AND THE SPEED OF CONSTRUCTION
1984. School of Technological Management, University of Bradford, 74pp.
Limitations on conventional means for controlling a construction project are considered to be capable of resolution by the use of a project manager (director). The project director has the responsibility and authority to make or delegate all decisions needed to achieve the project objectives within the target costs and completion time authorized.

395
A. Walker
PROJECT MANAGEMENT IN CONSTRUCTION
1984. Granada, 206pp.
Designed to provoke a re-evaluation of the effectiveness of the organization structures used in the management of construction projects. The client's role is distinguished and examined and a model of the construction process is developed, as is a method of analysing and designing project organization structures. Against this backcloth a variety of organizational forms available for the implementation and management of construction projects are considered in terms of their contribution to the fulfilment of the client's objectives.

394
J. Franks
BUILDING PROCUREMENT SYSTEMS – A GUIDE TO BUILDING PROJECT MANAGEMENT
1984. CIOB, 71pp.
The various non-traditional forms (including BPF) of contracting are considered in turn, the advantages and limitations of each being identified. This is then followed by a comparative assessment. Finally there is a section of literature covering all systems.

393
R.F. Moore
RESPONSE TO CHANGE – THE DEVELOPMENT OF NON-TRADITIONAL FORMS OF CONTRACTING
CIOB Occasional Paper No. 31, 1984, 26pp.
A résumé is given of the reasons underlying the change from traditional to non-traditional forms of contracting having greater contractor involvement. Particular attention is paid to design–build, turnkey and management contracting. The response of firms to these new techniques is evaluated by means of

a survey which provides some hard data on the uptake.

392
Construction Industry Research and Information Association
A CLIENT'S GUIDE TO MANAGEMENT CONTRACTS IN BUILDING
1984, 12pp.

391
BPF SYSTEM
Building 1984 *266* June 15, pp. 28–33
Contributions on the new system of building management cover the advantages/limitations, the philosophy of the adapted ACA form for use with BPF systems and application of the system to two real projects.

390
B.D. Phillis
QUANTITY SURVEYOR AS PROJECT MANAGER
Building Economist 1984 *23* June, pp. 7–9
The skill requirements of a project manager are compared to those of a quantity surveyor.

389
R.A. Hartland
PROJECT MANAGEMENT TODAY
Consulting Engineer 1984 June, pp. 18–19
The changing role is examined of the project manager and how he copes with the conflicting interests of the design team and client.

387
M.R.K. Garnett
JOINT VENTURES
Arbitration 1984 *49* May, pp. 326–31
The basic principles of joint ventures are outlined.

386
T.A.N. Precott et al.
FOYLE BRIDGE: ITS HISTORY, AND THE STRATEGY OF THE DESIGN AND BUILD CONCEPT
Proc. ICE 1984 *76(1)* May, pp. 351–61
The history of the River Foyle crossings and the events leading up to the decision to go to a design-and-build contract are outlined. How the contract was drawn up, the bids received and the assessment of the tenders and the award of the contract are described.

385
B.P. Wex et al.
FOYLE BRIDGE: DESIGN AND TENDER IN A DESIGN AND BUILD COMPETITION
ICE Proc. 1984 *76(1)* May, pp. 363–86
The positions are described of the contractor and designer in design and build tender procedures and compares them with their respective roles under normal UK tendering practice. The setting up of the R.D.L. Graham joint venture for the construction of the bridge is also covered.

384
L. Stace
BPF SYSTEM A PERSONAL VIEW
Chartered Surveyor Weekly 1984 7 April 5, p. 29
It is argued that the BPF approach is wrong in trying to eliminate BOQ since it is the contract which is at fault.

383
J. Pain
CONCENTRATING THE CONTRACTOR'S MIND
Building 1984 *226* April 27, pp. 32–3
Arguments are made to demonstrate the inadequacies of traditional forms of contracting. Greater responsibility for the contractor would encourage finishing the job on time.

382
W.H. Alington
COMMUNICATIONS FOR RUNNING MULTI-CONTRACT PROJECTS FROM A CONSULTANT'S OFFICE
Paper to AIB/NZIOB Conference 'Communication in our industry', Christchurch, New Zealand, March 1984, pp. 75–84
The organization of 'separate trades' contracts is discussed with reference to the monitoring of the contracts, the documentation and the supporting computer systems.

381
A Sidwell
BUYING REFURBISHED BUILDINGS
Building Technology & Management 1984 22 April, pp. 22–6
Means of procurement by traditional firm price contracts, cost reimbursement contracts, management contracts, single trades or AMM contracts, partnership agreements, and serial contracts are discussed. A summary is provided of the advantages and limitations of each.

380
M.V. Manzoni
PROJECT MANAGEMENT – NOW AND IN THE FUTURE
Paper to Chartered Quantity Surveyors 13th Triennial Conference, London, April 1984, 17pp.
It is suggested that improvement of the industry will be achieved only by means of an organization structure which ensures that each part of the industry provides the development and training of its own discipline and executes its own work without undue sub-letting. After describing the principal contribution a contractor can make, a comparison is made of traditional contracting with management contracting.

379
C. Davies
EXHIBITION OF SPEED
Building 1984 266 March 23, pp. 30–2
Bovis's design–build approach to the construction of the Scottish Exhibition Centre is outlined.

378
B. Heaphy
BEHIND THE FEE SYSTEM
Building 1984 266 March 16, pp. 28–30
The advantages of the management fee contract are described.

377
L. Clements
KESSOCK BRIDGE DESIGN AND BUILD CONTRACTS AND PROPOSALS FOR MANAGING SIMILAR CONTRACTS
ICE Proc. 1984 76 (Part 1) February, pp. 23–34
Events leading up to the planning and adoption of the design-and-build form of contract are reviewed. The aims, problems and achievements are described and proposals put forward for modified procedures which could be adopted for managing similar projects in the future.

376
H. Walton
PROJECT MANAGER: A CAPITE AD CALCEM
Project Management 1984 2 February, pp. 31–5
The skills and qualities of a project manager are evaluated in terms of the environments in which he may operate and the tasks to be performed.

375
H. Try
UNPALATABLE MEDICINE FOR THE BUILDING TEAM
Building Technology & Management 1984 22 February, pp. 3–4

A personal response to the British Property Federation's manual for building design and construction.

374
G. Testa
OLD ORDER CHANGETH. . . . ?
Chartered Quantity Surveyor 1984 6 January, p. 212
Two forms of non-traditional approach to contracting are outlined. One is a 'single source responsibility service' in which the clients spatial, functional, cost and time requirements are managed by the architect, with input from the contractor, until the main elements of the client's needs are established and the cost plan and programme frozen. Full responsibility then passes to the contractor with provision for input from the design team. The second approach involves a multi-disciplinary team with the general contractor as team leader in joint venture with a services contractor.

373
E. Haltenhoff
INNOVATIVE CONTRACTING – A TREND
American Professional Constructor 1984 8 Winter, pp. 6–10
The four variant forms of construction management as practised in the US are described.

1983

372
N.M.L. Barnes
BUILDING MORE FOR LESS – A COST AND PERFORMANCE STUDY
Proc. JLO Annual Conference 1983 'Building for recovery – new clients, new markets'. Birmingham, 3pp.
Objectives of the study leading to the BPF manual are summarized.

371
R.W. Woodhead
METHODOLOGICAL APPROACH TO PROJECT MANAGEMENT
Proc. 9th CIB Congress. Stockholm 1983. Volume 1b. Renewal, rehabilitation and maintenance, pp. 25–36
A methodological approach is presented to project management which focuses on the consideration of management functions, decision processes, and the role of managers. In this way basic project management concepts can be developed that have general validity.

370

W.J. Diepeveen
PROJECT MANAGEMENT AND ITS IMPACT ON THE MANAGEMENT OF PARTNER ORGANIZATIONS
Proc. 9th CIB Congress. Stockholm 1983. Volume 1b. Renewal, rehabilitation and maintenance, pp. 11–23
Project management wants to ensure efficient management of the construction process. It makes use of management techniques that guarantee the coordination of the activities of the different project partners such as the client, the architect, the consultants and the builder. The end result of a well-organized construction process should be a building of optimum quality for the client. On the one hand the project partners should satisfy the needs of the client in a most effective way, but on the other hand they must keep an eye on the demands of continuity and rentability in their own organizations, be it an architects' partnership, a consultancy or engineering practice or a building firm. The best building may be harmful for the demands of their home organization. Each partner has a divided responsibility, divided between his own interests and the interests of the client as seen through the eyes of a team of individual partners that may have never met before and who also may have conflicting interests. The two processes run simultaneously. Both the project and the partners' organizations have their own demands for an effective management. The construction process asks for an optimum project management and the partners' own organization at home must be guaranteed by an optimum business organization. The two may come into conflict and we will see how the two may be developed in harmony and what measures will be needed to do it.

369

J. Bennett
PROJECT MANAGEMENT IN CONSTRUCTION
Construction Management and Economics 1983 *1* Winter, pp. 183–197
A conceptual framework for project management in construction is proposed. It comprises two distinct phases. The first is strategic, being concerned with client objectives, project description and organization. The second is concerned with the execution of basic construction tasks. The essential nature of these concepts and of relationships between them is described. The need to regard projects as hierarchies is discussed. The paper concludes that within construction projects, management, design and construction strategies must be matched and then given expression in clearly defined tasks. Creating and maintaining that consistent framework is project management.

368

R. Thomas et al.
AUTHORITY STRUCTURES FOR CONSTRUCTION PROJECT MANAGEMENT
ASCE Journal of Construction Engineering and Management 1983 *109(4)* December, pp. 406–22
A primer on authority structures is presented. The basic corporate organizational forms are described and construction examples are given. The basic authority structures for project management are also described. These forms are the functional, pure project, and matrix. For each form, the advantages and disadvantages as they relate to the project manager's ability to support the project are cited. Nine factors that influence the choice of authority structure are discussed. The role of the project manager is described. His effectiveness as a manager is related to the organizational form, hierarchy within the organization, authority gap, management style, and the ability to resolve conflict. Six principles for developing a project organization and selecting a project manager are given.

367

B. Waters
BPF SYSTEM
Building 1983 *265* December 16, pp. 25–30
The main proposals of the British Property Federation in regard to procurement are described, the reasons underlying their introduction being outlined. A critique of the proposals is also included.

366

R.O. Powys
PROFESSIONAL CONSTRUCTION MANAGEMENT – THE AUSTRALIAN PRIVATE SECTOR
Building Economist 1983 *22* December, pp. 326–9
The concept is discussed of project management and management contracting, reference being made to recruitment, fees and the position of the architect.

365

A.T. Brett-Jones
BARCHESTER LOW RISE: A CASE STUDY OF A MANAGEMENT CONTRACT FOR REMEDIAL WORK TO A LARGE HOUSING SCHEME
Construction Management and Economics 1983 *1* Autumn, pp. 91–117
The case study discussed involved detailed evaluation of the defects; a pilot contract; a management contract approach; cost monitoring and performance monitoring; post contract cost control; innovative use of temporary shelters.

364

P.W.G. Morris
PROJECT MANAGEMENT ORGANIZATION

Construction Papers 1983 *2(1)*, pp. 5–18
Current concepts of the organization of large projects are reviewed. The origins of project management are described and the essential patterns of organization found on projects are detailed. In conclusion some practical lessons of project organization are given, drawn from a variety of international projects.

363
J. Berny and R. Howes
PROJECT MANAGEMENT CONTROL USING REAL TIME BUDGETING AND FORECASTING MODELS
Construction Papers 1983 *2(1)*, pp. 19–40.

362
G. Ridout
CONTRASTING BUILDING MENUS FAVOUR AFTER-TASTE AT TWO BOOT HOTELS
Contract Journal 1983 *316* December 15, pp. 16–17
The progress is shown to be significantly different on two equal-sized hotels, one on a traditional contract with a steel frame and the other a management contract with precast concrete.

361
H. Knoepfel
SYSTEMATIC PROJECT MANAGEMENT
International Journal of Project Management 1983 *1* November, pp. 234–41
A set of conceptual models for the management of projects on the basis of the physical system of constructed facilities is presented. The purpose, structures, boundaries, environment and objectives of these models and some of the application procedures are discussed.

360
O. Hogberg and A. Adamsson
SCANDINAVIAN VIEW OF PROJECT MANAGEMENT
International Journal of Project Management 1983 *1* November, pp. 216–19
The effects are discussed of cultural variations in project management. Based on the experiences of project organizations and project control systems, some concepts for management and control are presented. The importance of realistic forecasting is emphasized.

359
G.P. Gilbert
STYLES OF PROJECT MANAGEMENT
International Journal of Project Management 1983 *1* November, pp. 189–93
The factors that a project manager needs to take into account are discussed and the case is made for a greater emphasis to be placed on leadership.

358
N. Davis
CONSULTANT QS AND PROJECT MANAGEMENT
Chartered Quantity Surveyor 1983 *6* November, pp. 132–3
Guidance is given on the possible methods of remuneration for project management services.

357
B. Waters
BALANCED APPROACH
Building 1983 *265* November 4, pp. 28–30
The design–build approach to the construction of a speculative office block is outlined. It is claimed that the approach strikes the right balance between architectural and commercial pressures.

356
Southern Counties Joint Consultative Committee for Building
MANAGEMENT IN CONSTRUCTION
Proceedings of a meeting held on 26 October 1983, 27pp.
The management of building projects is considered from three viewpoints:
   The traditional approach, by R. Paul
   Project management in practice, by A. Massey
   Management contracting and its variants, by G.S. Rendall.

355
R. Cecil
KEEP THE PROFESSIONALS
Building 1983 *265* August 19, p. 25
The argument is challenged that building consultants should be subject to the same kind of contractual sanctions as builders.

354
N. Parkyn
MARKETING MANAGEMENT
Building 1983 *265* August 19, pp. 29–31
BDP's philosophy in regard to its project management services is explored.

353
J.F. Woodward
PROJECT MANAGEMENT EDUCATION LEVELS OF UNDERSTANDING AND MISUNDERSTANDING
Project Management 1983 *1* August, pp. 173–8
The teaching of project management both in-house and at academic establishments is reviewed.

352
CONSULTANTS ON THE LINE
Building 1983 *264* July 29, p. 22

It is argued that the architect could help stem the tide towards non-traditional forms of contracting by imposing some of the disciplines on himself that are accepted by the contractor. These could include the imposition of a design programme and a warranty of fitness for purpose.

351
C. Davies
STUDIO IN STORE
Building 1983 *264* June 3, pp. 36–8
The construction of a TV studios conversion let on a management contract is briefly discussed.

350
C. Davies
ARCHITECTS WITH A PACKAGE DEAL
Building 1983 *264* May 20, pp. 30–5
A. Epstein & Sons offer a package deal, the difference being that the firm is one of architects not a builder. The firm's basic approach and its application to Sainsbury's supermarket in Cromwell Road, London are described.

349
A. Ashworth
CONTRACTUAL METHODS USED IN THE CONSTRUCTION INDUSTRY
Building Trades Journal 1983 *185* May 12, pp. 24, 29
An outline is given of the principles of management contracts, turnkey operations and serial contracts.

348
J. Franks
ASSESSING THE ALTERNATIVE SYSTEMS FOR MANAGING THE BUILDING PROCESS
Building Trades Journal 1983 *185* May 12, 40pp.
An assessment is made of traditional contracting, management fee and package deal.

347
R. Ormerod
SUCCESSFUL EXPERIMENT
Building 1983 *264* April 15, pp. 34–7
MEPC's design–build office scheme carried out by Henry Boot is described, particular attention being given to the management aspects.

346
J. Bennett and R. Flanagan
MANAGEMENT OPTIONS
Building 1983 *264* April 8, pp. 32–3
New forms of contracting are seen as being of advantage to the client. The background to these new forms is traced and an outline given of the principles of project management, design-and-construct and construction management (management contracting).

345
C. Davies
FASTBUILD SYSTEM
Building 1983 *264* April 1, pp. 31–4
The management of a design build contract is outlined, particular attention being given to the role of the architect within the team. Lack of an adequate client's brief resulted in £100,000 of additional work.

344
C.B. Tatum
ISSUES IN PROFESSIONAL CONSTRUCTION MANAGEMENT
ASCE Journal of Construction Engineering and Management 1983 *109(1)* March, pp. 112–19
The use of professional construction management has increased rapidly since the introduction of this form of organization in the early 1960s. Despite this widespread use questions concerning the scope, definition, and differences in implementation of this project delivery system remain. An ASCE technical committee has investigated these questions and disseminated information concerning professional construction management through technical sessions at ASCE meetings, published papers, and a speciality conference. This paper summarizes the results of these activities and provides references of the literature available regarding the development and use of professional construction management.

343
A.C. Sidwell
EVALUATION OF MANAGEMENT CONTRACTING
Construction Management and Economics 1983 *1* Spring, pp. 47–55
The paper discusses the main features of the system of management contracting which has developed in the UK in the last decade and evaluates these in relation to those elements of the building process thought to influence project success. Data from a number of case studies are examined to establish the time saved and other advantages of using this system.

342
J. Franks
CONSTRUCTING A BRIDGE BETWEEN CLIENT, ARCHITECT AND BUILDER
Building Trades Journal 1983 *185* February 10, pp. 28–9
The concept of project management is discussed.

341
J. Franks
SEPARATE CONTRACTS SYSTEM
Building Trades Journal 1983 *185* January 27, pp. 22–3

The separate contracts system is basically where the architect lets contracts to individual trades rather than to a general contractor. The advantages and limitations of such a system are discussed.

340
SPECIAL REPORT, PROJECT MANAGEMENT
Chartered Surveyor Weekly 1983 2 January 13, pp. 84–5, 87, 89, 93
The report includes a number of separate contributions including an outline of the RICS project management diploma course; the role for chartered surveyors; computer aids; and the financial/time benefits.

339
J. Franks
USING THE DESIGN AND BUILD SYSTEM
Building Trades Journal 1983 *185* January 6, p. 14.

338
J.F. Woodward
PROJECT MANAGEMENT: OCCUPATION OR VOCATION?
Project Manager 1983 2 January, pp. 2–3.

337
H. Darnell and M.W. Dale
TOTAL PROJECT MANAGEMENT: AN INTEGRATED APPROACH TO THE MANAGEMENT OF CAPITAL INVESTMENT PROJECTS IN INDUSTRY
1983. Asset Management Group (BIM), 43pp.

336
J. McKinney
MANAGEMENT CONTRACTING
CIOB Occasional Paper No. 30, 1983, 14pp.
An evaluation is made of management contracting based on a review of the existing literature. The case is argued for the management contractor to be selected from contracting rather than the design professions. Following an outline of the development and growth of management contracting, attention is given to its market and the question of accountability when used in the public sector. Some useful guidance is given on the selection and operational stages before the final section which sums up the advantage and limitations.

335
Construction Industry Research and Information Association
MANAGEMENT CONTRACTING
Report No. 100, 1983, 44pp.
The use of management contracting in the UK construction industry, predominantly in the building, process plant and offshore sectors is described. A review of construction management in the USA is also included. Management contracting is becoming more popular but in the UK it is still in an evolutionary phase. The problems with management contracting are identified and areas where improvements in practice could be made are indicated. The report is based on visits to 52 firms and organizations, 39 in the UK and 13 in the USA. Thirteen case studies are included, illustrating a variety of approaches to the management of construction projects. Potential weaknesses are identified. Provided these are recognized it is concluded that the various forms of management contracting can offer viable and flexible contractual relationships for projects where time is important, especially where there is a likelihood of insufficient design information being available at the stage when a main construction contract would normally be let. They are also suitable where there is a need to coordinate a considerable number of construction contractors and suppliers. Management contracting offers potential for improved management of design and construction, particularly where a client has insufficient resources or expertise to concentrate on these crucial aspects of managing a project.

334
British Property Federation
MANUAL OF THE BPF SYSTEM FOR BUILDING DESIGN AND CONSTRUCTION
1983, 99pp.
The system is geared to both conventional and non-traditional methods of procurement and it acts as a guide to the formal and informal team relationships. The main management functions of controlling time, cost, standards and performance are handled by a Client's Representative. For pre-tender design and specifications a Design Leader is appointed but the contractor is also allocated a proportion of the design to facilitate buildability. The system is in five stages but is flexible, allowing clients to decide where the dividing line between stages should be drawn. An adjudicator is appointed to deal quickly with disputes.

333
Construction Industry Research and Information Association
CLIENT'S GUIDE TO TRADITIONAL CONTRACT BUILDING
1983, 12pp.

1982

332
J. Franks
PACKAGE DEAL SYSTEM HAS ALL THE CLIENTS' BUILDING NEEDS

Building Trades Journal 1982 *184* December 2, pp. 24, 28
The principles of the package deal are outlined.

331
J. Franks
MANAGEMENT FEE CONTRACTS AND TWO STAGE TENDER SYSTEMS
Building Trades Journal 1982 *184* November 18, pp. 37, 39.

330
D. Hammond
PROJECT MANAGEMENT: WHAT'S IT ALL ABOUT?
Contract Journal 1982 *310* November 11, pp. 34–5
The concept of project management is outlined.

329
J. Franks
TRADITIONAL SYSTEM OF MANAGING THE BUILDING PROCESS
Building Trades Journal 1982 *184* November 4, pp. 50, 52.

328
I. Atkinson
INDUSTRY PUTS FPL ON PROJECT MANAGE-MENT MAP
Contract Journal 1982 *309* November 4, pp. 14–16
The approach is outlined of Fairclough Projects Ltd to management contracting in the industrial sector.

327
H.S. Kaden
INTERNATIONAL CONTRACTING
Proceedings of the CIB W–65 mini-symposium. The problems of organization and management of construction in developing countries and international contracting. November 1982. Istanbul, pp. 3.1.1–3.1.12
Attention is given to the role of the World Bank's procurement choices for the client and the salient points to be considered by a contractor on seeking an overseas contract.

326
A.C. Sidwell
PROJECT MANAGEMENT: CONSIDERATIONS FOR INTERNATIONAL CONTRACTING
Proceedings of the CIB W–65 mini-symposium. The problems of organization and management of construction in developing countries and international contracting. November 1982, Istanbul, pp. 111/1.1–1.14
The major variables likely to be encountered with an international project are discussed in addition to the problems posed by social, cultural, political, economic and educational differences. A case study is presented to illustrate the cultural role that the project management team plays. In conclusion four principal characteristics are highlighted which are particularly demanding of the project manager if success is to be achieved.

325
B. Waters
CONTRACTUAL SYSTEMS COMPARED: TWO HAMPSHIRE SPORTS BUILDINGS
Architects Journal 1982 *176* October 20, pp. 67–74
The two contractual arrangements examined are design-and-build, and a managing contract, i.e. one in which the contractor was able to compete for packages of work.

324
LUDER VIEW ON THE MANAGING ARCHITECT
Contract Journal 1982 *309* September 2, pp. 10–12
The architect's role in project management is explored.

323
P. Carolin
DESIGNING FOR BUILDABILITY
Architects Journal 1982 *176* August 11, pp. 32–3, 38, 41
The organization is described of a management contract carried out by Wimpey for civic offices, emphasis being given to the architect's role.

322
I. Atkinson
CONTRACTOR BUILDS MANAGEMENT SER-VICE FOUNDED ON TRUST
Contract Journal 1982 *307* June 24, pp. 12–14
Higgs & Hills approach to management contracting is outlined.

321
BUILDING METHODS AND MANAGEMENT
Financial Times Survey 1982. June 30, 8pp.
Among the subjects covered are management contracting, brick and timber frame, steel-framed construction and a design–build contract for Findus's Newcastle Plant.

320
I. Atkinson
'MOTIVATE AND MANAGE' IS THE DAVID WOOLF STYLE
Contract Journal 1982 *307* May 13, pp. 16–17
Woolf Project Management's approach to management contracting is discussed.

319
I. Atkinson
SMOOTHING THE PATH OF DEVELOPMENT

Contract Journal 1982 *307* May 6, pp. 12–14
Trollope and Colls approach to management contracting is discussed.

318
P. Sharp
MANAGEMENT OR FEE OR BOTH?
Chartered Quantity Surveyor 1982 *4* May, pp. 307–9
A review is made of the place for fee and management contracting.

317
G. Trickey and J. Sims
DOES THE CLIENT GET WHAT HE WANTS?
Quantity Surveyor 1982 *38* May, pp. 86–8
A summary is given of two talks given at the 1982 Building Industry Convention. Particular attention is devoted to the traditional methods of procurement and how those fail to meet the client's requirements.

316
LAING TEAM CONFIDENT OF RESTORING SUCCESS
Construction News 1982 April 15, pp. 18–19
An interview with the Chief Executive of John Laing, Leslie Holliday, which covers the future of the Group, the approach to training, Super Homes development, and management contracting.

315
P.D. Titmus
DESIGN AND BUILD IN PRACTICE
Building Technology and Management 1982 *20* April, pp. 9–12
The case for the design-and-build approach to contracting is discussed, it being argued that one of its most important characteristics is the increased willingness of parties to find rapid solutions to problems and to overcome difficulties. Responsibilities are clearly defined, thereby leading to a minimum of misunderstanding.

314
A.L.Y. Lewis
RECRUITMENT OF PROJECT MANAGEMENT STAFF
Project Manager 1982 *2* April, pp. 15–17
Some information is given on job specification, responsibilities, conditions of employment and recruitment.

313
A. Walker
LINEAR RESPONSIBILITY ANALYSIS
Chartered Quantity Surveyor 1982 *4* March, pp. 228–30
Linear responsibility analysis is a tool which project managers use to design an appropriate organization structure at an early stage.

312
BUILDING EFFICIENTLY: HOW THE AMERICANS MANAGE IT
RIBA Journal 1982 *89* March, pp. 32–3
Two articles explore project management and the advantages of the North American approach to contracting.

311
C.B. Tatum
PROFESSIONAL CM: THE ARCHITECT ENGINEER'S VIEWPOINT
ASCE Journal of the Construction Division 1982 *108* (CO1). March, pp. 177–8 (Discussion).

310
H.S. Crowter
NEW JCT DESIGN/BUILD CONTRACT – 1981
Quantity Surveyor 1982 *38* March, pp. 42–4
A commentary is provided on the major articles and conditions.

309
N. Barratt
MANAGEMENT CONTRACTING TO PROVE ITS WORTH AT HEATHROW'S NEW TERMINAL
New Civil Engineer 1982 February 25, pp. 12–14
The background is outlined to the development, advantages and current use of management contracting. The British Airports Authority is to let the construction of terminal 4 as a management contract.

308
DIRECT AND DESIGN
Building 1982 *262* February 26, pp. 24–5
A profile is given of the design/build organization the JT Group.

307
H.S. Crowter
NEW JCT DESIGN/BUILD CONTRACT – 1981
Quantity Surveyor 1982 *38* February, pp. 25–7
A commentary is provided on the new form as it relates to professional advisers, design liability and VAT.

306
F.C. Graves
QUANTITY SURVEYOR AND PROJECT MANAGEMENT
Quantity Surveyor 1982 *38* February, pp. 28–32
The benefits of project management and the functions of the project manager are discussed.

305
B. Waters
CONVERSION ON THE FAST TRACK

Building 1982 *262* January 15, pp. 24–6
The conversion of an hotel to offices is described briefly, attention being given to the contractual arrangements which involved a project management organization at inception and dealt with the costing and advising on the programme implications of alternative designs. The project management organization saw its role as client's agent, with the client contracting with 40 contractors using a modified AIA contract.

304
D. Sudjic
RICHARD ROGERS LTD: FAST TRACKING IN WALES
RIBA Journal 1982 *89* January, pp. 31–3, 36–7
The construction is described of a microchip factory built in just over 15 months using a management contractor.

303
Aqua Group
TENDERS AND CONTRACTS FOR BUILDING
1982. 2nd edition. Granada, 100pp.
Forms of contractual arrangement are described.

302
B. McGhie
IMPLICATIONS OF PROJECT MANAGEMENT
Proceedings 3rd Bartlett Summer School. 1981. Production of the built environment. 1982, pp. 3.1–3.9.

301
Chartered Institute of Building
PROJECT MANAGEMENT IN BUILDING
1982, 36pp.
Combines two previously published papers:
– Project management in building, issued as Occasional Paper No. 20
– Education for project management in building.

300
K.F. Branu
PROJECT MANAGEMENT
Building Technologists 1981–82, *8*, pp. 17–23
Attention is given to instructions; the design team; appointment of consultants; and client/project manager liaison.

1981

299
L.W. Murrway et al.
MARKETING CONSTRUCTION MANAGEMENT SERVICES

ASCE Journal of the Construction Division 1981 *107* December, pp. 665–77
A survey of ninety-five construction management firms and two hundred and twenty-two construction management clients was undertaken to assess marketing practices and preferences. Forty-nine firms and forty-six clients responded to the survey. An analysis of the firm's responses indicated that the most important determinant of contract awards was the amount of general experience of the firm. Clients stressed the importance of the quality of services provided by the firm. Clients desired more information to assess the quality of the firm's proposed project manager. A marketing model is developed to assist construction management firms in positioning their marketing efforts. The model focuses upon the project manager, the project team, and requires that the firm include information to enable the clients to evaluate the flexibility of the firm's solutions to the clients' construction management problems.

298
PROJECT MANAGEMENT AND MANAGEMENT CONTRACTING – THEIR FUTURE ROLE
Building Technology and Management 1981 *19* October, pp. 11–12.

297
N. Davis
PACKAGE DEAL SERVICE AND FEES
Chartered Quantity Surveyor 1981 *4* October, pp. 60–1
The scope of quantity surveyor's services in relation to package deals is discussed and proposals are made on establishing fees for these services.

296
A. Yates
OLD RELATIONS IN NEW CLOTHES
Chartered Quantity Surveyor 1981 *4* October, p. 64
The principles of management fee contracts and their particular strengths are discussed.

295
M. Barnes
PROJECT MANAGEMENT BY MOTIVATION
Proc. PMI/Internet Joint Symposium 'The World of Project Management' Boston, USA. September 1981, pp. 341–6
The motivation factors are examined which are in some of the main sectors of project management – client's decisions, design, contracts and construction.

294
R.M. Davis and H.G. Irwig
PROJECT MANAGEMENT SERVICES: EFFECTIVENESS IN BUILDING CONSTRUCTION

Proc. PMI/Internet Joint Symposium 'The World of Project Management' Boston, USA. September 1981, pp. 318–30
The evolution of the need for project management is discussed and the nature of the project manager's responsibilities are reviewed.

293
L.W. Murray and H.T. Moody
PROJECT MANAGER IN MARKETING PROFES-SIONAL SERVICES
Proc. PMI/Internet Joint Symposium 'The World of Project Management' Boston, USA. September 1981, pp. 364–73
The role is discussed of project managers in the marketing strategy of firms selling professional services. Market surveys exploring this role for project management and for process engineering design and construction are examined.

292
E.G. Trimble
MOTIVATION OF CONTRACTORS IN MEDIUM TECHNOLOGY PROJECTS
Proc. PMI/Internet Joint Symposium 'The World of Project Management' Boston, USA. September 1981, pp. 257–61
The incentive value of different types of contractual arrangements are outlined.

291
Junior Liaison Organization
THOSE SUCCESSFUL PRACTICES. HOW DO THEY DO IT?
Conference held at St Edmund Hall, Oxford, September 1981, 40pp.
The only substantial summary is that of the paper by T.W. Fleming on management contracting. The points covered are the type of project, design involvement, time, sub-letting, work packages, value for money, cost control, incentive to the management contractor, fees and industrial relations.

290
D. Byron
ROLE OF THE ARCHITECT IN NEW FORMS OF CONTRACTING SERVICES
Building Technology and Management 1981 19 July/August, pp. 13–4
Particular attention is given to design–build projects.

289
H.G. Irwig, R.M. Davis
CONSTRUCTION MANAGEMENT SERVICES IN BUILDING CONSTRUCTION: USE AND EFFECT-IVENESS IN THE USA
Proceedings of the CIB W–65 3rd Symposium on Organization and Management of Construction.

Dublin, July 1981, Volume I, pp. A.1.234–A.1.251
A nationwide survey of 200 repeat purchasers of commercial, industrial and institutional buildings in continental USA and Canada to evaluate the pattern of usage and the degree of effectiveness of professional construction management services is reported. Analysis of the data reveals that:
– the use of construction management services is associated with projects of high complexity and value and moderate budget constraints. These characteristics do not, however, appear to be relevant in influencing either the type of construction managers utilised or the conditions of engagement.
– Although a very wide range of functions were regarded as primary responsibility areas for construction managers, only those concerned with the scheduling of construction, the negotiation and management of construction contracts, and the provision of preliminary budgets and cost projections were functions in which construction managers were generally perceived as being helpful.

288
T.M. Lewis
THE ROLE OF THE PROFESSIONAL CON-STRUCTION MANAGER
Proceedings of the CIB W–65 3rd Symposium on Organization and Management of Construction. Dublin, July 1981, Volume II, pp. C.2.228–C.2.238.

287
R. Fish
TENDERING AND CONTRACT PROCEDURES
Chartered Quantity Surveyor 1981 3 July, pp. 388–9
Tendering practice for industrial engineering contracts is discussed, reference being made to documentation, type of contract, conditions, contractor selection, and tender appraisal.

286
J.M. Hutcheson
PROJECT MANAGEMENT ACROSS CULTURAL BARRIERS
Proceedings of the CIB W–65 3rd Symposium on Organization and Management of Construction. Dublin. July 1981, Volume II, pp. C.1.52–C.1.67
A series of case studies and first-hand experiences in developing and undeveloped countries are outlined. An evaluation is made of the construction problems encountered in these case studies with a view to synthesizing lessons for project management. Human relations, legal, financial and other aspects are contrasted with their relationships in project management in countries with different cultures. Studies of overheads encountered by consultants and constructors operating away from their homeland are highlighted.

285

P.T. Pigott

APPLICATION OF THE SfB SYSTEM TO PROJECT MANAGEMENT

Proceedings of the CIB W–65 3rd Symposium on Organization and Management of Construction. Dublin. July 1981, Volume I, pp. A.1.409–A.1415.

284

A. Walker

ANALYSING BUILDING PROJECT MANAGEMENT STRUCTURES

Project Manager 1981 2 July, pp. 6–11

A method (linear responsibility analysis) is described by which post-mortems can be carried out on building projects which allow the organizational causes of deficiencies in the outcome of projects to be identified.

283

G. Smith

TENDERING PROCEDURES SCRUTINIZED. ESSEX COSTS THE ALTERNATIVES

Chartered Quantity Surveyor 1981 11 June, pp. 356–7

The cost effects of alternative tendering procedures, based on questionnaire and interview, are evaluated. Data are provided on the frequency of use of different procedures (competitive; negotiated; two-stage; cost plus fee; design-and-build), frequency of use of procedures for specialist works, average difference in pricing levels for main contract procedures, cost to client, total tendering costs, and average tenderer's costs for each from submitting a tender.

282

J.A. Ramsay

PROFESSIONAL CM: THE ARCHITECT: ENGINEER'S VIEWPOINT

ASCE Journal of the Construction Division 1981 107 June, pp. 408–9 (Discussion)

Views supporting the project management concept are expressed.

281

P.W.T. Pippin

PROJECT MANAGEMENT: THE THIRD DISCIPLINE IN ARCHITECTURAL PRACTICE

Architectural Record 1981 June, pp. 63, 65

It is argued that project management is of equal importance to design and production. The basic aims of a project manager and the advantages of project management are discussed.

280

V. Ireland

MODELLING THE BUILDING PROCESS. 4. SEQUENTIAL LUMP SUM TENDERING VERSUS PROJECT MANAGEMENT

Chartered Builder 1980/81 31 Summer, pp. 73, 75–8

A critique is made of general systems theory from which the action approach is stated and a model developed which can be applied to design, tendering and construction. A model representing project management is also developed.

279

DESIGN AND BUILD – THE QS OPPORTUNITY

Quantity Surveyor 1987 37 May, pp. 95–6.

278

D. Pritchard

QS VIEW OF MANAGEMENT CONTRACTING

Construction News Magazine 1981 7 May, pp. 13–14

The advantages and limitations of management contracting are summarized, the type of project for which it is particularly suitable being identified.

277

TALKING THE CONTRACT THROUGH

Building 1981 260 April 23, pp. 28–30

A group discussion is reported on the building industry's ability to meet the client needs, the significance of contractual arrangements being paramount.

276

R. Mortimer

DESIGN AND CONSTRUCT, ITS GROWTH, SHORTCOMINGS ETC.

Paper to RICS Quantity Surveyor 12th Triennial Conference, April 1981, 5pp.

275

H. Davis

ADVANTAGES OF MANAGEMENT CONTRACTS – APPARENT OR REAL?

Paper to RICS Quantity Surveyor 12th Triennial Conference, April 1981, 10pp.

The basic principles of management contracting are considered, reference being made to some projects built using the arrangement. Disadvantages and advantages are indicated.

274

J.B.G. Carpenter

UK SYSTEM OF CONSTRUCTION PROCUREMENT AND WHAT IS WRONG: HOW TO IMPROVE

Paper to RICS Quantity Surveyor 12th Triennial Conference, April 1981, 16pp.

It is suggested that projects go wrong because the actual tasks peculiar to the project are not clearly identified. This failure prevents appropriate procedures being developed for the project. Particular attention is given to the roles, assumed and actual, of all participants to the building process.

273
A. Walker
MODEL FOR THE DESIGN OF PROJECT MAN-AGEMENT STRUCTURES
Quantity Surveyor 1981 *37* April, pp. 66–71
The salient features of the model, the methodology and the results obtained are identified and discussed.

272
P.G. Cheesman
WHAT IS PROJECT MANAGEMENT AND WHO ARE PROJECT MANAGERS
Project Manager 1981 *2* April, pp. 19–21
The scope of project management and the project manager's role are discussed – the functions of a project manager are given as an appendix.

271
J.F. Woodward
TRAINING FOR PROJECT MANAGEMENT
Project Manager 1981 *2* April, pp. 17–19.

270
T. Farrow
IN PLACE OF STRIFE
Building 1981 *260* March 27, p. 47
An outline is given of the principles of project management.

269
R. Flanagan
CHANGE THE SYSTEM
Building 1981 *260* March 20, pp. 28–9
Some of the arguments for non-traditional forms of letting contracts are presented.

268
A.P. Carpenter
DESIGN AND CONTRACT PROCEDURE COMPARISONS
Building Economist 1981 *19* March, pp. 217–25
A review is made of the RICS report comparing the UK and US construction industries and at the same time a comparison is made of the selling price and achieved times of the Australian industry.

267
H. Schlick
PROFESSIONAL CM: THE ARCHITECT: ENGIN-EER'S VIEWPOINT
ASCE Journal of the Construction Division 1981 *107* March, pp. 158–9 (Discussion).

266
R. Moxley
DESIGN/SUPERVISE/BUILD
Architects Journal 1981 *173* February 25, pp. 359–63

Practical application is demonstrated of the AMM approach to building in which the architect was involved on a day-to-day basis on site, and no middle-man main contractor was employed.

265
T. Frost
UNCONVENTIONAL ALTERNATIVES
Quantity Surveyor 1981 *37* February, pp. 30–1
Some thoughts are expressed on the variety of contractual arrangements available to clients and on the value of the QS in giving appropriate advice.

264
Lam Cheok Weng
TURNKEY CONTRACT PROFESSIONAL VIEWS
Building Technologists 1981–82 *8*, pp. 118–25
The views are expressed of Malaysian personnel.

263
Bovis Construction Ltd.
SELECTION OF A MANAGEMENT CONTRAC-TOR FOR THE PUBLIC SECTOR
1981, 13pp.

262
CIRIA
CLIENT'S GUIDE TO DESIGN BUILD
1981, 12pp.

261
G. Peters
PROJECT MANAGEMENT AND CONSTRUC-TION CONTROL
1981. Construction Press, 131pp.
Concerned primarily with client-orientated project management, chapters are included on contracts, decision making, programme planning, materials procurement, project control and monitoring and project estimating.

1980

260
I. Fraser
AMM CASE STUDY, DESIGNING AND BUILD-ING A PRIMARY SCHOOL
Architects Journal 1980 *172* December 10, pp. 1163–6
AMM (Alternative Methods of Management) has the architect as full-time designer and project controller. With no general contractor the client employs specialist contractors and trades directly through the architect. The aims are speed and quality through rapid communication and close control of work. Aspects of the specific project discussed include the

contractual approach, the role of the job architect, insurances, contracts, valuations, programming, tendering, and site works. Speed and quality were achieved. Areas requiring closer attention on subsequent jobs would include cost control, manpower planning and supervision levels.

259
J. Dressler
CONSTRUCTION MANAGEMENT IN WEST GERMANY
ASCE Journal of the Construction Division 1980 *106* December, pp. 477–87
In Germany, both professional construction management and construction management techniques have been refined during the last two decades. Increasingly, modern management techniques to plan and control time, resources, and costs of construction processes are used by owners and by the construction industry. A brief overview is given on the status of the German construction industry within the German economy. Project management techniques commonly used in the country are reviewed. Emphasis is given to the velocity diagram. Construction management concepts are presented as used on several large construction projects in Germany. Differences with regard to various owners will be illustrated.

258
R.J. Christesen and C.B. Tatum
LABOUR RELATIONS CONSIDERATIONS ON PCM PROJECTS
ASCE Journal of the Construction Division 1980 *106* December, pp. 535–49
Implementation of effective labour relations programmes is essential for successful professional construction management (PCM) projects. This paper identifies elements of such programmes and proposes responsibility assignment. Implementation tasks and actions to integrate the contractor programmes are also examined. To provide a background of relevant construction industry characteristics, an overview of industry scope and organization is presented. Specific objectives are then defined for labour relation programmes on PCM projects. Tasks and method of implementation, including both the initial project programme and those of each specific contractor are examined. Suggestions are also included for avoiding common problem areas by anticipation and early resolution. To further highlight the unique requirements of labour relations programmes on PCM projects, essential differences from other forms of organization are reviewed.

257
H.I. Davis
ADVANTAGES OF DESIGN AND BUILD TO THE PRIVATE EMPLOYER

Paper to Company Communications Centre Seminar, 'Joint Ventures', London, 25–26 September 1980, 15pp. (Summary)
In discussing the advantages of design and build contracts reference is made to risk, conflict of interest and communication and responsibility. Examples are given to illustrate the cost benefits of the approach.

256
D.A. Macniven
MONITORING A MANAGEMENT CONTRACT
Chartered Quantity Surveyor 1980 *3* September, pp. 52–3
Brief details are given of a quantity surveyor's experience of a management contract. Difficulties associated with the number of sub-contractors and associated delays are mentioned. The major benefit resulting from the use of a management contract was that design time available was maximized by the programming of work packages and obtaining competitive tenders for each of the sections of the work.

255
D.S. Barris
GUIDELINES FOR SUCCESSFUL CONSTRUCTION MANAGEMENT
ASCE Journal of the Construction Division 1980 *106* (CO3) September, pp. 237–45
Some of the somewhat controversial and undefined areas of the professional construction management approach are reviewed. The discussion and suggested guidelines include the assignment of liabilities and risk, labour relations considerations, compensation and fee structures, forms of contract, organizational concepts and licensing considerations. A discussion of the responsibilities and qualifications of each of the team members (designer, owner, and construction manager) is included. To be successful, the three-party team must have the proper individual qualifications and each team member must respect and appreciate the skills and professionalism of the other.

254
B.C. Paulson Jr. and A. Tsuneo
CONSTRUCTION MANAGEMENT IN JAPAN
ASCE Journal of the Construction Division 1980 *106* (CO3) September, pp. 281–96
Components of the industry that are described include public works agencies, trade and professional associations, approximately half a million contractors, private owners, banking, and trading groups. Other sections of the paper give more detail on ranking and prequalification of contractors by public and private owners, selection of bidders, factors affecting project design and construction, project management, specialty contractors, and methods and techniques for project control. Although many factors

would ease acceptance of professional construction management approach, three potential obstacles include: (1) close interdependencies between general contractors and their subcontractors; (2) ambiguities in contract administration related to 'Confucian sense of social obligation'; and (3) legal restrictions preventing commencement of projects before all plans and specifications have been completed and approved by building officials. Nevertheless, there is strong interest in adapting this method to Japanese conditions.

253
A. Heaphy
CONTRACTS IN THE USA
Building Technology and Management 1980 *18* July/August, pp. 29–32
Following a short assessment of the development of the US construction industry and current developments, attention is given to contractual arrangements. Reference is made to lump sum, cost plus, guaranteed maximum, design–build, and construction management contracts. Services offered by the contractor under the latter contract are described in some detail.

252
J.L. Lammie and D.P. Shah
PROJECT MANAGEMENT – PULLING IT ALL TOGETHER
ASCE Transportation Engineering Journal 1980 *106* July, pp. 437–51
New innovative managerial techniques employed in a US Rapid Transit Authority allowing control and coordination during the first phase of the project are discussed.

251
S.B. Tietz
WHEN TIME IS OF THE ESSENCE ...
Structural Engineer 1980 *58A* July, pp. 225–8 (Discussion)
The discussion relates to reducing the time to get the design to tender stage, reference being made to package deals and management contracts.

250
F. Perryman
DEFINING THE ROLES OF THE DESIGN ENGINEER AND CONTRACTOR, PART 2
QS Weekly 1980 June 26, pp. 8–9
Methods of tendering are indicated that are particularly applicable to designers and contractors. Responsibilities in relation to coordination are considered before attention is given to pre- and post-tender cost control.

249
N. Heayes
MANAGEMENT CONTRACTING SURGES FORWARD

Contract Journal 1980 *295* June 26, pp. 21–3
An overview is given of the current status of project management, some of its advantages and the scope of its application being discussed by practitioners.

248
C.B. Tatum et al.
PROFESSIONAL CM: THE ARCHITECT/ENGINEER'S VIEWPOINT
ASCE Journal of the Construction Division 1980 *106* June, pp. 141–53
The professional construction management form of organization is gaining increased usage because of distinct advantages offered on certain types of projects. The paper examines the viewpoint of the architect/engineer (A/E) serving as a member of the CM team under this delivery system. The role of the A/E, including differences in A/E performance as contrasted with the traditional form of project organization, is considered in detail Key A/E tasks during each phase of the project are identified. Elements of effective A/E performance, including responsiveness, responsibility, field organization, and design documents are analysed. The writers conclude that the potential benefits of this project delivery system can be best realized by a precise definition of the A/E role. The A/E must be both aware of differences in performance under this system and receptive to construction input from the CM. Practical application of the concepts presented from the A/E viewpoint lies in avoidance of common problems on CM projects and the full support of the PCM team.

247
M. Spring
PACKAGED WITH DESIGN
Building 1980 *238* May 23, pp. 28–30
The factors leading to a medium-sized industrial client choosing a package deal for its new factory are identified. Consultant quantity surveyors were asked to compile a draft building specification and to assist in selecting the contractor. Advantages of the approach as they were found in practice are outlined.

246
F.A. Hammond
CONTRACTUAL SYSTEMS
Paper to CICC Conference, 'Financial policy and control in construction projects' London. 15/16 May 1980, pp. 25–35
Some thoughts are expressed on the role the client should play in determining his requirements and in selecting the contractual arrangement best suited to his purpose. This is followed by a summary of the basic principles of the design-and-build, traditional, management contracting, and project management approaches to letting a contract.

245
M. Snowdon
PROJECT MANAGEMENT
ICE Proc. 1980 *68* Part 1, May, pp. 309–12.

244
J. Wesselman et al.
MANAGING SUPER PROJECTS IN THE PUBLIC SECTOR: THE PUBLIC AGENCY CONSULTANCY
Paper to ASCE Annual Convention. Portland, April 14–18, 1980, 16pp.
Programme management is where the public agency delegates the authority for management and technical services to contractors who then operate under close monitoring by agency personnel. The advantages of this approach are described with reference to client and consultant relations, relations with receiving agencies, relations with the public, and efficiency and cost effectiveness.

243
G.M. Gans
CONSTRUCTION MANAGER AND SAFETY
Paper to ASCE Annual Convention, Portland April 14–18, 1980, 18pp.
A variety of approaches to safety are described for application with the professional construction management system. Some of the current problems in performance, legality and regulatory interpretation which accompany these approaches are discussed.

242
T. Frost
AND NOW FOR SOMETHING COMPLETELY DIFFERENT
Quantity Surveyor 1980 *36* April, pp. 62–4
The experiences reported of a QS acting as project manager for the construction of a Chaplaincy Centre for the campus of Bristol Polytechnic. The role was to organize and coordinate the construction, to liaise with the Manpower Services Commission (grant provider) and other external organizations, and to provide regular cost and progress information to the trustees.

241
R. Winsor
IS GOD A PROJECT MANAGER?
Project Manager 1980 2 April, pp. 16–17
An architect identifies four principles of good project management as being a clear objective, a plan of action, healthy relationships, and effective communication.

240
P. Taylor and P. Cox
GETTING A BUILDING BUILT

Chartered Builder 1980 *29* April, pp. 29–31
Basic procedures for a number of methods of tendering are outlined. These include selective and negotiated tendering, open selected tendering, management contracting, and fixed fee tendering.

239
F. Wai
PROJECT MANAGEMENT IN HONG KONG
Quantity Surveyor 1980 *36* February, pp. 20–2
The role of the project manager is described, and the advantages discussed of employing this approach.

238
M. Snowden
PROJECT MANAGEMENT
Quantity Surveyor 1980 *36* January, pp. 2–4
A background is given to the understanding of project management. It is seen as a series of the following ten steps. Establish the background to the project; define the objectives; determine the criteria for success; draw up an action plan; establish base for control; mobilize resources; set up required organization; monitor progress, control and set to work.

237
Bovis Construction Ltd
BUILDING BUSINESS. THE CLIENT'S GUIDE TO CONSTRUCTION
1980, 14pp.
Details are given of the fee and management type contracts operated by the company, the advantages to the client being identified.

1979

236
C.J. Liddle and A.J. Wallace
PROJECT MANAGEMENT OF CONSTRUCTION WITH RESPECT TO PROCESS INDUSTRIES AT HOME AND ABROAD
Structural Engineer 1979 *57A* December, pp. 401–6
A comparison is made of project management at home and abroad. After describing the growth of consultancy in the process industries, culminating in the multi-discipline management consultant, the point is made that, for major industrial projects, the process engineer fulfils the function that the architect contributes to home-based building projects. The accepted duties of project management are then described.

235
J.W. Rogers
PROJECT MANAGEMENT A MANAGING CON-TRACTOR'S APPROACH
Structural Engineer 1979 *57A* December, pp. 407–9
A managing contractor's (Taylor Woodrow) approach to project management in the UK is described. The importance of the role of the client is emphasized and the general functions and sequence of operations of the project manager are identified. Coordination of design disciplines for multi-discipline projects is stressed, together with the need for an effective system for the control of changes or modifications. It is suggested that the contractor is ideally suited to develop a project management capability. Finally, five factors are listed which are considered essential to a satisfactory outcome to the services provided.

234
D.J. Dickinson
PROJECT MANAGEMENT THE CLIENT'S VIEW
Structural Engineer 1979 *57A* December, pp. 410–14
The role of the client is discussed in the management of his own projects. The terms of engagement of a professional service are considered and some of the ways are discussed by which the written word of the contracts is no longer adequate. An 'in-house' set of conditions of control is referred to which places more responsibility on the client and the contractor than on the team of professionals. The relative success of this approach over 10 years is discussed.

233
D.S. Barrie
TRADE CONTRACTORS' VIEW OF CONSTRUC-TION
ASCE Journal of the Construction Division 1979 *105* (CO4) December, pp. 381–7
Conclusions are reached through the use of questionnaires obtained from contractors who have performed on construction management projects. A tabulation of the results shows the comments about the projects surveyed were favourable from the speciality contractors. Less favourable comments were received about design changes or modifications made after award of the contract. Following a work plan, awarding contracts in an ethical manner and pre-qualifying contractors is necessary for a successful project.

232
K.A. Kettle
PROPOSED CONSTRUCTION MANAGEMENT
ASCE Journal of the Construction Division 1979 *105* (CO4) December, pp. 367–80
A specification is presented for use in Agreements for construction management services. Precise wording is used throughout, and definitions provided for words that might result in variable interpretations. A cover sheet provides a brief review of the use of the specification together with necessary inclusions in the Agreement between the Owner and the Construction Manager.

231
A.C. Paterson
IMPORTANCE OF PROJECT MANAGEMENT
Structural Engineer 1979 *57A* December, pp. 399–400
An overview is given of the role of British consultants acting as project managers overseas.

230
N. Evans
ON-SITE MANAGEMENT TODAY
Paper to Interbuild Seminar, Birmingham, 5 December 1979, 4pp.
Consideration is given to management contracting, i.e. the organization of construction by selected subcontractors, reference being made to the services involved, and the operation of a management contract.

229
PETER TROLLOPE PUTS UP A SOUND CASE FOR PROJECT MANAGEMENT
Construction News 1979 November 1, p. 19
The case for project management is argued and it is maintained that it is in the areas of overall performance – time, budget and quality – that project management will make its biggest contribution. It will provide the overall coordination and control of the project in the pre-contract and construction stages, bringing clarity of thought and discipline to decision making.

228
G. Goulden
BUILDING ON DESIGN
Building 1979 *237* November 16, pp. 36–7
The structure and operation are described of the Shepherd Design Group which offers a comprehensive design-and-build service.

227
A. Walker
APPROACH JTO THE DESIGN OF PROJECT MANAGEMENT STRUCTURES
Quantity Surveyor 1979 *35* October, pp. 537–9
The potential is considered of thinking about construction projects in systems terms and the significance is discussed of the contingency theory in the understanding of project management.

226
H.R. Beaton
PROJECT CONTROLS MANUAL v MACHINE

Paper to ASCE Convention, Atlanta, October 22–6, 1979, 14pp.

Systems available to the project manager to assist in the initiation, management and completion of a project are discussed in relation to the five major phases of the project – project definition; engineering and design; procurement; construction; project management. Two areas are examined where the project manager does not receive significant support from the computer – financial and timing controls.

225

E.B. Smith and M.F. Fishette

CONSTRUCTION MANAGEMENT IN THE MIDDLE EAST

Paper to ASCE Convention, Atlanta, October 23–5, 1979, 22pp.

The basic components of project management and the particular requirements of Saudi Arabia are discussed. Potential problem areas such as logistics, project mobilisation, communications, and local customs, are identified.

224

J. Hinckley

LESSER DESIGN AND BUILD – MORE A WAY OF STRIFE

QS Weekly 1979 October 4, pp. 8–9

An interview is reported with Harvey David, MD of Lesser Design and Build, which considers the advantages of the design-and-build approach and its future prospects.

223

C.B. Tatum

EVALUATING PCM FIRM POTENTIAL AND PERFORMANCE

ASCE Journal of the Construction Division 1979 *105* September, pp. 239–51

A set of criteria for evaluating the potential and performance of professional construction management (PCM) firms is proposed. Based on the work of the ASCE Committee on PCM, these criteria relate to a task list of PCM services. The criteria, both subjective and objective, cover each of the five phases of most construction projects. Following suggestion of criteria, a methodology for PCM evaluation is presented. This methodology includes defining the extent of evaluation required, obtaining the necessary information, and performing the evaluation. Both selection of a PCM firm for a future project and evaluating a PCM on an active project are addressed. Practical application of the criteria defined, in both selection and evaluation, is reviewed.

222

J.D. Madsen

PROFESSIONAL CONSTRUCTION MANAGEMENT SERVICES

ASCE Journal of the Construction Division 1979 *105* June, pp. 139–56

A full range of professional construction management (PCM) tasks are identified that may be utilized on major construction projects. This listing is based on the work of the ASCE committee on PCM. Identification of the essential tasks of a professional construction manager, as a basis for measuring performance, was the primary purpose of this work. Basic attributes of an effective PCM firm are presented. The functional PCM tasks are divided into the five phases of major construction projects; (1) conceptual planning; (2) programme planning; (3) design construction; (4) close-out; and (5) start up. For each of these phases, the primary PCM services and tasks are identified. Examples are included where appropriate. Practical application for selection of a firm, evaluation of a firm on an active project, or self-auditing by a PCM firm, is discussed. The successful PCM firm must be multi-disciplinary, include all control functions, and provide a broad spectrum of management, engineering, construction, systems and legal expertise.

221

C. Reed

CM IN FEDERAL BUILDING CONSTRUCTION

Constructor 1979 *41* June, pp. 33–5

An outline is given of how construction (project) management is used by federal building agencies in the US. Reservations are expressed of the practice where the architect retained to design a project also acts as construction manager.

220

R.P. Maher

COMPLEX PROBLEMS WITH SEPARATE CONTRACTS SYSTEM

ASCE Journal of the Construction Division 1979 *105* June, pp. 129–37

Contracting systems used in the construction industry today are presenting new and complex problems and those engaged in the industry should be aware of them. The construction management concept used to produce construction today has adapted the separate contract system to implement its purpose. The concept, which itself is relatively new, is adapting an old system in different ways without looking to the legal, technical, and management problems involved. It is using these systems in a number and at a rate at which the slower processes of law cannot keep pace. Three major problems are presented here.

They are not solved because the solutions wait on the law. The purpose of this paper is hopefully to serve as a signal or reminder to the industry and to bring to the industry's notice some of these problems in the hope that its members will recognize them and act accordingly.

219
RIGHT FORM OF DESIGN AND CONSTRUCT?
Contract Journal 1979 239 June 21, pp. 25–7
A discussion with the deputy executive of the IDC Group is reported which covers the need for a contract for package deal contracts, particularly for industrial buildings.

218
M. Barnes
GROWTH OF INDEPENDENT PROJECT MANAGEMENT
Proc. Company Communications Centre Seminar. 'Tendering and Contracting in the UK', London, April 1979, pp. 25–9
Brief consideration is given to the skills and attitude of the project manager and the project manager's contract.

217
G.C. Trickey
PROCEDURES FOR TENDERING AND CONTRACTING
Proc. Company Communications Centre Seminar. 'Tendering and Contracting in the UK', London, April 1979, pp. 14–24
The development of the design and build method of contracting is discussed and compared with the traditional approach. Minimum ingredients to be contained within a design-and-build contract are identified and some guidelines are presented on tenders and tender evaluation. Finally, consideration is given to contractual responsibilities.

216
G.H. Brown
CASE STUDIES OF INTERNATIONAL TENDERING METHODS AND FORM OF CONSTRUCTION CONTRACTS
Paper to CICC Easter Conference 1979 'International Construction', University of Nottingham, April 5 and 6, pp. 53–7
A form of contract is described for a design-and-build project in Saudi Arabia involving the construction of 1664 flats in 32 high rise towers. A comparison is made with the FIDIC form of contract.

215
R. Penwarden
OVERSEAS PROJECT MANAGEMENT
Paper to CICC Easter Conference 1979 'International Construction', University of Nottingham, April 5 and 6, pp. 111–23
The organization necessary to execute the works following the award of an overseas design-and-construct contract is described. The various head office organizational functions and controls are set out which are employed in coordinating the design, materials procurement, sub-contractors work, and the roles and functions of the construction organization carrying out the works.

214
D.S. Barrie
TRADE CONTRACTOR'S VIEW OF CONSTRUCTION MANAGEMENT
Paper to ASCE Convention and Exposition, Boston, USA, April 2–6 1979, 11pp.
An assessment is made, from the specialist subcontractor's viewpoint, of project management. It is concluded that design changes after award cause most of the major problems in construction; responsibilities should be closely defined; contracts coordinated by the owner directly must be fully integrated into the programme so that interfaces can be both described in tender documents and coordinated during construction; information must pass through the project manager.

213
D.B. Neff
OWNER'S VIEW OF OVERCOMING PROJECT PROBLEMS
Paper to ASCE Convention and Exposition, Boston, USA, April 2–6 1979, 18pp.
Following an outline of the difficulties faced by an owner in getting a building built, consideration is given to types of client, the six main phases of a project, and the various contractual arrangements available, the advantages and disadvantages of each being indicated. The value of project management is discussed and the role and functions of a project manager are described.

212
C. Popescu
PITFALLS OF GSA-CMCS SOFTWARE
ASCE Journal of the Construction Division 1979 105 (CO1) March, pp. 95–106
General Service Administration has implemented a phase construction management approach for new Federal construction. Phase construction involves the overlapping of design and construction activities in a carefully planned, executed, and controlled order. In response to the above change, GSA adopted a modified IBM-CPM package. The system itself is

made up of modules or groups of reports that are structured by type of information and by management level. As a result of information at two universities, pitfalls of this GSA-CMCS are presented. At the present time, the construction industry is in need of a good CPM project management and control system accessible to all contractors and educators at a low cost – GSA-CMCS does not fulfil this general requirement at the present stage.

211
P.E. Emmett
ALTERNATIVE METHODS OF MANAGEMENT. PROGRAMMING: RESPONSIBILITIES AND TECHNIQUE
Chartered Quantity Surveyor 1979 *1* February, pp. 52–3
AMM is a form of project management in which the architect and QS retain their traditional relationships with the client and work through a main contractor, or preferably with a number of specialist contractors. It facilitates communication and gives better control of quality, cost and time. The system of estimating and programming adopted by AMM – based on statistical information and the cost/time method of estimating – is described.

210
MANAGEMENT CONTRACTING: HENRY BOOT'S NEW APPROACH
Construction News 1979 January 18, pp. 14–15
An interview with David Woolf, managing director of Henry Boot Construction discusses the company's approach to management contracting with particular attention to client satisfaction, time, types of suitable job, cost savings, sub-contractors and possible developments.

209
Associated General Contractors of America
OWNER'S GUIDE: BUILDING CONSTRUCTION CONTRACTING METHODS
11pp.
An outline is given of contractual arrangements, including lump-sum contracts, cost-plus contracts, guaranteed maximum or upset price contracts, construction management contracts, design–build contracts and turnkey contracts.

208
PROJECT MANAGEMENT IN ACTION
Chartered Builder 1979 *26*, pp. 65–8
An outline is given of the construction of a hospital in Queensland. The project management system employed allowed the design to be developed to a stage where detail adequate for competitive tendering was attained. At this point design was frozen.

In this way design and construction develop progressively so that the basic building components are constructed parallel to design and development of later components.

207
M. Snowdon
PROJECT MANAGEMENT
ICE Proc 1979 *66* (Part 1), pp. 625–33
Based on the concept of a capital project being an instrument of change, the management steps of a project are analysed and shown to be wider than is commonly supposed. Because of this perspective it is possible to emphasize the early stages of activity and the sponsor's role throughout. As well as retaining normally available design and construction resources, the sponsor has to ensure that management resources are adequate; project manager selection and training are touched upon.

1978

206
P.F. Rad and M.C. Miller
TRENDS IN USE OF CONSTRUCTION MANAGEMENT
ASCE Journal of the Construction Division 1978 *104* (CO4) December, pp. 515–23
Construction management generally refers to a contractual relationship whereby an owner secures professional management services of a large multi-discipline firm for a specific construction project. This newly found market for construction management services has created a proliferation of designer, constructor, and management firms competing for construction-management contracts, each offering their own version of construction-management services. An analysis of the data provided in the top contractor and designer firm listings for the past six years showed that the use of construction management grew throughout the design-construct industry by 9 per cent between 1971 and 1976. Currently, 50 per cent of the design firms are more likely to offer construction-management services as well. Larger firms are more likely to offer construction-management services although this service is more common to the engineer–architect design firms.

205
L. Clements
KESSOCK BRIDGE DESIGN AND BUILD CONTRACT PROCEDURES
Structural Engineer 1978 *56A* December, pp. 345–6; Discussion 1980 *58* February, pp. 52–8

The requirements are determined for design-and-build tendering and the procedures associated with them are identified; the discussion includes contributions from unsuccessful tenderers.

204

G. Suhanic

PROJECT MANAGER CAN DELIVER HIS CAPITAL COST PROJECT IN 16 WAYS

Trans. 5th Int. Cost Engineering Congress, Utrecht, October/November 1978, pp. 158–63

Sixteen different ways by which a client may procure a building from lump sum, design/build to lease/purchase – are delineated and defined in relation to each other and the client. An indication is given of the role of the cost engineer.

203

C.O. Bonar

EFFECTIVE TOOLS FOR PROJECT MANAGERS

Trans. 5th Int. Cost Engineering Congress, Utrecht, October/November 1978, pp. 199–206

The increasing relevance of project management is discussed before consideration is given to the essential activities in the areas of risk assessment; organization structuring and project responsibility definition; application of selective controls based on risk assessment; control of changes to scope, contracts and responsibilities; and the control and use of management reserves.

202

D.N. Mitten

CONSTRUCTION MANAGEMENT ON COMPLETED PROJECTS OF THE GSA IN CONTRAST WITH TRADITIONAL CONTRACTING

Trans. 5th Int. Cost Engineering Congress, Utrecht, October/November 1978, pp. 85–93

A comparison made on five specific projects of the actual design and construction time using construction management (CM) and similar projects using traditional methods. It was found that CM was a superior organizing and controlling technique and that GSA realized savings of 23.1 per cent of construction cost when using CM combined with phased construction.

201

K. Brown

HALF-CENTURY OF BOVIS FEE

Construction News Magazine 1978 4 October, pp. 38–9, 41–3, 53–5

The development is traced of Bovis Construction with particular reference to its fee system. Mention is made of the close association with Marks and Spencer and details are given of some other contracts let under this system.

200

K.A. Godfrey Jnr

PROFILE OF THE DESIGN/CONSTRUCTION COMPANIES

Civil Engineering 1978 47 October, pp. 131–6

An outline is given of the development of design/construct, particular reference being given to the approach by such as Koppers Co., Fluor and Ebasco Services.

199

B.J. Peachey

CONSTRUCTION PROJECT CONTROL

Paper to RICS Annual Conference, Harrogate, 26–9 September 1978, 18pp.

The functions are described of the project manager (controller) reference being made to agreeing objectives, selection of the professional team, briefing, programme compilation, and the design solution. Contractual management is then considered, with due regard being paid to contractor selection, communication and programming. A project management organization diagram is presented as an appendix.

198

R. Porter

DESIGN/BUILD NEEDS CAREFUL THOUGHT AND PREPARATION

National Builder 1978 59 September, p. 322

The design/build concept is considered in relation to the requirements of the contractor, legal requirements and the developing market.

197

H.I. Davis

BOVIS METHODS OF CONTRACTING

Paper to DHSS Regional Quantity Surveyors Association Conference 'Alternative contractual methods', Newcastle-upon-Tyne, 22 June 1978, 14pp.

An outline is given of the Bovis fee system, its advantages being highlighted and some examples of its use indicated.

196

S.J. Jenkins

DEVELOP AND CONSTRUCT CONTRACTING

Paper to DHSS Regional Quantity Surveyors Association Conference 'Alternative contractual methods', Newcastle-upon-Tyne, 22 June 1978, 7pp.

Following an outline of the background to develop-and-construct, the technique as currently applied is described. The design team take all decisions regarding site layout and development and produce the specification based mainly on performance requirements. The contractor is selected on single-stage tendering with BOQ for site development and externals the contractor's firm price for each type of dwelling for super-structures, and the price per block for substructures. The successful tenderer develops his design in collaboration with the design team.

195
K. Thain
CONSTRUCTION PROGRAMME MANAGE-MENT
Paper to DHSS Regional Quantity Surveyors Association Conference 'Alternative contractual methods', Newcastle-upon-Tyne, 22 June 1978, 20pp.
The project management service offered by Heery-Farrow is described, its advantages and limitations to the client being identified. Particular attention is given to the development of a compatible brief, contracting for design services, time/cost control, reporting and the on-site management team.

194
J. Christopher
ARCHITECTURE OR BUSINESS
Building Design 1978 May 12, p. 2
The advantages of the 'design-and-build' approach to contracting are assessed from which it is concluded that it has its place but not at the expense of the practice committed primarily to architecture.

193
P. Lord-Smith
PACKAGE DEAL CONTRACTS
Architects Journal 1978 *167* May 3, pp. 388–9 (Correspondence)
Reference is made to two new RIBA (JCT) 'package deal' contracts and to the accompanying Practice Notes. The implications of the RIBA giving its approval to this form of contract are discussed.

192
I. Peters
PROJECTING THE QS AS MANAGER
Building 1978 *234* April 14, pp. 73–4
The functions of the project manager are described, the qualities and training of the QS which suit this role being identified.

191
D. Stephenson
MANAGEMENT CONTRACTING OVERSEAS THE PROBLEMS TO BE FACED
Construction News 1978 April 27, p. 22
A report of a conference organized by the Export Group for the Constructional Industries covers the concept of project management, responsibilities, fee arrangements and selection.

190
R. Saville
SURVEYING THE FUTURE

Building 1978 *235* April 14, pp. 67–8
An interview with the President of the RICS QS Division, David Male, is reported. It covers such topics as advertising, merger with the IQS, education and project management.

189
J.B.G. Carpenter
CLIENT'S VIEW OF THE CONSTRUCTION PROJECT MANAGER
Paper to RICS, Chartered Quantity Surveyor 11th Triennial Conference, London April 1978, 5pp.
Consideration is given to the scale or type of project where a project manager is needed, the client's requirements, the responsibilities of the project manager, and the suitability of quantity surveyors for this role.

188
D. Johnston
IMPROVE YOUR RISK MANAGEMENT AVOID DESIGN LIABILITY
Constructor 1978 *60* April, pp. 24–6
Some means are discussed by which US develop-and-construct or construction management contractors are attempting to reduce excessive liability for design faults.

187
B.J. Hill
DESIGN AND CONSTRUCT: A CASE STUDY
Paper to RICS, Chartered Quantity Surveyors 11th Triennial Conference, London, April 1978, 15pp.
A commentary is given on a major government contract for services accommodation where the builder was responsible for the provision of all working drawings from the client's original design drawings and specification. The contractor then had to build the project to a predetermined budget to which he was already committed. The apparent advantages gained by the client, builder, consultants and specialist sub-contractors are discussed in full before consideration is given to ongoing management and financial controls.

186
C. Davies
PACKAGE DEAL: POST OFFICE
Architect 1978 *124* March, pp. 37–40
An architectural appraisal is made of the Liverpool central Post Office constructed by a package dealer. The involvement of design consultants is indicated.

185
W. Turner
DESIGN AND TENDER PROJECTS
Heating and Ventilating Engineer 1978 *52* March, pp. 12–13

The implications of a contractor being invited to design and tender for the services of a building are considered from the contractor's and client's viewpoint. Limitations to the procedure are identified and some suggestions made whereby they can be avoided.

184
H. Dawson
MANAGEMENT CONTRACTING: PRINCIPLES OF OPERATION IN SAUDI ARABIA
Middle East Construction 1978 3 March, pp. 78–9.

183
FUTURE DEVELOPMENT: THE CLIENT'S DILEMMA. PART 2
Quantity Surveyor 1978 34 March, pp. 112–21
A report is given of a conference, detailed summaries being provided of the following papers:
Commercial client's aims and experience, by W.J. Mackenzie, which discusses the client's philosophy in relation to his projected building, the client's role, and improvements required in regard to administration, time and workmanship. Public sector client's aims and experience, by J. Boyce, which considers procurement – serial tendering and design–build, consortia, efficiency of the industry, and professional services.
Part performance of the industry and the need for change, by R. Warren-Evans, which deals with the standard form of contract in relation to defects, professional fees and integrated design and payment systems.

182
E. Reid
JOB MANAGEMENT: AN ALTERNATIVE METHOD
Architects Journal 1978 167 February 22, pp. 355–7
The alternative method of management (AMM) evaluated has two fundamentals; it gets the architect back full time on site as the designer and project controller and it allows the various specialist contractors and trades to be employed by the client directly through the architect. It is concluded that AMM is suited mainly to projects over £350,000 and to rehab projects. It does enable projects to be completed faster than average and gives a close control on cost.

181
FUTURE DEVELOPMENT: THE CLIENT'S DILEMMA. PART 1
Quantity Surveyor 1978 34 February, pp. 87–96
The aim of the conference reported was to examine the construction market from the viewpoint of both client and industry; to investigate the different forms of contract procurement, assess their performance, and provide a basis for discussion whilst at the same time clarifying the client's criteria and constraints. Individual contributions are given by R. Warren-Evans on the client's needs, by O. Luder on the architects' role, by F. Smith on the QS's role and by L.P. Whiting on the package deal.

180
J. Franks
PROJECT MANAGEMENT 10 ORGANIZATIONS, PROFESSIONAL BACKGROUND AND TRAINING
Building Trades Journal 1978 175 February 3, pp. 12, 14–16, 18, 23
An outline is given of non-conventional methods of tendering including the package deal, a turnkey contracts, management contracting, design-and-construct, and of the functions and responsibilities expected of the project manager – including contributions taken from the literature. Finally, consideration is given to existing facilities for the training of project management.

179
ALTERNATIVE METHOD OF MANAGEMENT
Building 1978 234 January 27, pp. 67, 69–70
A live case history of the use of the Alternative Method of Management (AMM) has been carried out by BRE. Applied to a rehabilitation job, it was chosen primarily because of the need to meet a tight time schedule. AMM involves the setting up of an office on site where the architect/manager who is to run the project resides full time, and the overlapping of the many activities as possible. The performance of AMM is evaluated, from which it is concluded that speed and quality control are achieved without reduction in standards.

178
ARCHITECT AND PROJECT MANAGEMENT
Building 1978 234 January 27, pp. 72–4
A discussion is presented on the AMM approach to project management. Educationalists regarded it as one of a number of possible alternative approaches which must be reflected in any educational approach. Nevertheless, there was research backing for the effectiveness of this system of project management by architects.

177
DESIGN/BUILD. A DIFFERENT SOLUTION?
Building 1978 234 January 20, pp. 68–9, 71, 73–81, 83, 85–90
A series of articles is presented to provide a rounded picture of the package deal approach to construction.

'Hallmark of real change' by R. Warren Evans argues that the system offers a hope for improved performances and indicates the limitations of conventional methods.

'Form of contract' by M. Barnes looks at those significant points for consideration in the development of a standard form of contract, particularly in relation to design responsibility.

A 'Growth Pointers' analyses the extent of the package deal and its potential.

'Company profile' by S. Ashley examines the experiences and attitudes of IDC Ltd.

'Customer appeal' by D. Pearce discusses the advantage and limitations of the client.

'Value for money' by R. Budd illustrates the economic advantages of the package deal and demonstrates the uninspired and mundane design that often results.

'Quality of design' by R. Moxley considers that the design suffers for the sake of economy and that architect-directed design/build is often the best solution. 'Pitched just right' by M. Spring suggests that it is possible to introduce innovative design.

176
W.J. Ryder and J.H. Mercer
PROJECT MANAGEMENT
Proc. of ICE Conference 'Management of large capital projects' London 1978, pp. 69–82; Discussion, pp. 83–95
Aspects of project management discussed include contractor selection, contractual conditions, running the job, controlling the design phase, controlling expenditure, the role of the project manager in cost control, controlling the programme and variations.

175
D.S. Barrie and B.C. Paulson, Jr
PROFESSIONAL CONSTRUCTION MANAGEMENT
1978, McGraw-Hill, 453pp.
The book is based on US practice and is in three main parts – construction industry and practice; professional construction management in practice; and methods of professional construction management. Within these sections there are chapters dealing with the nature of the industry; development and organization of a project; preconstruction site investigation, planning scheduling, estimating and design; bidding and aware; selecting a construction manager; project planning and control estimating; cost engineering; procurement; value engineering; quality assurance; and safety and welfare.

174
RICS
PLACING ORDERS FOR MAJOR CONSTRUCTION WORKS

1978, 6pp.
Methods available to clients for contracting building works are outlined. Reference is made to contractor selection, tendering procedures, types of contract and conditions of contract.

173
RICS
DESIGN AND BUILD. PACKAGE CONTRACTS: WHO REPRESENTS THE CLIENT?
1978, 4pp.
A guidance leaflet giving information on the operation of a package deal and what role the QS may serve.

172
Higgs and Hill
INTRODUCING THE HIGGS AND HILL MANAGEMENT FEE SERVICE
1978, 12pp.
The project management approach adopted by the company is outlined and examples given of building work carried out under the service.

1977

171
DESIGN/CONSTRUCT. TECHNICAL PIONEERING BY DESIGN/CONSTRUCT FIRMS
Civil Engineering 1977 47 December, pp. 76–9
Brief details are given of the projects, particularly in the industrial field, carried out by design/construct firms. Advantages claimed for the technique are summarized.

170
G. Brooke
PROJECT MANAGEMENT IN THE HEALTH SERVICE – THE PROBLEMS AND POSSIBLE SOLUTIONS
Hospital Engineering 1977 31 December, pp. 16–20
Having established a definition of project management and the level at which it is practised in the health service a number of problem interfaces are examined. These include those existing between departments and that between the project team and outside consultants and contractors. Finally some suggestions are made in relation to developing the concept of project management.

169
PROJECT MANAGEMENT IN THE HEALTH SERVICE – INVITED CONTRIBUTIONS

Hospital Engineering 1977 *31* December, pp. 21–5
Personal views by five individuals are presented on the concept of project management.

168
PROJECT MANAGEMENT IN THE HEALTH SERVICE – OPEN FORUM
Hospital Engineering 1977 *31* December, pp. 225–6
A summary is presented of the main points raised during discussion.

167
J. Rawlinson and M. Hodgetts
PROJECT MANAGEMENT
Building Economist 1977 *16* December, pp. 131–5
The concept and operation of project management are discussed in relation to selection of objectives, establishment of systems, appointment of personnel and organizations, development of work functions and targets and implementation, monitoring and control.

166
P. Knowland
ROLE OF THE PROJECT MANAGER
Hospital Development 1977 *5* November/December, pp. 16–17
The case for the appointment of a project manager to exercise direct control on behalf of the client on project costs and economy. An outline is given of the project managers tasks and duties.

165
D.C. Fulcher
PROJECT MANAGEMENT AND THE QUANTITY SURVEYOR IN AUSTRALIA
Quantity Surveyor 1977 *34* November/December, pp. 56–8
Following definitions of the terms 'project manager' and 'construction manager' the recent development of project management is outlined. The role of the quantity surveyor is then discussed in relation to the cost management and budgeting control services he can provide to project management.

164
W.D. Padget
WHY CONSIDER THE NEED FOR BETTER MANAGEMENT OF HEALTH BUILDING PROJECTS?
Hospital Engineering 1977 *31* November, pp. 4–6
It is assumed that the NHS has to ensure that there is no waste of its limited resources and that there is evidence that this has not been achieved in a number of large projects. The concept of project management should be examined further to establish whether it will improve the management of such projects in the future.

163
F.C. Graves
MANAGEMENT. THE NATIONAL EXHIBITION CENTRE COMPARED WITH THE HEALTH BUILDING PROJECTS
Hospital Engineering 1977 *31* November, pp. 6–8, 11–12
The work of the author as project manager for the NEC is described, the terms of reference for the job and pre- and post-contract activities being highlighted. Some comparisons are made between how it is considered project management should work and how it is not working in the health service.

162
J. Franks
PROJECT MANAGEMENT 9. WORK INVOLVED FROM THE TENDER TO COMPLETION
Building Trades Journal 1977 *174* November 18, pp. 30, 32, 34, 36
The tasks of the project manager are discussed in relation to obtaining tenders, managing the works in progress, controlling costs, handing over and analysing the project.

161
F.C. Graves
CLIENT'S CONTRIBUTION TO A SUCCESSFUL PROJECT MANAGEMENT OPERATION
Proc. Conference Associates Seminar 'Helping the client to build' South Africa, November 1977, pp. 55, 57.

160
E.C. Wundram
AMERICAN APPROACH TO CONTRACTING
Paper to CICC Conference 'Management in the Construction Industry' London, November 1977, pp. 81–92
A review is made of the common methods of contracting in the USA each method being analysed in terms of definition, selection method, advantages and cautions. The trend to project management is discussed and explained in some detail. Finally, the major differences between British and US contracting are summarized.

159
M.P. Nicholson
CAN A SMALL FIRM INNOVATE?
House Builder 1977 *36* November, pp. 451–3
It is suggested that with the development of contracts of the package deal type the builder has a greater interest in innovation since he is intimately associated with the design. The advantage of architects being allowed to become directors of building firms in this respect are indicated. The concept of innovation is discussed further in relation to prefabricated components, the basis for delays on site,

consumer reaction, regulations compliance and time and financial limitations.

158

E.W. McCanlis

CONTRACTUAL OPTIONS IN THE UK

Paper to CICC Conference 'Management in the Construction Industry' London, November 1977, pp. 99–111

The financial responsibilities of a contractual situation and the characteristics of contracts are seen to be reflections of project circumstances. The process of arranging a contract is shown to be compounded of separate processes of defining contractual responsibilities, obtaining an offer and selecting a contractor. Each of them are examined in turn. Contracts are classified into types but seen to be composite. The nature of an offer is explored and different types noted and the selection of a contractor is analysed from four viewpoints. Finally, the importance of choosing contractual options, as a function of project management, is related to other aspects of management.

157

S. Kaplan

PROJECT MANAGEMENT: THEORY VERSUS MANAGEMENT

Proc. Conference Associates Seminar 'Helping the client to build' South Africa, November 1977, pp. 29, 31, 33, 35, 37–45

The philosophy of project management is expressed before consideration is given to a number of models illustrating number of concepts relative to project management.

156

E. Finsen

ARCHITECT AND PROJECT MANAGEMENT

Proc. Conference Associates Seminar 'Helping the client to build' South Africa, November 1977, pp. 21, 23, 25, 27

The relationship between architect and project manager is discussed, the point being made that project management can benefit projects of relatively moderate size. However, this may not be warranted, particularly if the architect is management oriented.

155

F.C. Graves

NATIONAL EXHIBITION CENTRE, BIRMINGHAM, AS AN EXAMPLE OF PROJECT MANAGEMENT

Proc. Conference Associates Seminar 'Helping the client to build' South Africa, November 1977, pp. 12–15, 17, 19, 21

An outline is given of the project, reference being made to the terms of reference and pre- and post-contract activities.

154

F.C. Graves

SCOPE AND POTENTIAL OF PROJECT MANAGEMENT IN THE BUILDING INDUSTRY

Proc. Conference Associates Seminar 'Helping the client to build' South Africa, November 1977, pp. 3, 5, 7, 9

Consideration is given to defining project management, sources of project managers, functions of project managers, relationships with client and professional team, service agreements; fees and professional indemnity; and recruitment, training and education.

153

J. Franks

PROJECT MANAGEMENT 8. ESTABLISHING GUIDELINES AND PRINCIPLES FOR PROJECTS

Building Trades Journal 1977 *174* October 28, pp. 42–4

The tasks of the project manager are enumerated and described in check list form.

152

J. Franks

PROJECT MANAGEMENT 7. DESIGNING, CONSTRUCTING AND DELIVERY TO THE CLIENT

Building Trades Journal 1977 *174* September 30, pp. 10, 12

The approach to designing the project is considered and the tasks of the contract manager specified in broad terms. The organization is outlined of a typical management contracting organization and consideration is given to the problems associated with the closing down of a project.

151

K. Szöke

BUILDING ECONOMICS

Proc. 7th Triennial Congress 'Construction Research International', Edinburgh, September 1977, pp. 167–77

In the introduction the position is reviewed of the construction industry in the national economy with special regard to the close interdependence between the general economic situation and the functioning of the construction sector. The impact of recent changes in the economic conditions and policies on the development of the construction industry is discussed briefly regarding both market and planned economies. The conclusion is drawn that while in advanced market economies – due to the recession on the construction market – the process of industrialization in the construction field has been slowing down, planned economies are invariably heading towards increasing the share of industrialized construction in the total output of the industry. In the second part a few examples are given to illustrate the influence of national/local conditions on the economics of the construction industry. Some general problems affecting the economics of construction are discussed and it is stated that the 'conflicting interests' of the client, the contractor and the designer should be harmonized and, as a reasonable way of facilitating the harmonization, the application of value analysis methods is recommended. A brief review is given on value analysis/engineering (VA) and on the pre-requisites of its application in the construction process. The feasibility of implementing VA is discussed in relation to the traditional and rationalized contracting systems. It is stated that package deal and negotiated contracts provide more favourable conditions for the implementation of VA. Attention is called to certain methodological and information communicational problems concerning the implementation of VA in the construction field.

150

D.S. Barrie and G.L. Muler

PROFESSIONAL CM TEAM DISCOVERS VALUE ENGINEERING

ASCE Journal of the Construction Division 1977 *103* (CO3) September, pp. 423–35

The state of the art of traditional value analysis and value engineering methods are reviewed and summarized as developed and utilized by a number of practitioners and agencies on public works. While significant savings have been achieved in the public sector, the value engineering concept has achieved less widespread acceptance in the private domain. The three-party professional construction management concept has facilitated the development of a simplified programme based upon the elimination of adversary relationships often present in the private sector along with the utilization of the original designer to analyse the technical acceptability of proposed value engineering savings. The simplified approach has produced significant savings on a number of projects and offers promise for increased utilization on design–construct and turnkey projects as well.

149

J. Franks

PROJECT MANAGEMENT 6. APPLYING THE PRINCIPLES ON CONSTRUCTION PROJECTS

Building Trades Journal 1977 *174* August 12, pp. 38–42

Referring to practical examples that tasks of the project manager are seen as mainly being directed towards coordinating, directing, organizing and controlling-planning the project, recruiting the team, estimating the project cost, designing the project, construction, handing over, and dissolving the team. The first three of these functions are discussed.

148

PROJECT MANAGEMENT: THE CASE FOR A CODE OF PRACTICE

ICE Proceedings 1977 *62* (Part 1) August, pp. 489–502 (Discussion)

A number of individual views are expressed on the concept of project management and on the proposal for a code of practice.

147

H. Wattin

METAMORPHOSIS OF A PROJECT MANAGER

Project Manager 1977 *1* July, pp. 14–15

The project manager is discussed in the terms of evolution, reference being made to the type of project managed; staff responsibilities; functions; acquiring skills and personal qualities.

146

J. Franks

PROJECT MANAGEMENT 5. HOW THE SYSTEM WORKS WITH THE PROJECT MANAGER

Building Trades Journal 1977 *174* July 8, pp. 20, 22, 24, 26, 28

The role and functions of the project manager for the NEC is described to illustrate the principles of the system in practice. This is followed by an analysis of the organization of a building design partnership, and finally the role of project management in the organization of turnkey nuclear power projects is discussed.

145

S.H. Wearne

TEACHING PROJECT MANAGEMENT

Project Manager 1977 *1* July, pp. 16–17

Brief comments are offered on educational needs, scope of courses, courses offered and the future.

144

A. Bond

SUGGESTED COMPUTER SYSTEM FOR PACKAGE DEAL BUILDING CONTRACTS

Quantity Surveyor 1977 *33* June, pp. 199–203

It is argued that the full potential of the computer cannot be realized with the present system of contracting but that it can be achieved where the greater part of the design-and-construction work is carried out by one organization. The applications of a computer within the package deal concept are then described.

143

A.C. Maevis

PROS AND CONS OF CONSTRUCTION MAN-AGEMENT

ASCE Journal of the Construction Division 1977 *103* (CO1) June, pp. 169–77

With an increase in the size and complexity of construction projects a need has arisen for a more professional approach to the overall management of these projects. Construction management has grown out of this need. A series of case histories is presented, both successful and unsuccessful. In the analysis and conclusion a series of ground rules are presented describing the owner's and the construction manager's responsibility in the process.

142

J. Franks

PROJECT MANAGEMENT 4. USA CONSTRUCTS BUILDINGS QUICKER THAN BRITAIN

Building Trades Journal 1977 *173* May 27, pp. 16, 18, 20, 22

The concept of project management as practised in the US is described. This is followed by a brief comparison between the contracting organization in the UK and US and an analysis of the reason for failure. Finally, the organization of contracting as effected by the Public Building Service is discussed. In this system the client is played by the project manager and the architect is occupied with the design and with the packaging of working drawings and specifications to fit the most advantageous grouping of separate construction contracts selected.

141

J. Sims

WHERE OUR SYSTEM GOES WRONG

Building 1977 *232* May 6, p. 73

It is argued that the present system of contracting mitigates against efficiency. Although the system is better, more flexible and sophisticated than that used in the USA therein lies its disadvantages since this removes the essential element of discipline. One of the main factors limiting efficiency is regarded as the letting of contracts on incomplete design information.

140

J. Franks

PROJECT MANAGEMENT 3. GREATER INVOLVEMENT IN EUROPEAN CONSTRUCTION WORK

Building Trades Journal 1977 *173* April 22, pp. 22, 24, 26, 28

A survey is made of the construction processes in France, Germany and Sweden to illustrate the principal differences between the organization structures used. This survey is made with particular reference to design, construction organization and control; cost control; and construction and contract procedures. Finally the situation in these countries is compared with the European countries to ascertain the state of the art of project management in Europe generally.

139

PROJECT MANAGEMENT

Chartered Surveyor 1977 *109* April, pp. 290–2

General principles are set out that are likely to apply in project management, particular attention being given to the definition of project management, sources of the project manager, project management services, relationships, service agreements, fees and professional indemnity, and recruitment and training. Finally, a check list is presented which represents the main points which a project manager should ensure are dealt with either personally or by other members of the professional team.

138

CHANGING BUILDING INDUSTRY

Construction 1977 *49* April, pp. 21, 40–1

This overview of the trends in the US building industry considers the impact of insurance – liability and completed operations cover in particular – the building systems approach adopted by the General Services Administration for public buildings, and management contracting.

137

R.W. Evans

PROPERTY AND PROPER ECONOMY. CAN THEY BE RECONCILED IN LOCAL AUTHORITY HOUSE PRODUCTION?

Chartered Surveyor Building and Quantity Surveyor Quarterly 1977 *4* Spring, pp. 38–9

The argument is advanced that conventional tendering procedures on the basis of full drawings, bills of quantities and competitive selection have three major defects. These are that 20 per cent of the expenditure is outside control; they are weak in controlling actual expenditure; and they contain no management check on contract extensions and variations. Non-conventional methods, it is argued, should not be ignored since they can be controlled by use of the generic performance specification.

136

J. Franks

PROJECT MANAGEMENT 2. THE REVIVAL OF THE PROJECT MANAGER IN CONSTRUCTION

Building Trades Journal 1977 *173* March 25, pp. 20, 22, 24

The development of management contracting and of the project manager in particular in the 1960s is discussed with reference to the appropriate literature.

135

F. Hotson

HOUSING. DESIGN AND BUILD. A MONEY SAVER FOR LOCAL AUTHORITIES

Building Trades Journal 1977 *173* March 25, pp. 10–12, 14

The design-and-build approach adopted by Shanley Contracting is described and its application to local authority contracts is discussed. It is claimed that the tendering system allows rapid start and completion of a project within the housing cost yardstick and yet to Parker Morris Standards.

134

J. Franks

PROJECT MANAGEMENT 1. NEW ROLE OF CO-ORDINATOR IS STILL EVOLVING

Building Trades Journal 1977 *173* February 25, pp. 11–12, 14, 16

Views from a number of sources are gathered to explore what is meant by project management, and these are considered in relation to the conventional relationships between the members of the building team.

133

P. Makepeace

PLATFORM: PACKAGE DEALS

Building Design 1977 February 18, p. 18

The cost and time effectiveness of package deals is challenged, arguments being presented in favour of the architect-controlled project.

132

A.C. Sidwell

PROJECT MANAGEMENT AND MEASURE-MENT IN SWEDEN

Building Technology and Mangement 1977 *15* February, pp. 14–15, 25

Following a short outline of the Swedish building industry, consideration is given to the responsibility for building failure and the provision of quantity surveying services. The management contracting system (byggledare) is described, its main advantages being highlighted.

131

M. Snowdon

PROJECT MANAGEMENT: THE CASE FOR A CODE OF PRACTICE

ICE Proc. 1977 *62* (Part 1) February, pp. 43–50

The wide issues embraced by the term 'project management' are acknowledged but limits are suggested for the purpose of discussion. It is suggested that formalization of some of the activity within the concept could improve the professionalism of the work, strengthen the links between the academic and the practical, provide a firmer base for training and experience and improve the understanding which is necessary to establish optimum organizations. A preliminary scope for a code of practice is suggested as a basis for presenting the case.

130

D.O. Pedersen

DESIGN CONSTRUCTION PROJECTS: GETTING VALUE FOR MONEY

Build International 1977 *5* January/February, pp. 24–33 (in English and French)

The application of value analysis techniques are described in relation to project management contracts. Value analysis can be employed to choose from several proposals on the basis of a comprehensive assessment of quality and cost (and time); to guide the design toward defined goals; and to improve communicating between client and designer.

129

D.O. Pedersen

DESIGN CONTRACT PROJECTS: GETTING VALUE FOR MONEY

Building Research and Practice 1977 *5* January/February, pp. 24–33 (in English and French)

Value analysis techniques are described as they are applied in Scandinavia to promote new building methods, improve design and contracting procedures and provide better value for money to the client.

128

G. Trickey

DEVELOP AND CONSTRUCT

Architects Journal 1977 *165* January 26, pp. 177–8

Develop-and-construct contracts are those in which the architect prepares sketch designs from the brief, determines site layout, disposition of building on site and the individual plan forms. The contractor develops this proposal, making final choices of materials and details, before submitting his tender. Advantages of the system are evaluated and some reservations expressed. It is concluded that efficiency can be best improved by builders concentrating on site management and by architects becoming more sensitive to the requirements of efficient construction when developing their designs.

127

M. Snowdon

MANAGEMENT OF ENGINEERING PROJECTS

1977, Newnes-Butterworth, 134pp.

Attention is given to project management, regarded as 'the achievement of an objective by the creation of a new or the modification of an existing capital asset', and considered to cover the total project from concept through to commissioning. Chapters are included on setting the scene; the anatomy of a project; management needs; planning the action; monitoring and controlling the action; people; and looking forward. Appendices deal with the time value of money; risk analysis; and project date for a chemical plant and swimming bath.

126
S. Goldhaber, C.K. Jha and M.C. Macedo Jr
CONSTRUCTION MANAGEMENT PRINCIPLES AND PRACTICES
1977, John Wiley and Sons, 312pp.
The concept of construction (project) management (CM) is introduced and defined and this is followed by a description of those principles and practices that make the concept work. Chapters are included on methodologies; advanced computer-based scheduling and cost control techniques; value management; field organization; contractual aspects; case studies; and outlook for CM.

1976

125
D. Barclay
FUTURE ROLE OF THE QS
Building 1976 231 November 12, p. 110
The view is expressed that not only is the QS profession unsuited to an expansionist role (into management contracting) but an investigation of their present activities and eventual curtailment to meet modern methods would improve generally the overall performances of the industry. Two areas of concern which are discussed relate to services, particularly bill preparation, and to fees.

124
R.P. Harris
TIME ELEMENT (PART 2)
Quantity Surveyor 1976 33 November, pp. 69–75
Consideration is given to the relative performance of architect-designed and package deal contracts in terms of construction time, post-completion time and overall time. The financial implications of time are discussed with reference to cost as a function of time, project details and times, construction prices, and optimum time. It is concluded that if the client is seeking to occupy his factory within the shortest possible time, then the package deal will generally be the most appropriate.

123
R.P. Harris
THE TIME ELEMENT (PART 1)

Quantity Surveyor 1976 33 October, pp. 49–55
An analysis is made of competitive tender and package deal alternatives for traditionally constructed factory buildings with the aim of establishing the time performance of each system and the ramification of such findings. Initially, consideration is given to client priorities and constraints from which it is concluded that clients give a high priority to the time element. This is followed by a report of the investigation of the time period of the pre-construction period of the contracts. From this it is concluded that a package dealer would provide a higher probability of achieving programmed design dates.

122
M.V. Manzoni
CONSTRUCTION OF THE NATIONAL EXHIBITION CENTRE
Polytechnic Seminar 'Professional Project Control', Birmingham, October 6, 1976 pp. 74–8
The role of the project controller during the construction phase is briefly discussed under the headings construction difficulties, specific and contractual problems, definitions, and functions.

121
E.D. Mills
DESIGN OF THE NATIONAL EXHIBITION CENTRE
Proc. City of Birmingham Polytechnic Seminar 'Professional Project Control', Birmingham, October 6, 1976, pp. 68–71; Discussion, pp. 72–3
Some general comments are made on the initiation and construction aspects of Centre, the problem areas being highlighted.

120
B.G. Lund
INTRODUCTION TO THE NATIONAL EXHIBITION CENTRE
Proc. City of Birmingham Polytechnic Seminar 'Professional Project Control', Birmingham, October 6, 1976 pp. 61–7
The historical background to the NEC and its evolution in its present form are outlined. The process of preparing the brief is described and this is followed by an analysis of the reasons for employing a project manager. The lessons gained at NEC are discussed with particular reference to coordination of a large design team and the need for complete control and discipline against a background of full cooperation from all concerned and a rigid financial control.

119
A.F. Adair
PROJECT MANAGEMENT AND PROJECT CONTROL

Proc. City of Birmingham Polytechnic Seminar 'Professional Project Control', Birmingham, October 6, 1976, pp. 17–38; Discussion, pp. 39–41

The role of project management is seen as being responsible for a project from inception to completion and as such being responsible for the preparation of a plan which will enable the objectives of the project to be achieved. The second phase of the project manager's role is controlling the project when the plan is implemented. Team management structures are considered prior to a closer examination of the role and need for a project manager. Finally, skills and abilities of the project manager are analysed.

118
A.G.J. Desssewffy
IN SEARCH OF THE 'IDEAL' CONSTRUCTION CONTRACT
Building Economist 1976 15 September, pp. 69–78
Recent developments are outlined in the documentation and administration of building and civil engineering contracts, particular reference being made to British practice under the headings – lump-sum contracts (including two-stage tendering, negotiated and serial tendering, management contracting, package deals, formula price adjustment) and cost reimbursable contracts (fixed fee and prime cost contracts and target and cost reimbursable contracts). The relevance of these procedures to the Australian building industry is discussed.

117
D.S. Barrie and B.C. Paulson Jr
PROFESSIONAL CONSTRUCTION MANAGEMENT
ASCE Journal of the Construction Division 1976 102 (CO3) September, pp. 425–36
The findings and conclusions of ASCE's Task Committee on Management of Construction Projects are reported. Definitions of 'professional construction management' and 'professional construction manager' and the reasoning behind them are explained. The responsibilities are then described of the professional construction manager and his requirements in the planning and execution phases of a project. Professional construction management differs from conventional design–construct and traditional separate contractor and designer approaches in that there are by definition three separate and distinct members of the team (owner, designer, and manager) and the professional construction manager does not perform significant design or construction work with his own forces. Professional construction management is not necessarily better or worse than other methods of procuring constructed facilities. However, the three-party-team approach is certainly a viable alternative

to more traditional methods in many applications, as its increasing use demonstrates.

116
J. Johns
PROJECT MANAGEMENT
Building Economists 1976 15 September, pp. 87–93
This paper is presented in the form of a conversation between three project managers and discusses the role of the project manager and the reasons for his appointment by the client, and some typical problems.

115
L.G. Krantz
MANAGEMENT IN HIGH RISK AREAS
Quantity Surveyor 1976 33 September, pp. 26–9
The need for owner-oriented project management is considered prior to a discussion of the requirements for better management tools, particular attention being given to deficiencies in conventional schedule and cost analysis.

114
WHO'S IN CHARGE HERE?
Building 1976 230 June 25, pp. 92–3
The basic advantages of management contracting are examined to draw attention to some of its limitations. In conclusion it is stated that the contractor is suited to a more prominent part than the principles of project management consultancy permit.

113
A.V. Kocass and G. French
CONSTRUCTION MANAGEMENT
Paper to the 25th Conference of the Building Science Forum of Australia (NSW Division) Sydney, June 9 1976, 8pp.
Project management as offered by a contracting organization is described, reference being made to method and terms of engagement, contractual arrangements, documentation, client's brief and budget, time, cost and finance control, team selection and construction and commissioning of the project.

112
K.A. Hawson, R.G. Brookes and G.A. Sutherland
PROJECT MANAGER (CLIENT)
Paper to 25th Conference of the Building Science Forum of Australia (NSW Division) Sydney, June 9 1976, 12pp.
The presentation is in the form of discussions between the three authors. They consider the role of project manager/client (i.e. project managers appointed to client's staff) and why clients make this appointment. Some of the problem areas are identified.

111

I. Turner

PROJECT MANAGEMENT SERVICES

Paper to the 25th Conference of the Building Science Forum of Australia (NSW Division) Sydney, June 9 1976, 11pp.

The role of the project management consultant is outlined, his evolution, the advantages and disadvantages, and the methods employed being considered. Attention is then given to contractual arrangements, the client brief, documentation and construction.

110

T. Crow and R. Hammond

MANAGEMENT CONSULTANT PROJECT MANAGEMENT

Paper to 25th Conference of the Building Science Forum of Australia (NSW Division) Sydney, June 9 1976, 12pp.

The case is argued for the management consultant to improve the coordination of and communication between members of the building team. The detailed role of such consultants is described, reference being made to benefits, basis of engagement, client's brief, sketch plan, design development, working drawings, construction and commissioning.

109

W.J. Diepeveen

PROJECT MANAGEMENT THROUGH BUILD-ING TEAMS

Proc. CIB Symposium on Organization and Management of Construction Washington, May 1976a, pp. 36–49

The value is discussed of the use of matrix organization to coordinate the functions of the building team members. It makes use of the optimal motivation of each member by treating him as an equal and independent expert, responsible for his own work, but acting with others in a team in the interest of an optimal project constructed during the course of an optimal process. A matrix organization is a mixed structure. Carrying on from this concept, project management (management contracting) is considered, the structure being identified and management of the process outlined.

108

D.J.O. Ferry

DEVELOPING TRENDS IN THE PROCUREMENT OF BUILDINGS

Building Economist 1976 14 March, pp. 216–20

The organizational problems of the client in acquiring a building are considered and those factors are identified which have led to conventional contractual arrangements being regarded as less than satisfactory.

Alternative methods discussed are negotiated contracts, the package deal and management contracting. Each method is evaluated, its advantages and limitations being indicated.

107

Associated General Contractors of America

CONSTRUCTION MANAGEMENT CONTROL PROCESS

1976, 6pp. (9 flow charts)

Guidelines are presented to indicate the normal processes to be followed on a CM project. The process is represented by the following three flow charts:

Division of responsibility for performance

Responsibility flow

Project control by the construction manager.

106

A. Walker

PROJECT MANAGEMENT – A REVIEW OF THE STATE OF THE ART

1976, IQS, 76pp.

A review is made of recent developments in the structure of the arrangements for the management of construction projects on behalf of the client. It considers the role and responses of project management from inception through the life of the building. The current state of development of project management as a separately identifiable function is considered through interviews with 18 organizations and conclusions are drawn in respect of the art and the possible directions project management may take. Developments in project management are considered against the performance of conventional processes.

105

US General Services Administration

USING CONSTRUCTION MANAGEMENT FOR PUBLIC AND INSTITIONAL FACILITIES

1976, 73pp.

A study of the use of project management (PM) by state and local agencies has shown that it has achieved general acceptance and that most users (73 per cent) would consider using it again. The usefulness of PM increases in proportion to project complexity and cost; the total PM approach can be used on a cost effective basis for complex projects with costs of $3 million and above. On the other hand individual features, such as value analysis, may yield real cost benefits on projects costing $1 million or less. The several forms of PM are described and a guide is provided to public administrations to allow them to determine whether or how they want to use PM.

104

N.H. Heayes

TAKING THE WRAPS OFF THE BUILDING 'PACKAGE'

Contract Journal 1976 *270* April 29, pp. 24–5
A general look is taken at recent developments in non-traditional contractual procedures, such as develop and construct, and the package deal. Early involvement of the contractor in the contract is discussed.

103
G.T. Heery and E.M. Davies
CONSTRUCTION PROGRAMME MANAGEMENT
Building Technology and Management 1976 *14* April, pp. 22–6
Construction programme management is defined as 'that group of management activities over and above normal architectural and engineering services related to a construction programme, carried out during the pre-design, and construction phases, that provides control of time and cost in the construction of a new facility'. The professional manager is thereby one who associates with the client to apply the proper combination of management techniques to achieve time and cost control. The role of this project manager is classified into ten basic components which are each considered in turn; pre-decision programming and budgeting; selection of designers and preparation of design contracts; pre-design project analysis; early cost and methods analysis; integrated cost control procedures; design review and approvals; time control procedures; computer assisted scheduling; management of tender/award; management during construction.

102
L.J. Brown
APLICATION OF MANAGEMENT METHODS IN DESIGN/CONSTRUCTION
Proc. CIB Symposium on Organization and Management of Construction Washington, May 1976, pp. IV.85–IV.95
An outline is given of the contractual procedures employed by the Canadian Department of Defence. They are fixed price contracts:
(i) traditional (design–bid–build)
(ii) proposal call (performance specification: bid–design–build).
and construction management contracts:
(i) project management/construction management
(ii) design–bid–build sequentially
(iii) design–bid–build with pre-tendering.

101
D.C. Aird and V.K. Handa
CREATING FLEXIBILITY IN A CONVENTIONAL DESIGN/CONSTRUCT ORGANIZATION
Proc. CIB Symposium on Organization and Management of Construction

Washington, May 1976, pp. 1–15
The development processes involved with a design/construct organization responsible for the construction of fossil-fuelled and nuclear power stations are described. A matrix organization – part functional, part profit type – was selected; the advantages and limitations of this organization are outlined.

1975

100
H. Buteux
DESIGN AND BUILD THE SSHA'S ANSWER
Architects Journal 1975 *162* December 3, pp. 1169–70
The Scottish Special Housing Association's methods described are claimed to speed up housing contracts by using the design team to accelerate pre-contract documentation. It involves transferring the decision on forms of construction from the contractor to the design team and by rationalizing the details used in house building – using an open-ended library of standard details.

99
G.S. Birrell
'BUYING' A NEW BUILDING: THE US MANAGEMENT APPROACH
Chartered Surveyor Building and Quantity Surveying Quarterly 1975/76 *3* Winter, pp. 23–8
The requirement of a client for a new building is used to explore the methods employed to ensure its constitution. Attention is devoted to the selection of the project team, comprising in this case separate design and construction firms. In addition a construction manager representing the client was appointed. Following on, consideration is given to the selection of bidding sub-contractors, project control during design and construction, sub-contractor control on site, and interim payments to sub-contractors. Finally, those major points are discussed, which lead to successful management of 'buying' a building.

98
S.E. Smith et al.
CONTRACTUAL RELATIONSHIPS IN CONSTRUCTION
ASCE Proc. Journal of the Construction Division 1975 *101* (CO4) December, pp. 907–21
The different types of contractual relationship in the US are considered from the owner, consultant, contractor and legal viewpoints. Principal relationships considered are general contractor, turnkey, construction manager and independent prime contracts.

97

A.H. Barraclough

FEE TYPE CONTRACTS

Building 1975 *229* November 28, p. 78

Experience, up to the conclusion of the pre-contract stage, is reported of the Department of Architecture and Planning of Leeds City Council providing most of the architectural services for a fee-type contract. Particular aspects discussed include contract options, estimate of prime cost, interviewing contractors, and the spread of tenders received.

96

SHOULD RIBA TIE IN WITH THE PACKAGE DEAL?

Contract Journal 1975 *268* November 27, p. 22

It is considered that the cost of construction is too high, and that the refinements that the separation of design and construction entails can no longer be afforded. It is suggested that the RIBA should revise its rules of conduct by allowing its members to become company directors.

95

M.J.D. Keatings

SOLVING THE COMMUNICATION PROBLEM

Building 1975 *229* August 29, pp. 43–5

It is considered that the trend in the development of the JCT standard form of contract has been a progressive transfer of risk from the contractor to the employer, exemplified by the relative lack of involvement of the architect during construction. Areas of difficulty identified are associated with design to coordination and nominated sub-contracts. It is advocated that on large or complex projects the client should appoint his own project manager. Consideration should also be given to the suitability of the JCT form of contract.

94

K. Manson

LIABILITY IN A PACKAGE DEAL CONTRACT

Building Trades Journal 1975 *170* July 25, pp. 14, 16, 18

The case is reported of *Greaves & Co (Contractors) v Baynham, Meikle & Partners* from which the following conclusions are drawn:

(a) Where there is a package deal contract the contractor is liable to the client if the building is not reasonably fit for its intended use.

(b) Architects/engineers are obliged to use reasonable care and skill in their professional duties.

(c) In such circumstances a professional man in his duties implies a warranty that the design will be fit for the intended purpose.

(d) A contractor employing a professional whose designs are not fit for the purpose may be able to

obtain indemnity for the cost of works to prevent and rectify damage.

93

SURPRISE PACKAGE

Architect 1975 *12* July, pp. 16–18

The P.O. Telecommunications Centre at Carlisle was constructed under a package deal contract by IDC Limited, and completed in 32 months – half the usual time.

92

H. Cruickshank

QUANTITY SURVEYOR/CONTRACTOR BARRIER: SOME HOME TRUTHS

Chartered Surveyor Building and Quantity Surveying Quarterly 1975 *2* Summer, pp. 45, 47–9

It is considered that the standard competitive system of placing contracts is the central cause of existing barriers, and evidence is presented to support this view. To resolve the situation it is suggested that the consultant must persuade the client of the value of more accountable integrated design construction teams and contract procedures.

91

REPORT OF NON-TRADITIONAL METHODS OF CONTRACTING

Building Economist 1975 *14* June, pp. 1, 3–13

This report was prepared by Australian IQS Contractual Relations Committee. It covers the conventional forms of contract – lump sum and cost reimbursement – and attempts to assess the relative merits and disadvantages in relation to non-traditional methods; particular attention being given to the problems of the design team, public accountability and pre-contract consultative services. Appendices provide suggested principles for selecting a contractor; details of the factors considered in determination of price; and details of non-traditional contractual methods – provisional lump-sum and negotiated contract types.

90

CONSULTANTS ENGINEERS LIABLE TO CONTRACTORS IN PACKAGE DEAL

Times 1975 May 16, p. 8

On appeal it was held that in the case of *Greaves & Co. (Contractors) Ltd v Baynham. Meikle and Partners* that contractors are entitled to a declaration of liability and an indemnity from consultants for the cost of work necessary to prevent and rectify damage to a building built under a package deal contract.

89

W. Amos and P.M. Worthington

MULTI–DISCIPLINARY PROJECT MANAGEMENT

ICE Proceedings 1975 *58* (Part 1) May, pp. 305–10
The various aspects are summarized that establish the viability of project management. One view is expressed that specialists and project management should receive the same opportunities and rewards, thereby promoting the concept of matrix management – the practice where a consultant reports to a superior in his own firm on technical and administrative matters and to the client on matters concerning the project. A need for formal training in project management is identified.

88
D.D. Patterson
PROJECT MANAGEMENT AND THE ENGINEER
ICE Proceedings 1975 *58* (Part 1) May, pp. 205–11
With complex projects clients are requiring more detailed information on programme/performance and expenditure/budget and in consequence the engineer has to develop monitoring techniques to supply these data. The interaction of the activities of project managers, client, contractors and engineers is reviewed with particular reference to the obligations imposed by the General Conditions of Contract.

87
M. Barnes
PROJECT MANAGER – A MAN OR A MYTH?
New Civil Engineer 1975 May 29, p. 22
It is considered that if the American view of project management as a new and definable concept is correct then it must differ from the British attitude since it does not appear to embrace any new techniques, relying as it does on the application of conventional techniques for cost control and planning and scheduling. Consequently it is suggested that its strength must lie in attitudes – the completion on time and within a budget being pre-eminent aims which are not merged with those of producing an elegant or functional design. Indications are given that there will be an increased demand in the UK for project management as clients stress the importance of conserving time and money.

86
M. Laing
PACKAGE DEAL – THE COMPLETE ANSWER?
Paper to IOB/PSA Conference 'Getting buildings designed and built – can we afford today's ways?' London, April 1975, 11pp.
The importance is stressed of providing buildings that represent the best possible value for money. The package deal, applied to suitable projects, is considered to meet this aim provided that the client who does not regularly buy new buildings, retains independent professional advice. Package deals can increase the efficiency with which a project is completed and substantial savings can be obtained from

bringing design into the area of competition and by giving proper consideration to the most effective method of construction. Package deals are widely used abroad and increasingly so in the UK – the contractor has a responsibility to see that they are used to benefit the client and the community.

85
R.I. Northern
CLIENT MANAGED PROJECTS – A COMPLETE SERVICE
Paper to IOB/PSA Conference 'Getting buildings designed and built – can we afford today's ways?' London, April 1975, 7pp.
Based on practical experience the aspects of project management discussed include the client's responsibilities, the function of the project manager, the alternative forms of contract, selection, integration of the building team, monitoring techniques, and final appraisal of the completed building.

84
W. Amos
INTRODUCING THE SUBJECT
Paper to IOB/PSA Conference 'Getting buildings designed and built – can we afford today's ways?' London, April 1975, 7pp.
The current interest in project management is reviewed. This is followed by an outline of the organization of project teams and analysis of the four stages involved in the building process which require special skills and involve different proportions of the total cost. The client's role is briefly considered prior to a summary of the methods of dealing with the management of projects. Attention is drawn to various fields of activities by listing the action programme of the PSA as a typical example of the amount of involvement in a client/designer organization. Finally the services are suggested that clients should receive from the industry throughout the building process.

83
A.F. Sampson
CONSTRUCTION MANAGEMENT – THE GSA APPROACH
Paper to IOB/PSA Conference 'Getting buildings designed and built – can we afford today's ways?' London, April 1975, 19pp.
The GSA (General Services Agency) provides for the civilian agencies of the US Government a system for the management of property and records, including construction and the operation and protection of buildings. One division of the GSA is the Public Buildings Service and an account is given of the management techniques employed by the service, as developed over the past five years. The current state

of the US building industry is indicated and some thoughts expressed on future trends in the built environment.

82

G.T. Heery

CONSTRUCTION MANAGEMENT IN ACTION

Paper to IOB/PSA Conference 'Getting buildings designed and built – can we afford today's ways?' London, April 1975, 8pp.

Attention is focused on the services of the independent construction manager (US practice) and details are given of how the manager utilizes the time/cost control system from pre-design through to occupancy. Specific case histories are reviewed which illustrate the scope of projects, the schedules and cost accomplished and the construction management plan in relation to phasing, etc.

81

A.T. Brett-Jones

'WHICH BUILDER?'. TENDERING PROCEDURES AND CONTRACTUAL ARRANGEMENTS

Paper to RICS 10th Triennial Conference of Quantity Surveyors, London, April 1975, 17pp.

It is advocated that tendering is an essential and key factor in the economic use of building resources and that decisions on tendering are essentially matters of professional advice, which is primarily the responsibility of the quantity surveyor. Clients too often regard themselves as expert in tendering, a function which may have as great an effect as design-decisions on the resources used in a building project. In considering the economic use of building resource four main aspects are identified: the contractor's effect on design; production cost savings; continuity; and risk. The significance of public accountability in formulating tendering policy is also indicated. The principles and application of negotiated and competitive tendering and fixed price and cost reimbursement contracts are discussed and some alternative forms, such as the package deal, identified. It is suggested that a tender should be evaluated not only in terms of the price offered but also in terms of the investment to be made and the potential saving if continuation contracts are negotiated. Such savings would need to be quantified by the identification and measurement of productivity. The close involvement of the client and the need to control sub-contractors tends towards the management contracting situation. In this the quantity surveyor would play a significant role.

80

K. Terry

CONTRACTUAL ARRANGEMENTS AND TENDERING PROCEDURES IN THE BUILDING INDUSTRY

Build 1975 *11* April, pp. 12, 14–15

An outline is given of the most common forms of contractual arrangements and tendering procedures.

79

W. James

PROJECT MANAGEMENT

Building Economist 1975 *13* March, pp. 200–4

Project management is discussed in relation to eight sections defining the function. These sections involve:

(a) Defining and obtaining the client's agreement to physical and financial objectives, priorities, delegation of power to the project manager, requirements as to frequency of reports etc. and terms of appointment.

(b) Selection and appointment of consultants capable of achieving the client's objectives.

(c) Settling terms of appointment of all consultants and the forms of agreement for executing the works.

(d) Checking and coordinating budgets and programme, formulation of global budget, monitoring and reporting progress.

(e) Organizing and reporting on arrangements for running and maintenance of the finished works.

(f) Reporting at completion of works on the financial outcome of the project.

78

T. Mitchell

IN PRAISE OF PACKAGE DEALS

Building Design 1975 February 21, pp. 20–1

The management approach of IDC Consultants to package deals is outlined and some practical examples of the advantages of the system indicated.

77

P. Grafton

QS MARK II THE NEW HORIZONS

Building 1975 *228* February 14, pp. 66–7

Some individual thoughts are expressed on the quantity surveyor as project manager and on the general contribution the RICS can make to planning and construction.

76

A.P. Grant

ECONOMICS OF THE PACKAGE DEAL

Building 1975 *228* January 31, p. 68 (Correspondence)

The advantages, in particular for industrial building, of the package deal are outlined.

75

DOE

DEVELOP AND CONSTRUCT

1975, HMSO, 44pp.

The develop and construct procedure is divided into eight stages with the design and construct phases overlapping. The architect remains responsible for the design but the contractor is given a share of the professional effort required for detailed work and can begins site work while this is continuing. The work is carried out using the contractor's own building method whereas the architect's skill is employed in producing type plans for all the buildings and arranging them on the site. The professional effort of the contractor lies in adapting his method to the type plans and to the site in a manner acceptable to the architect. Significant time savings are made using the procedure. Following a case study, flow charts are presented illustrating the sequence of operations-feasibility, sketch design, working drawings and specifications, bills of quantities, tender period, evaluation and acceptance of tender, develop, construct.

74

O. Lindgrew et al.
EARLY TENDERING FOR PLUMBING INSTALLATIONS ACCORDING TO THE FEE METHOD
National Swedish Building Research Summary R19: 1975, 2pp.
This summary considered the early negotiation of plumbing contracts by the fee method. Indications are provided of the time savings achieved and other aspects of the report such as the assessment of the relative proportions of labour, material and other costs, and product group breakdown for different contracts.

73

Hillier Parker May and Rowden
PROPERTY DEVELOPMENT – SUMMARY OF PROFESSIONAL AND ESTATE SERVICES
1975, 24pp.
A brochure providing some reasons for the use of management contracting and some examples of where it has been successfully employed.

72

G.T. Heery
TIME, COST AND ARCHITECTURE
1975, McGraw-Hill, 212pp.
A definitive system is discussed for time and cost content that may be applied within any programme of requirements, quality level or design goal. The time/cost control system can be employed by the architect/engineer or by the construction manager. Both approaches are considered. Commencing with fourteen case histories further chapters deal with a management approach to the construction programme: the client; introduction to time/cost control system; pre-design project analysis; systems approach to design; cost-control system; time control, contract time provision and extension rulings; use of CPM and scheduling techniques; phased, separate and transferable contracts; bid and negotiations

management; and construction management in the construction phase.

71

NEDO:
THE PUBLIC CLIENT AND THE CONSTRUCTION INDUSTRIES
1975, HMSO. 126pp.
It is found that public clients tend to view each project in isolation rather than in relation to their on-going programmes of work. This does not make for the most efficient use of clients' or contractors' resources. Studies showed that value for money is construed too narrowly and sought largely in the wrong place – it is looked for primarily at the letting of individual projects. The end of 'stop-go' policies is called for and the Government is urged to adopt policies to foster greater stability in demand, and to keep a watchful eye upon the supply of funds. The important role of the client is stressed. Design-and-construct contracts were found to perform well and the advantages were established of the contractor participating in the pre-construction phases. Open tendering is condemned and two-stage tendering is advocated for one-off projects of large scale or complexity, 'design and construct' for repetitive projects; and serial tenders for continuous programmes of similar projects. A look is taken at payment and disputes on construction contracts and although limited remedies only are advanced it is recommended that a mini-tender could be used whereby the contractor, faced with a major variation, quotes an inclusive price for its execution, the client being given the option of accepting the price or of pricing the variation under the conventional procedures. The provision is also suggested of calling in an independent expert to ascertain the facts in a dispute.

1974

70

PSA WAY – DEVELOP AND CONSTRUCT
Building 1974 227 November 15, pp. 141, 143
The develop and construct procedure described involves contractors offering tenders on the basis of site layouts, plan types and performance specifications. The successful tenderer is given possession of the site while the contractor in parallel prepares the working drawings which are vetted by the project architect. One of the main advantages is the overall time savings from sketch design to completion and the early involvement of the selected contractor. The eight conventional stages involved in the contract are outlined.

69

A. Massey

PROJECT MANAGEMENT – A NEW APPROACH

Paper to IOB Annual Conference, London, November 1974, 5pp.

The basic parameters of project management are defined and the value of this type of service to the client described. Education and training requirements are indicated and future prospects discussed.

68

G.B. Wheeldon

FACTORY BUILDING – ADVANTAGES OF THE PACKAGE DEAL

Building Trades Journal 1974 *168* October 25, pp. 28, 31, 33–35

The principles of operation of a package deal contract are described and the advantage to both client and builder summarized.

67

W. James

PROJECT MANAGEMENT

Chartered Surveyor, Building & Quantity Surveying Quarterly 1974 *2* Autumn, pp. 1–4

A definition is given of project management in relation to a construction-development project. This definition is classified into eight sections and these are discussed separately. They involved (a) establishing the clients requirements (b) selecting and appointing consultants able to achieve the clients objectives (c) settling terms of appointment of all consultants and the forms of agreement for executing the works (d) checking and coordinating initial individual budgets and programmes, and testing their validity (e) organizing and reporting on arrangements for running and maintenance of finished works, including documentation (f) reporting at completion of works on the financial outcome of the project.

66

S. Lucas

TIME SAVING AT A FAIR PRICE

Building 1974 *227* September 13, pp. 123, 125

Following an outline of the disadvantage that can be experienced by competitive tendering the benefits of negotiated contracts, package deals and the management fee system are summarized. It is considered that whereas the client is unlikely to get a cheaper building he is likely to be occupying it much quicker.

65

W.T. Shaw

MANAGEMENT CONTRACTORS? OR 'BRASS PLATE' BUILDERS?

Surveying Technician 1974 *3* June, pp. 8–10

The differences in contracting between pre- and post-war contracting are outlined and some possible reasons for these are indicated. A schedule is presented of the make-up of a contract sum for a contract in the 1930s compared to one of today which illustrates the considerable reducation in the work carried out directly by the contractor.

64

J.R. Lowe

POINTS AGAINST PACKAGE DEAL

Construction News 1974 March 28, p. 8 (Correspondence)

One main criticism is the inability to use the strengths of specialists to the best purpose. This is reinforced by the view that an independent consulting engineer can provide a better service.

63

G.R. Hill

AGAINST THE PACKAGE DEAL

Construction News 1974 March 14, p. 29

Construction News 1974 March 21, p. 10 (missing illustration)

It is claimed that the vast majority of package deal contracts are typified by a low standard of design and value for money. Costs are considered to be 10–20 per cent more expensive than a conventional contract plus professional fees. Particular attention is given to the apparent inadequate specification found with such contracts.

62

P.W.G. Morris

SYSTEMS STUDY OF PROJECT MANAGEMENT – 2

Building 1974 *226* February 1, pp. 83–4, 87–8

The systems approach to project management is discussed with particular reference to integration, coordination and control, the overall coordination of design and production, and production.

61

P.W.G. Morris

SYSTEMS STUDY OF PROJECT MANAGEMENT – 1

Building 1974 *226* January 25, pp. 75–6, 79–80

Research is reported on the various types of design/production interface which exist in building using analytical techniques belonging to organizations and systems theory. The case studies presented cover a traditional contract, two negotiated contracts and three where there was closer involvement of design and construction such as management fee, and management contracting.

60
J.C. White
IMPROVED BUILDING PROCUREMENT MEANS A CHANGED BUILDING PROCESS
Industrialization Forum 1974 *5(1–2)*, pp. 39–43
Related to US practice the broad process problems experienced by the client, designer, contractor, sub-contractor, and the manufacturer are outlined. Limitations in the traditional bidding process are considered and some alternatives – negotiated contract, phased bidding and construction – are indicated: both require project management.

59
S. Thake
PROCUREMENT AND PRODUCTIVITY – THE SCOPE FOR CHANGE
Industrialization Forum 1974 *5(1–2)*, pp. 9–18
It is suggested that although competitive bidding procedures dominate in the public sector it is necessary to change them, in order to benefit from the potential for continuity. Obstacles to efficiency are traced to instability, discontinuity, and the lack of uniform contract conditions. Serial and continuity contracts allow for greater productivity, and industrialization is highly desirable, in terms of improved and reduced cost of buildings.

58
G. Wigglesworth and D. Wisdom
PROCUREMENT METHODS THEIR EFFECT ON THE INDUSTRIALIZATION OF BUILDING
Industrialization Forum 1974 *5(1–2)*, pp. 19–28
Organizing demand for building through procurement policies is discussed with reference to the public sector housing, and educational fields. It is concluded that system building did not receive sustained orders to amortize plant costs and consequently contractors returned to traditional methods of house building. The number of closed systems for educational building is felt to have defeated long-term objectives, the influence of such systems on the process of industrialization generally is regarded as small.

57
M. Green
IN PRAISE OF THE PACKAGE DEAL
Construction News 1974 January 24, p. 28
The advantages of the package deal are outlined.

56
Associated General Contractors of America
CM FOR THE GENERAL CONTRACTOR – A GUIDE MANUAL FOR CONSTRUCTION MANAGEMENT
1974, 161pp.

An examination is made of the differences between construction (project) management (CM) and traditional contractual methods. Sections include an overview of CM; selling CM services and negotiating the contract; planning and scheduling; estimating and budgeting: CM control system; procurement and construction. Appendices provide details of the function of the CN during planning and construction phases; a standard form of contract; and a standard form of sub-contract.

55
CPRE
DEVELOPMENT CONTROL PACKAGE BUILDINGS
1974, 34pp.
Weaknesses in countryside planning and development controls are identified. It is estimated that some 80 per cent of all agricultural buildings will contain a package element within 20 years. In most cases the design will offer no flexibility, yet planning procedures are concerned with building appearance only after an application has been submitted. Consequently it is considered that controls must be exercised at the blueprint stage before costly manufacturing processes have been set up. It is suggested that a central agency be set up to publish criteria and principles for design and to award certification for finishes and cladding.

1973

54
J. Dunaway
MANAGEMENT CONTRACTS – A PSA VIEW
Construction (DOE) 1973 December, pp. 29–30
The principles of management contracting and its advantages are discussed.

53
P.W.G. Morris
ORGANIZATIONAL ANALYSIS OF PROJECT MANAGEMENT IN THE BUILDING INDUSTRY
Build International 1973 *6* November/December, pp. 595–616
The way in which the systems approach can help a project management function and the kinds of forces which shape a particular projects information requirements are studied. Attention is paid to the problems of bridging the design–construction gap and organization theory is used to examine the pattern of co-ordination and control in the building process.

52

N. Cameron and P. Pearson

PLANNING AND CONTROLLING 'DESIGN AND CONSTRUCT' PROJECTS

Building 1973 *224* April 13, pp. 115–16, 119–20

The building and equipping of new offices under a package deal contract is described with reference to the design brief and placing the contract, client's management procedure, working procedure, main contractor's role, cost control and project planning.

51

J. Carter

TECHNICAL STUDY. INTEGRATED DESIGN AND CONSTRUCTION: ESSO MOTOR HOTEL AT BRISTOL

Architects Journal 1973 *157* March 21, pp. 707–14

Looks at an integrated design and construction project and shows how a package deal provided, arguably a quicker answer than more traditional methods. The project, a 156-bedroom motel, has air-conditioned conference accommodation for 400, a restaurant for 200 and a one-acre (0.4ha) artificial lake. Progress month by month is tabulated at the end of the article.

50

J. Carter

MANAGEMENT CONTRACTING: THE HORIZON PROJECT

Architects Journal 1973 *157* February 14, pp. 395–400

The management contracting procedures employed, with Bovis Fee as the management contractor, in the construction of a cigarette factory are described with the events being given in diary form.

49

COMPETITION v NEGOTIATION – MANAGEMENT CONTRACTING

Architectural Design 1973 *43(3)*, p. 197.

48

MAKING A CONTRACT – THE PACKAGE DEAL

Building Trades Journal 1973 *166* February 16, pp. 22, 24, 28

The package deal contract is examined in the context of larger projects and an outline given of some of the necessary procedures in its negotiation.

47

RICS

THE CHARTERED QUANTITY SURVEYOR AND PACKAGE CONTRACTS

1973 (Pamphlet)

Disadvantages of package deals are summarized although it is accepted that under certain circumstances the system can be advantageous to the client.

It is stated that considerable evidence is available to show that the appointment of a quantity surveyor by the building owner results in substantial financial savings to the owner.

46

MUNTER PROJECT – DRAFT OF DOCUMENTATION FOR EARLY TENDERING

National Swedish Building Research Summary R74: 1973, 2pp.

It is considered that existing recommendations in Sweden are not adjusted to invitation of tenders and contracting resulting in package deal contracts or early tendering. Draft instructions are outlined for the drawing up of documentation for contracts between client and contractor.

45

J.B. Cannel

PACKAGE DEAL AND THE PROFESSIONS

Chartered Surveyor – Building and Quantity Surveying Quarterly 1973 *1* September, pp. 7–9

The package deal concept is evaluated and the conclusion made that there is no evidence of the final cost or contract time under a package deal being very different from those found with traditional methods. Without proper control by the client it is suggested that the cost could be significantly higher.

1972

44

J. Carter

MANAGEMENT CONTRACTING

Architects Journal 1972 *156* December 13, pp. 1371–1374

The climate is assessed for the development of management contracting, described as the appointment of the contractor to join the design team to assist in working out the design, programme the work and run the job on site. This is followed by an outline of how the contract is managed and a discussion of the responsibilities carried by the respective members of the team. Finally the advantages to the design team and the contractor are evaluated.

43

J. Anderson

CHARTERED SURVEYORS AND THE PACKAGE DEAL

Chartered Surveyor 1972 *105* October, pp. 173–4

A report is given of a survey to establish the types of service and advice given by surveyors to clients when retained to assist and advise on package deal projects. Following an outline of the package deals available and the services offered by the contractors, replies to questions are reported dealing with the problems encountered in relation to the form of contract, difficulties with variations and extras, control exercised by client's surveyor, defects liability period, methods of payment, and fee scale.

42

E.V. Broadbent

TRENDS IN CONSTRUCTION MANAGEMENT

Building Services Engineer 1972 *40* June, pp. 75–8

The problems are discussed which arise from the traditional separation of development, design and construction and in particular of the harmful effects of divided responsibility. The benefits of package dealing in mitigating some of these problems are presented.

41

J. Chisholm

AGAINST THE PACKAGE DEAL

Architect 1972 May, pp. 49–50

The main criticism of the package deal is that it contributes to a further lowering of architectural standards which are unlikely to improve when the main criteria for new building is predetermined cost and speed of erection.

40

W.J. Shergold

COMPUTER AIDS IN CONTRACT LETTING AND CONTROL FOR CIVIL ENGINEERING AND BUILDING CONTRACTS

Paper Seminar on Tendering Procedures, April 1972, 20pp.

Following an outline of the types of contract available, e.g. package deal, lump sum, and measurement, the provision of a schedule of rates is discussed in relation to its computerization.

39

J.A. Summers

UNITED KINGDOM/FRENCH TENDERING PROCEDURES

Paper RICS 'Anglo-French Collaboration in Property Development and Management' Conference, Paris, April 1972, 4pp. (in English and French).

An outline of UK tendering procedures only is given.

38

CONSTRUCTION MANAGEMENT: PUTTING PROFESSIONALISM INTO CONTRACTING

Construction Methods and Equipment 1972 *54* March, pp. 59–75

Guidelines are presented for practising construction management which comprises project planning,

design and construction as integrated tasks within a construction system consisting of the client, construction manager and architect/engineer. The team works from project inception to completion, interactions between cost, quality and completion schedule being carefully examined so that a project of maximum value to the client is realized in the most economic time scale. Directly related to US practice some personal views of the advantages obtained are presented.

37

N.P. Golds

CURRENT CONTRACTING METHODS

Construction (DoE), 1972 *(1)* March, pp. 23–37

Following a brief outline of the historical development of the current contractual arrangements, the various forms of tender and contract at present in use are examined.

36

A.E. Thomas

MANAGEMENT CONTRACTING

I0B Site Management Information Service Paper No. 46, 1972, 6pp.

The benefits of management contracting are discussed which as a result of involving the management team at the design stage can lead to greater site efficiency and improve the client's chances of gaining from a competitive situation, since all works are quoted for, including those normally included under the main contractor's services. The concept is highly flexible and there is virtually no type of scheme on which it would be anything but beneficial. A lower limit of £250,000 may be necessary to ensure economic viability.

35

W.B. Foxhall

PROFESSIONAL CONSTRUCTION MANAGEMENT AND PROJECT ADMINISTRATION

1972, AIA and Architectural Record, 114pp.

Professional construction management is seen as the coordination of the skills that allows the project to run orderly and with the greatest efficiency: it must be a professional service since it participates in a role of agency towards the client rather than drawing on the profit margin in a construction contract. The component skills and functions are identified and related to the central professional requirements of time, cost and quality control.

34

Architects in Industry Group

THE ARCHITECT AND THE PACKAGE DEAL – A CASE FOR PROPER RECOGNITION

1972, 4pp.

This report considers the concept of package deals, its advantages and limitations, and the role of the architect and quantity surveyor. It recommends that the RIBA should give greater recognition to the package deal as a legitimate form of practice for its members; that the JCT should produce a form of practice appropriate to the particular requirements of the package deal; and that notes for guidance be produced for those intending to operate within or use the package deal system showing the rights and obligations of the participants and the advantages and limitations of this type of contract.

33
J. Lundeberg
ARCHITECTS AND PROBLEMS – A STUDY OF THE INITIAL STAGE OF A PACKAGE DEAL CONTRACT
National Swedish Building Research Summary R37: 1972, 2pp.
This study, based on tape-recorded material of four meetings, covers observation and analysis of the sequence of events and solutions found to problems during the initial stage of work on the tender document. One interesting facet is the conflict between the architects' and contractors' systems of assessing a situation.

32
CONSTRUCTION MANAGEMENT. PART 2 – THE MAN BEHIND THE CONCEPT
Construction Methods and Equipment 1972 *54* April, pp. 110–18
The attitude of individuals in the US construction industry to the concept of management contracting and in particular the general contractor's viewpoint are expressed. The application of management contracting to three projects is considered and the results of each operation examined.

31
Associated General Contractors of America
CONSTRUCTION MANAGEMENT GUIDELINES
1972, 10pp.
A simple guide is given to construction (project) management (CM), the formation of the CM team, selection and functions.

1971

30
D.R. Harper
EVALUATION OF ALTERNATIVE METHODS OF CONTRACTOR SELECTION

Paper to UMIST Conference at International Building Exhibition, London, November 1971, 2pp.
The developments which have made competitive tendering less and less attractive and led to the introduction of other forms of contractor selection are summarized.

29
R. Jones
GROWTH AND DEVELOPMENT OF PACKAGE DEALS
Building Trades Journal 1971 *163* July 30, pp. 12–13
It is suggested that from the contractor's viewpoint he will take the best from the professional side and match it with his own abilities in the management, coordination and economic fields. The components of the package deal are described and the benefits to the client outlined. Marketing of the service is also discussed.

28
J. Weller
PACKAGING THE FACTORY FARM
RIBA Journal 1971 *78* May, pp. 194–9
The reasons are discussed for the firm entrenchment of the package deal in farm building. It is considered that the central role of package deal building in agriculture reflects a revolution which must take place in other spheres of specialized design and construction, and is bound to have profound implications for architects.

27
R. Jones
GROWTH AND DEVELOPMENT OF PACKAGE DEALS
Paper, Institute of Marketing, Construction Industry Market Group Meeting, May 1971, 11pp.
The various parts comprising the package deal concept and the marketing of this service are described. In the ensuing discussion the place of the architect was considered and differing views were expressed regarding whether the architect should be employed within the contractor's organization.

26
NEGOTIATED HOUSING – WHAT'S IN STORE FOR THE PACKAGE DEAL?
Surveyor 1971 March 12, pp. 28–9
The current situation in the public sector where the negotiated contract has virtually disappeared is discussed in relation to the deleterious effect that it is having on system builders.

25
G. Ericson
VALUATION OF TENDERS AT PACKAGE DEAL CONTRACTS

National Swedish Building Research Summary R24: 1971, 2pp.

A system is described to enable the client to make a choice from a number of tenders. Applied to a project for one-family houses it was found that in this case mathematical evaluation systems of this type do not give unambiguous results due to uncertainty of weighting and marketing when differences between the tenders are small.

24

Association of Professional Engineers of the Province of Ontario

PERFORMANCE STANDARDS FOR PROJECT MANAGEMENT AND SCALE OF FEES FOR PROJECT MANAGEMENT SERVICES

1971, 11pp.

The standards of performance to be expected for the management of planning, design, construction, and commissioning of a capital project within a cost budget and prescribed time schedule are described.

1970

23

J. Carter

PACKAGE DEALS 3: CLIENTS AND CONCLUSIONS

Architects Journal 1970 *152* November 25, pp. 1263–5

Comments on their reasons for choosing a package deal are given by a number of clients who have had industrial buildings constructed. Although the selection of a package dealer was based on varying factors it did appear that dealing with the one organization was significant; of particular importance was the impression that there was a lack of specialization among architects in this field in contrast to an increasing number of package dealers. In conclusion it is considered that the private architectural practice as a building management organization is no longer economically viable and nor is it able to provide a specialist service for an increasing demand. This implies that the contractor will become increasingly the client's first contact and leader of the building team, perhaps leading to the architect becoming a 'space and planner-subcontractor'. To retain his position there needs to be a repeal of the directorship ban altogether with a revaluation of the architect's education to remedy the urgent and essential need for a common understanding between architects and builders. As an immediate measure the setting up

by architects of contracting organizations is proposed with the RIBA providing an advisory service for members.

22

J. Carter

PACKAGE DEALS 2: PORTRAITS OF FIVE FIRMS

Architects Journal 1970 *152* November 18, pp. 1203–7

General details are given relating to the structure and operation of four unnamed package dealers and The Building Design Partnership.

21

J. Carter

PACKAGE DEALS 1: WHY PACKAGE DEALS?

Architects Journal 1970 *152* November 11, pp. 1155–6

Indications are that package dealing has increased considerably in the last few years and results of a limited survey show that one sixth of larger contractors provide an all-in service to the extent of 20 per cent or more of their turnover. The origins of the package deal are outlined and the reason for their present development considered in relation to the concept of the architect as an artist and as the client's adviser.

20

PROGRAMMED TENDERING FOR ALBERTA UNIVERSITY BUILDING

Building 1970 *219* August 21, p. 64

Under the procedure briefly outlined the contractor acts in a project management capacity calling and awarding contracts in consultation with the university. The procedure is expected to allow construction to begin 4–6 months earlier than normal.

19

REAL PACKAGE DEAL

Architects Journal 1970 *152* July 22, p. 169 (Editorial)

A new package deal service developed by E.E. Chivers & Sons does not simply combine design and building but is a true package deal. They find alternative means of financing the project and a choice of sites, and this is followed by recommending an architect and if necessary a quantity surveyor. It is considered that this sophisticated form of package deal is the real threat to the future of the architects' practice.

18

Lord Mais

ROLE OF THE QUANTITY SURVEYOR. THERE ARE NOT ENOUGH PRACTICAL PEOPLE

Illustrated Carpenter & Builder 1970 *161* July 17, pp. 17–20
An interview ranging over topics such as the amalgamation of the IQS and RICS, technician training, the future role of the quantity surveyor, and the effect of the package deal on the quantity surveyor in private practice.

17
O. Luder
OTHER SIDE OF THE PACKAGE DEAL
Construction Steelwork 1970 June, pp. 6, 8, 10
The reasons for the increase in package dealing are outlined. It is considered that the client loses two valuable advantages by deciding upon a package deal; the independent advice of the architect and the ability to obtain competitive tenders for the work. A suitable alternative put forward is to employ the services of an integrated design consortium and the contractor selected by negotiation or open tendering. Although mainly concerned with illustrating the potential disadvantages of the package deal the author accepts that it has its merits but makes a plea that the client consider every alternative before deciding by which method he should obtain his new building.

16
A. Wates
PACKAGE DEAL BY ANY OTHER NAME THAN WATES
Building Design 1970 June 26, pp. 6–7
An interview regarding Wates' contractor consultancy system which involves the contractor in bringing together a management and specialist team to provide a service to the developer or architect.

15
R.B. Hellard
TWO STAGE PACKAGE DEALS
Architects Journal 1970 *151* April 1, pp. 792–3
The new procedure proposed involves the design team forming part of a new multi-disciplinary management unit – 'the project management group' – which would, through its design team, prepare and design, obtain tenders from selected contractors, and then put in a comprehensive tender for the whole project. The client would be free to accept the tender or to reject it, pay the design fees only, and seek alternative tenders for building the group's design.

14
R.G. Orr
CASE FOR THE PACKAGE DEAL
Construction Steelwork and Metals 1970 March, pp. 24, 26–7

The main arguments for the package deal are discussed, with particular reference to marketing, specialization, responsibility, costs and price, and collaboration with consultants.

13
E.D. Jefferies Matthews
IF WE MUST HAVE PACKAGE DEALS ...
Construction News 1970, March 19, p. 10
It is considered that to fully safeguard the client's interest it is desirable for an architect to provide a brief in a form which enables the contractor to obtain a complete picture of the requirements and give him a sound basis for his estimates.

12
J.R. Lowe
THE CONSULTANT'S CASE AGAINST PACKAGE DEALS
Construction News 1970 January 8, p. 18
Examples are presented to illustrate the danger to the client of a package deal. It is shown that the client can obtain an inferior or unsuitable product and not necessarily in a shorter time. Although it is accepted that there is a place for package deals it is maintained that the use of a professional team will provide a better and cheaper design.

11
P. Janson
PACKAGE DEALS
National Swedish Building Research Summary R47: 1970, 2pp.
This study shows that with the package deal the client has little scope for controlling design rationally, and consequently there should be some compensation. Although lower prices are claimed by package dealing there is a danger that monopolies will be formed with the result that prices will increase.

10
Ministry of Public Buildings & Works
THE BUILDING PROCESS: A CASE STUDY FROM MARKS & SPENCER LTD
1970, HMSO. 60pp.
The way is described in which a large commercial organization meets its continuous need for new buildings or extensions to existing ones. The study is in six parts covering background information, the building programme, the building process – design and site operations, computer preparation and pricing of bills of quantities, and evaluation of the performance of the organization. Appendices give examples of monthly cost statement, budgetary data, form of contract between the company and its main

contractor, minutes of typical meetings, priced locational bills, item location and materials and labour scheduling.

9
General Services Administration – Public Buildings Service
CONSTRUCTION CONTRACTING SYSTEMS – A REPORT ON THE SYSTEMS USED BY PBS AND OTHER ORGANIZATIONS
1970, 150pp. (4 appendices)
An evaluation is made, in relation to experience gained by the American Public Building Service, of the conventional firm-price lump-sum contract and why in the interests of efficiency and productivity other forms of letting a contract needed to be examined. It is concluded that turnkey contracts can provide significant benefits on simple design projects and that management contracting is suitable for large and/or complex projects.

1969

8
R.G. Orr
CASE FOR THE PACKAGE DEAL
Construction News 1969 December 4, pp. 22–3

7
CLIENT EDUCATION IS KEY TO PACKAGE DEAL SUCCESS
Construction News 1969 *89* July, 10, p. 10

6
C.J. Platten
PACKAGE DEAL IN PERSPECTIVE
Architect and Building News 1969 March 13, pp. 36–9

5
L.W. Madden
PACKAGE DEALING
Building 1969 *216* February 21, pp. 147–8, 150
Studies have shown that the procedure is on the increase and for this reason it would be helpful to everybody if more design-and-build examples were exposed to public view. Aspects considered in particular are the place of outside consultants, work handled by architects, house design–build by contractors, hospitals design and build, LA's use of design–build and contractor's views on future.

4
O. Luder
PRIVATE ARCHITECT AND THE DEAL
Building 1969 *216* February 7, pp. 87–8
Reasons behind the growth of the package deal are summarized. It is believed that the private architect can offer better service than the package dealer but only if he is willing to make some radical changes in the method of practice.

1968

3
R. Bidgood
ARCHITECTS AND PACKAGE DEALS
System Building and Design 1968 October, pp. 63–6; 1969 January, pp. 43–6. 1969 May, pp. 51–4
The architect's involvement in various types of package deal are described and the methods of organization and implementation are discussed, together with the reasons why a professional practice could be packaged. The two main types of package deal are considered and the advantages to the participants indicated.

2
J. Gwynn
PACKAGE DEAL THREAT
Consulting Engineer 1968 *32* July, pp. 59–64.

1967

1
H. Hicks
MANAGEMENT AND THE PACKAGE DEAL
Proceedings 10B Annual Conference, Harrogate 1967, pp. 9–12
The philosophy of a package deal contractor is outlined and details provided of his method of operation. Advantages to the client and his safeguards are considered.

Index

ACA form of building contract, BPF edition 29
adjudicator 29
architect ix, 3, 6–14, 16, 20–3, 26, 32, 45–6, 53, 57–8, 61–3
architect/engineer 54
Australia 34

Banwell Report 1, 33
Basic Contractual Terms for PFIs 32
Belgium 53, 54
bills of quantities 11–14, 16, 17, 27, 29, 37, 41, 54
BOO (*see* build, own and operate)
BOOT (*see* build, own operate, and transfer)
builder (*see also* contractor) 6, 12, 13, 16, 19, 21, 22, 23, 42
building surveyor 21
build, own and operate (BOO) 29
build, own, operate and transfer (BOOT) 29
British Property Federation System 4, 11, 19, 21, 24–7, 51, 59, 62

CD 81 (*see* JCT Standard Form of Building Contract with Contractor's Design)
clerk of works 7, 28
client ix, 1–13, 16–34, 36, 39, 40, 42–6, 54, 56–63
client's representative 6–11, 25–8, 45, 57
Constructing the team 1
Construction Contracts Bill 2
Construction Industry Council 2
construction management 11, 15, 37, 39, 40, 47, 49, 50, 59
construction manager 15–18, 54
contractor ix, 1, 4, 8, 9, 11, 13–29, 32–4, 42, 43, 54, 63
cost benefit analysis 53

DBFO (*see* design, build, finance and operate)

Denmark 53
design-and-build 11, 19–24, 39–44, 47, 49, 51, 52, 54, 59
design, build, finance and operate 19, 29–32
developer 6, 38, 45, 46, 56, 58, 59, 62, 63
Domestic form of sub-contract 14, 24
DOM form of sub-contract (*see* Domestic form of sub-contract)
Department of the Environment 2

ECC (*see* Engineering and Construction Contract)
Emmerson Report 62
employer (*see* client)
employer's agent 21, 23
engineer 3, 7, 8, 10, 12, 13, 26, 32, 53, 54, 62
Engineering and Construction Contract 2, 8, 10, 14, 19, 24, 35
Engineering and Construction Contract sub-contract 14, 24
estate manager 8
Europe ix, 53
European Union 55

Faster Building for Commerce 7
Faster Building for Industry 36–7
fast-track ix, 15, 36, 38
France 53–5

general contractor (*see* contractor)
Germany 53–5

HM Treasury 30, 32

ICE Design and Construct Form of Contract 24
IFC 84 (*see* JCT Intermediate Form of Contract)
Institute of Civil Engineers 10
Italy 53

Japan 34
JCT (*see* Joint Contracts Tribunal)